THE CHARTIST IMAGINARY

THE CHARTIST IMAGINARY

*Literary Form in Working-Class
Political Theory and Practice*

MARGARET A. LOOSE

THE OHIO STATE UNIVERSITY PRESS
COLUMBUS

Library of Congress Cataloging-in-Publication Data

Loose, Margaret A., 1967–

The Chartist imaginary : literary form in working-class political theory and practice / Margaret A. Loose.

pages cm

Includes bibliographical references and index.

ISBN 978-0-8142-1266-0 (cloth : alk. paper) — ISBN 0-8142-1266-2 (cloth : alk. paper) — ISBN 978-0-8142-9370-6 (cd) — ISBN 0-8142-9370-0 (cd)

1. Politics and literature—Great Britain—History—19th century. 2. Chartism. 3. English litera-ture—19th century—History and criticism. 4. Literature and society—Great Britain—History—19th century. 5. English literature—Women authors—History and criticism. 6. Working class writings, English—History and criticism. 7. Political poetry, English—History and criticism. 8. Working class in literature. I. Title.

PR468.C43L66 2014

820.9'007—dc23

2014013225

Cover design by Thao Thai
Text design by Juliet Williams
Type set in Adobe Minion Pro

9 8 7 6 5 4 3 2 1

· CONTENTS ·

· ILLUSTRATIONS ·

• ACKNOWLEDGMENTS •

Petitioning among their fellows to support and identify with the People's Charter galvanized communities of people and conferred on them a unity of aspirations, identity, and effort. That sense of collectivity might seem antithetical to the solitary project of writing, but one of the saving revelations of working on this book was the breadth and warmth of other people's commitment to it and to me, the feeling of shared hope and the knowing sympathy of prolonged labor in similar endeavors. I have been deeply touched by the outpouring of support from all of my colleagues in the Department of Literature at the University of California, San Diego, and especially Kathryn Shevelow, Meg Wesling, Don Wayne, Nicole Tonkovich, Heather Fowler, Jin-kyung Lee, and Stephanie Jed. Jin and Stephanie have read drafts, raised questions, pushed me in new directions, and guided me in the arts of authorship with unfailing optimism and human kindness, and I feel so lucky to have them as allies. The Literature Department and the University of California, San Diego generously afforded me grants and teaching leave that made possible my writing and my research abroad. I also wish to give sincere thanks to the anonymous readers whose detailed, thoughtful feedback dramatically improved my manuscript. Thanks, too, to *Philological Quarterly* for permission to incorporate a revised version of my essay "Chartist Revolutionary Strategy" into chapter three.

My friends at the Dickens Project have likewise inspired and aided me professionally over the years, including in particular Tricia Lootens, John Jordan, Carolyn Williams, Elsie Michie, Carol MacKay, Teresa Mangum, Rebecca

Stern, Galia Benziman, and Miriam Margolyes, who graciously hosted me in her home while I conducted research at the British Library.

This project began and made some of its greatest progress under one of the finest teachers and scholars I have ever known, Florence Saunders Boos. Her exquisite ear for and delight in poetry renewed the joy of its study for me month after month, and her skill as a writer improved my own. In addition, her generosity in sharing her research on working-class women poets helped me learn about the abundance and range of their writing, and gave me leads to pursue in my own search for working-class Chartist women writers.

My family, and especially my mother Margaret M. Loose, has believed in me since my earliest memory, actively promoted my intellectual curiosity, cheerfully made sacrifices to enable my writing, and helped me maintain perspective about what I most value in life. Mimi Van Ausdall has steadily encouraged and heroically supported me in my work through all the years, and her example has taught me much about what it means to be a careful thinker and a humane teacher. Anne Myles too has lent me daily friendship and sympathy, moved me with superb writing, and stayed up late to go crazy talking with me about poetry. For over a decade Liz Corsun has been my friend and fellow traveler on Victorian roads, reading drafts of my work, suggesting new ideas, making me laugh, and sharing life with dogs. In more recent years my friend Teresa McGee has given me so much of her creative intelligence, patient confidence, and cheerful wisdom that I wonder if I would ever have finished this book without her.

To all of this community who have helped this book come into existence, I am more deeply grateful than a few paragraphs can tell.

• INTRODUCTION •

CHARTISM AND THE POLITICS OF FORM

While cycling in southwest Utah some years ago, I encountered pre-Columbian petroglyphs representing not only the sun, bighorn sheep, and dogs, but also people carrying things on their backs, holding tools, and perhaps gazing at their reflections in water. I still wonder about the ancestral Puebloans who scratched those nonutilitarian images into the red sandstone over a thousand years ago. When desert survival must have dominated everything about their lives, they made representational art. I am only the latest person to wonder why, but for those of us who teach and do research in the humanities, such questions and speculations are our *raison d'être*, the most compelling basis for why we do what we do and believe that it matters.

Sculpture, painting, music, narrative, and other arts seem to be part of our species being, as fundamental as finding water. The more I have thought and written about what function literature served for those variously educated nineteenth-century working people calling themselves Chartists, the more I have come to realize how absolutely essential it was for the existence of a political movement. It was not simply that imaginative writing expressed ideals or promoted community or demonstrated cultural refinement; it half *created* the people who created it. These marginalized people felt and affirmed their humanity—its range of emotional experience, its ability to imagine and remember, for instance—in the acts of reading and of writing creatively. In purely human terms, that was a crucial achievement for a group of people so often represented as subhuman, and who might even have felt themselves to be so when they were forced to devote all their energies and time to the

I

procurement of food and shelter. The sense of personal dignity and species belonging were not the only results, however.

Working-class writers also exercised their latent powers of postulating unrealized scenarios, strengthening or even generating their ability to conceive of altered social circumstances, to set political goals, to motivate and sustain themselves and others in aspiring to greater equality. As Sanders shows (*Poetry*), on their own account, reading (or hearing) and writing even simple poems or short stories in their local Chartist newspapers also made them intellectually hungry, stimulating self-education and a demand for living and working conditions more conducive to self-education. This was a geometrically cumulative, self-perpetuating, and self-fulfilling force, and it lies at the heart of what I mean by the "Chartist imaginary" of the book's title. Lucidly theorized by Mike Sanders[1] (with application specifically to poetry, though I am broadening its use somewhat here), the term refers to the "total qualitative transformation of consciousness" which results from contact with imaginative literature (13). Not merely through direct intervention in some specific political issue, Chartist writing awakened and shaped people's awareness of mismatch between professed ideals and reality, exercised their conceptual powers (literary and social), sharpened their appetite for more knowledge, more intellectual power, more dignity, more agency in the present to fashion a utopian future. The Chartist imaginary thus constituted and generated a unique kind of agency, one whose exact content could not be predicted because it was a kind of thinking rather than a precisely specified content. In the course of researching and writing about this movement and its literary culture, I have come to see art not simply as expression, reflection, symptom, or the other usual descriptions of its role, but as an agent that effects qualitative, cognitive (perhaps even neurological), and ultimately political change.

The task of the Chartist writers discussed in this book was successfully to embody their varying political concerns in the most effective formal or generic correlatives. Why did Massey use a dream vision romantic poem to discuss the passions? Why did Cooper compose an argumentative epic to expose the pretensions of religion? What about the novel form lent it to Wheeler's effort to imagine new routes to revolution? And why did Elizabeth La Mont designate a poem she wrote about acts of imagination "A Simile"? It might be that these choices seemed fitting, among other reasons, because poetry—the most familiar genre of literature for working-class people—evoked emotions and ideals, but the new genre of working-class fiction permitted a more spe-

---

1. In fact I borrow this term from chapter 1 of his *The Poetry of Chartism*, which anyone interested in a more extensive theorization of the abstract concept should read (6–37).

cific concern with how these ends could be achieved and the potential pitfalls along the way. Reformist and new ideas seek new forms and new channels for existing forms, so that the aim of political reform mandates an accompanying literary reform.

In the course of his critique of religion, Thomas Cooper in the *Purgatory of Suicides* attacked Gothic architecture for its habituation of the human mind to dimness and ignorance and its promotion of the acceptance of contradictions and improbabilities. By doing so, he made an audacious entry into the company of such elite aesthetic thinkers as Pugin and Ruskin, joining a contemporary debate that might have seemed to have little relevance to any but art critics. Yet Cooper saw in artistic buildings physical evidence of a cultural effort to inculcate deference to political injustices. For him, as for all of the Chartists this book will consider, art was a site of political debate, a realm in which people could perceive the relations of their world and think about ways of changing them. Cooper's example points to part of the reason it is necessary to examine the *politics* of Chartist literature: however removed from social reality art might sometimes seem, it was for the Chartists inescapably connected to it. Aesthetic choices served more than narrative or lyric ends, and to endeavor to assess those aesthetic choices without regard to their social effects yields an incomplete, and I would say unsatisfying, result.

The agitational and educational aims attached to the Chartist program informed genre selection, the choices of stanza forms and narrative devices, the diction, the rhyme schemes, the fictional settings and character development, and even the grammar of Chartist literature. In my view, reading politically heightens one's sensitivity to the formal features of poetry and fiction as well as enhancing the ability to explain them; it deepens one's engagement with literature regardless of agreement or disagreement with the principles or goals informing the work. As Ian Haywood has pointed out, "Chartism was a movement whose vision centred on a literary document [the People's Charter]" (*Literature* 1). That written expression of political goals united more laboring Britons than had ever been done before and conferred on the unprecedented collective its own name. The political and the literary, for Chartism, were inextricable.

Fortunately for posterity, the Chartists left a considerable body of writing that gives insight into the movement's goals and tactics, its disagreements, decisions, weaknesses, heroes, and more. That writing included newspaper articles, editorials, poetry, fiction, speeches, pamphlets, petitions, resolutions, meeting minutes, broadsides, correspondence, autobiographies, historical studies, and diaries. Yet the following chapters concentrate almost exclusively on creative writing—short stories, novels, and poems—even though such forms might not represent the most transparent articulation of Chartist poli-tics. They are, however, among the most interesting articulations of Chartist politics.

That judgment derives in part from the fact that literary conventions impose a certain necessity for crafting one's material, for condensing or expanding ideas or preoccupations according to generic norms, for a more-than-usually acute attentiveness to the role of language and form in conveying meaning. Chartist literary works also command interest because their very literariness represented a rebuttal to those who, like George Eliot, opposed working-class enfranchisement on the basis of their uncultured ignorance. Whether Chartists accepted or rejected middle-class standards of merit, and even if they disagreed that formal education should be a prerequisite for suf-frage, many Chartist writers regarded stylistic accomplishment as a powerful validation of the claims of their class. If working people could navigate the challenges of meter, or sustained character development, or the complex lay-ering of meaning, if they could write epics that placed Chartist aspirations at the fore of a nation's destiny, then they demonstrated an intellectual sophisti-cation that entitled them to equal participation in self-government. For many Chartists, the forms of their writing were in themselves political gestures, so that one cannot fully understand Chartist politics without attending to its lit-erary incarnation. It is therefore not only pleasurable but also vital to dwell on the politics of Chartist *literature*.

Chartist writers perceived no disjunction between politics and literature, because it was precisely the fact that they wrote in mixed genres, Spenserian stanzas, heroic couplets, and melodramatic novels that generated a cognitive dissonance within literary history and made Chartists into protagonists in Britain's national history and culture. Their example poses problems for some later Marxist theories that separated intellectual and manual laborers, aesthet-ics from politics. *The Chartist Imaginary* shows that working people were, in large numbers, also writing people, and that as thinkers and doers they were uniquely able to grasp the connections between economics and philosophy. Their writings demonstrated the incompatibility of liberal institutions and poverty and simultaneously contested their exclusion from governance and literary tradition.

Chartism was the first mass working-class movement in Britain, drawing into its ranks hundreds of thousands of men and women from every region of England, from Wales, Scotland, and Ireland, and representing a major-ity of the adult population of the nation. The people who wrote and read the works examined in this study were the pioneers of all subsequent self-organization on behalf of proletarian interests in Britain. Political parties,

trades unions, social campaigns, and strike committees would relate themselves, either by positive or negative example, implicitly or explicitly, to Chartism and its tactics, organization, demands, and results. As the foundation for
so much subsequent practice and debate for such a significant majority of the
British populace, the Chartist movement retains a compelling interest. There
had been unions, sporadic demonstrations, and Owenite cooperatives before
the late 1830s when Chartism was born, but this movement was unique for its
nationwide character and overwhelming popularity, its combination of political demands with the economic muscle of laborers, its working-class composition, and its literariness. Two recent and thorough books have updated
the accounts of Chartism in England and Scotland,[2] but a schematic history
of the movement will suffice here.

Following the failure of the first Reform Act (1832) to bring Britain's laborers more than the hated New Poor Law (1834) and the worsening of living conditions, family life, and the hours and conditions of labor that accompanied
increasing urbanization and "free trade," activists began in the late 1830s to
draft and organize around a document they called *The People's Charter*. Fired
by many grievances they felt would be addressed if they could gain a voice
in the governance of their nation, the Chartists, as they became known, dis-
tilled their ambitions into six generally democratizing points: universal adult
male suffrage, equal electoral districts, annual Parliaments, vote by secret
ballot, elimination of the property qualification for Members of Parliament,
and payment of Members of Parliament. Their primary method for achieving this goal followed the time-honored tradition of presenting petitions to
Parliament, which they did on three occasions: 1839, 1842, and 1848. Few leading Chartists were greatly surprised by their government's refusal to pass the
reforms they demanded, but as an organizing tactic that raised political consciousness by requiring focused discussion of a definite program in cities and
villages across the kingdom, the petitions were spectacularly successful. In
open-air meetings, at marches and demonstrations, in pubs and trades union
meetings and neighborhoods, working men and women acquired a more or
less cohesive collective identity, and the scope of their outlook and program
widened.

The Six Points never changed, but the introductions to Chartist petitions
and the debates in the pages of their national newspapers show intense col-
lateral interest in repealing the Act of Union with Ireland and the New Poor
Law, in reducing the hours of work, disestablishing the Church of England,

---

2. Malcolm Chase's *Chartism A New History* (2007) and W. Hamish Fraser's *Chartism in
Scotland* (2010).

abolishing or reforming the monarchy and standing army and police, instituting freedom of assembly and a system of national education, land reform, and other sweeping social changes. Most of these matters, and a consistent solidarity with international movements for democracy and revolution, filled the pages of the *Northern Star,* the weekly newspaper founded by Feargus O'Connor in 1837 and the leading periodical (of which there were many) of the Chartist movement. Memorialized by Chartists as "the Lion of Freedom," O'Connor stood at the head of the movement's numerous prominent figures. A polarizing personality, O'Connor worked tirelessly for the cause, and like nearly all of Chartism's leaders, he spent time in jail as the government's reaction to Chartism swung between cautious and hysterical.

An important source of such official panic were the events of 1839, including calls for a general strike, the Bull Ring riots in Birmingham, and especially the Newport Rising in South Wales, where thousands of armed people marched on the town to demand passage of the Charter and release of the arrested Chartist leader Henry Vincent. Marchers converged on a hotel that temporarily housed some other arrested Chartists, and at least seventy people were killed or injured by the soldiers inside. The rising was to be coordinated with similar actions in Yorkshire and Tyneside, which did not materialize, but the insurrectionary tone of Chartist rhetoric and journalism in the summer and fall of that year stoked the climate of unease. Massive arrests and repression followed, but sympathy and support for the Chartists grew by the time they presented their second petition to Parliament in 1842. When it, too, was rejected, many observers feared further insurrectionary activity, but while a wave of militant strikes, "plug-drawing," and some arming and drilling occurred, there was no repetition of Newport.

In fact, after serious government repression followed these events, Chartist energies after 1842 fragmented into distinct strands with decidedly less radical goals. "The New Move," as O'Connor christened the splintering "Knowledge Chartism," "Teetotal Chartism," "Church Chartism," and "Household Chartism" groups, was less politically focused and would divert adherents from their vital unity around universal male suffrage.[3] In addition, O'Connor himself launched his cherished Chartist Land Plan with the aim of settling workers on their own 4-acre plots in a thousand-acre estate with its own school and surgery. In its way, this too diverted attention from Parliamentary reform and contributed to the years of downturn between 1843 and 1846. Increased clarity and activity in 1847–48 led to the large demonstration on Kennington Common in London, which preceded presentation of

---

3. For a careful parsing of these strands, see Chase 168–78.

the final Chartist petition in April 1848. Despite its third petitioning defeat, the movement surged in late 1848 before unevenly developing and unraveling in the 1850s and finally disappearing. In its post-1848 configuration under the leadership of such figures as Ernest Jones, Chartism took a more socialist turn but never regained its previous strength and gradually passed out of existence.

Yet during the decade or two that it existed, the Chartist movement not only laid a foundation for later democratic and labor movements but also generated a substantial corpus of literature alongside and in dialogue with that written by their more privileged contemporaries. As one might expect, authorial decisions about aesthetic medium and its relation to political content vexed certain writers, Chartist and non-Chartist. Arguably the *locus classicus* of Victorian angst over the appropriateness of generic choice to convey political content and elicit reader response is Elizabeth Gaskell's 1848 social problem novel *Mary Barton*. In *Tainted Souls and Painted Faces* Amanda Anderson argues that *Mary Barton* is a contest, not simply between competing romantic and political plots but also between the genres of melodrama and social realism. The tale of youthful love and industrial strife demonstrates Gaskell's preference for the kind of sympathy which springs from personal contact between the classes, but it also reveals her anxiety lest her novel act as a kind of emotional pressure-valve to readers, giving them the cathartic satisfaction of having felt sympathy for her working-class characters without necessarily motivating what was to her that crucial next step of concrete personal action to ameliorate the conditions of their class.[4]

Her anxiety that her art will not result in social reform, that its melodrama and romance ultimately overshadow its reformist politics, is justified, I think, because of at least two facts noted by many critics: the representative of the political plot John Barton becomes increasingly shadowy and finally disappears from the last half of the book, and unable to solve the crisis it has movingly laid out, the novel ends with the improbable, sentimentalized ending of so many Victorian novels, capped with removal of all of the primary characters from the scene of economic and political struggle.

A similarly fantastic ending concludes Thomas Cooper's short story "Seth Thompson, the Stockinger" (1845), in which the struggling worker Seth is (temporarily, at least) delivered from his troubles by the wealth of an uncle to whose West Indian plantation he emigrates. The story reminds us that any

---

4. Elizabeth Gaskell's letters make clear her frustration with anonymous charity that was not case-specific, personal, and individualistic, for she complained of those who gladly gave money to her and her husband to use charitably but would not themselves visit the poor and minister to their needs.

too-rigid dichotomy between middle-class and working-class writers will founder on the basis of broadly inclusive evidence.[5] But the surprise inheritance/geographical solution here sharply diverges from much other Chartist fiction, one of the most interesting examples of which is also by Cooper. As noted by Haywood (*Literature* 9), the conclusion of his short story "'Merrie England'—No More!" (1845) absolutely falls apart in its final paragraph, but the explosion of the rules of grammar there shows a Chartist author struggling to adapt bourgeois fictional forms for radical ends. When it reaches its ending, the story breaks out of the dialogue among unemployed framework knitters which it has recorded and, in fragments connected only with dashes, directly addresses readers to tell them that there is no "tale" to end because the characters—and thousands like them—go right on in their "miserable round" of working when possible, starving when not, going in and out of the revolving door of the workhouse "Bastile," and finally it poses the question "What are your thoughts, reader?" Here is the final paragraph, the grammar of which is so intriguing:

> There is no "tale" to finish about John or his lad, or Jem and his wife. They went on starving,—begging,—receiving threats of imprisonment,—tried the "Bastile" for a few weeks,—came out and had a little work,—starved again; and they are still going the same miserable round, like thousands in "merrie England." What are your thoughts, reader? (59)

The schizophrenic predication of this paragraph subjugates the rules of representation to the imperative of social reform. Cooper shatters the coherent conclusion, and even the grammar in which that might be written, in an effort to make his story approximate the chaos and monotony of false starts and cyclical depressions in his characters' lives: his is a confusion, not a conclusion. Heaven, emigration, and latent aristocracy simply will not suffice as conclusions as long as they avoid or merely escape from social miseries not so magically relieved. In this instance Cooper contrasts with many middle-class reform writers, harmonizing literary representation with the Chartist demand for political representation to the extent that while one is denied, neither is the other possible. Even the aesthetic fails to provide a neat solution as long as social and political ones go untried. As Haywood explains, Cooper "cannot impose a resolution while the struggle [is] still taking place" and he

---

5. Rob Breton persuasively argues that even when they use the *deus ex machina,* Chartist writers consistently differ from middle-class ones by insisting through the device that "the only way to survive in an unjust world is through an unworldly intervention. Willpower and individual effort do not suffice" ("Ghosts" 560).

"pushes his realism to the limits of representation" (*Literature* 9). Cooper is not alone among Chartists in this respect, either, for of the works studied in this book alone, a significant number conclude ambiguously (by Somerville, Linton, Wheeler, "Argus," and Massey). Whether he was writing poetry or fiction, Cooper's political aims deeply influenced how he handled his medium.

There is an important respect in which Cooper's story resembles Gaskell's, though, and that is in the vital role each ascribes to the active response of their readers. Gaskell obtrudes political meditations into romantic moments, constantly endeavoring to nudge her readers away from passive reception. She insists on a realist, rather than melodramatic, reading of her central plot element (Carson's murder). Similarly, Cooper makes any conclusion to his tale impossible and then directly addresses readers, as if demanding from them the conclusion to the story. In both cases, it is reader intervention on which the authors rely to connect art and society. I would argue that the first step in such an activist engagement with literature includes systematic attentiveness to aesthetic forms.

For that reason, *The Chartist Imaginary* reads Chartist literature more for its literary techniques and engagements than for its historical accounts or overtly political themes, though those necessarily form part of my discussion. The book includes some familiar names from the Chartist canon such as Ernest Jones, W. J. Linton, Thomas Cooper, and Gerald Massey. But in every case it incorporates works by them that have received little or no scholarly attention, expanding the range of works from which our theories about Chartism should derive. Where their more standard works appear, my approach differs from other critics either in being more detailed or in steadily focusing on the importance of their literary form. In several instances, *The Chartist Imaginary* introduces works and authors either faintly known or completely unknown before: "Argus," Alexander Somerville, Mary Hutton, Elizabeth La Mont, the seamstress E. L. E, and numerous fictional and poetic pieces.

In *The Poetry of Chartism*, Mike Sanders rightly contends that the body of Chartist literature is significantly larger than our historically narrow focus on its most famous writers would suggest, and he sets about correcting this by discussing a broad range of poems that appeared in the columns of the *Northern Star*. Heeding his call to look beyond the usual writers and works, *The Chartist Imaginary*, as mentioned above, does so. Though very much aligned with Sanders philosophically and theoretically, the book differs from Sanders's by including works published outside the main Chartist newspaper, performing sustained analysis of other genres than poetry, and using a methodology more strongly interested in historical prosody. It also, of course, devotes an entire chapter to Chartist poetry by women. *The Chartist Imaginary* applies close formal scrutiny to Chartist oratory and journalism, short stories and novels, and poetry of varying lengths and forms, making it the first full-length account in some years to examine Chartist literature cross-generically.

Given the size of the contemporary readership of Chartist literature and the volume of poetry and fiction the movement produced, one might reasonably expect to find Chartist works represented in every survey or anthology of Victorian writing. This body of work was a major strand of the literary culture of mid-nineteenth-century Britain, yet it is conspicuous more for its absence than its inclusion in collections and discussions of 1840s and '50s writing. The explanation for such omission lies in part with the fact that much of— though certainly not all—Chartist writing appeared in ephemeral forms such as newspapers and magazines, rather than substantial volumes catalogued in the British Library collection. But some of the cause of such oversight probably lies with the implicit assumptions of those who compiled or wrote anthologies and literary histories. The evidence of their work reveals a tendency to believe that—regardless of their appeal to certain contemporary audiences— only those works directed at middle- and upper-class readers and written by authors from similar backgrounds could be works of enduring merit. Moreover, then as now, some scholars dismissed works with overt political intent without much thought for whether unequivocal allegiance to some cause or ideal necessarily entailed an uncomplicated or unsophisticated use of literary form. I would suggest, however, that any conception of Victorian literature minus Chartist literature can only be incomplete, and my intention here is to aid in a richer, more nuanced picture of what Victorian literature is. In particular, the "social problem" writings of Dickens, Gaskell, Disraeli, Kingsley, and Eliot should be balanced with writings by working people themselves, with their own self-representations and ideas for the betterment of England's oppressed. In addition, close attention to this *oeuvre* reveals its considerable aesthetic merit and interest. Demonstrating that Chartist literature can not only sustain but also solicit formal analysis is another of the goals of this book.

In general, the first chapter examines the interplay of poetic traditions in the formation of Ernest Jones's internationalist identity and argues that the trajectory of his political consciousness offers a microcosm of radical Chartism as a whole. Chapter two argues that through their literary forms, Chartist epics helped shape the identities and ambitions of the movement. Three divergent accounts of revolution compose chapter three, which looks at the variable impacts of generic hybridity in Chartist fiction. The fourth and fifth chapters focus on matters of gender and form, thereby connecting Chartist literary practices to the larger mid-Victorian preoccupation with the "Woman

Question" and enabling a more thorough discussion of this topic than critics have so far achieved. Chapter four surveys Chartist literary treatments of women and then argues that the very literary conventions one Chartist uses in his treatment of gender themselves communicate the claustrophobic position of women in matters of sex and marriage. Finally, the fifth chapter relies on extensive archival research to introduce some women's Chartist poetry and consider how for them poetic representation *was* political representation. By identifying the ways in which new views of social reality evoked an innovative reshaping of traditional literary forms, this book seeks to contribute to a larger project of vindicating the place of working-class literature in Victorian studies.

· I ·

Ernest Jones and the Poetics of Internationalism

Born in Germany to upper-class parents, how did Ernest Jones (1819–1869) come to be a "poet laureate" of a movement (Chartism) that was British and working-class? How did the young boy who disappeared from home for three days until his parents found him—pack tied on his back, making his way to join the Polish resistance to Russia—cross over from privileged schoolboy to Polish freedom fighter? In his later years as a practicing barrister in England, what explained his role as the champion and defender of Irish Fenian prisoners accused of killing a police officer? How is one to understand this son of a retired military officer, a veteran of Britain's anti-French fighting at Waterloo, organizing with French exiles and excoriating British militarism in his speeches and writings? The story of Jones's life and career is overwhelmingly one of such border-crossings as these, a chronicle of lifelong self-fashioning that refused the identities and loyalties prescribed to him by birth and custom.[1]

A similar insistence on choosing, rather than inheriting, one's identity distinguishes Jones's poetry as well. For example, in "Erin" (1847) the speaker refers to "the home of my fathers" in Ireland where he "play'd in [his] childhood," and calls on the British to join the struggle for repeal of the Act of Union (lines 46, 51).[2] Of course Jones, born in Germany and named after his

---

1. A rather more critical view of his self-fashioning forms the substance of Miles Taylor's 2003 biography of Jones.

2. This poem, published unsigned on pages 92–93 of the *Labourer* in 1847, could well be by

godfather (and Queen Victoria's uncle) the Duke of Cumberland, was not Irish but assumed that voice for poetic and political ends. *The New World* (1851) closes with a vision of the whole world speaking one common language and sharing the earth as one common home. And an "Epitaph" (1848) he wrote for the year 1847 asserts that "all men *are* brethren," without regard to origins in Spain, Italy, Poland, America, Asia, and other named countries and regions. The poem states that people's decision to *act* on that *de facto* brotherhood, their choice of a personhood liberated from narrow nationalism, is the prerequisite to genuine freedom. In each of these examples the poet takes for granted the exercise of an individual's volition: one's nationality and loyalties are a matter of personal selection rather than the accidents of birth or ancestry.

What is perhaps surprising about this emphasis on the individual and one's ability to define a personality for oneself is that it would seem to contradict Jones's broader intention to foster a mass, class-based identity that seeks social justice through collective action. For his poems to be effective as Chartist propaganda, should they not derive the sense of self from community and class instead of from the more inward-looking, Romantic notion of the solitary being whose personhood is a private matter? Undoubtedly there is a Romantic dimension to Jones's poetry, with frequent appeals to nature in its relation to the self, an idyllic countryside dotted with bright cottages, and generally less exalted poetic forms and language than had characterized much pre-Romantic writing. But there is also a pronounced emphasis on the wretched plight of industrial workers and the cultivation of an awareness of their collective interests and power. His poetry puts forward a class-based appeal to mass action for broad political ends. Less meditative than agitational, less interior than collective, his verse does not fit readily into the usual (if incomplete) categories of Romantic poetry.

Such categories describe only a part of Romanticism, which scholars such as Anne Janowitz have demonstrated. In her argument that readers should consider Romantic poetry dialectically, Janowitz explains that "in the romantic poetic were to be found elements of both traditional culture, with its sense of the centrality of a common voice, along with the developmental, self-authorising, autonomous subject of liberalism" (*Lyric and Labour in the Romantic Tradition*, 30). Sometimes Romantic poetry is solitary and medita-

---

someone besides Jones, who signed many poems he published in the journal. He did not sign all of this work, however, publishing without attribution his serial novel *The Romance of a People*, for example. Janowitz notes that the "poetry which appears in *The Labourer* was written for the most part by Jones himself," and supplemented by many from W. J. Linton (*Lyric and Labour in the Romantic Tradition*, 181).

tive, transcending context, and at other times it "polemically call[s] for a kind of poetical activism closely linked to social life" (ibid., 15). Thus it was precisely the individualist thrust of Romanticism that allowed aristocratic poets such as Byron and Shelley to opt for identification with alien classes and nationalities, as they famously did in both verse and life. The kernel of Janowitz's argument that promises the most for my analysis of Jones is her notion that the voluntarism implied by the lyric "I," the power to define oneself without reference to customary sources of identity (e.g., family, country, class, region), actually clears the path to the writer's transpersonal membership in communities different from those of his or her own birth. While seeming to liberate someone from being simply the latest instantiation of a pre-existing communal identity, Romantic individualism can also actually permit one to cross out of solipsism, nationalism, and classism into a powerful identification with other communities. It "unmoors" personal identity, allowing one to place himself in groups other than his inherited ones.

What this dual potential of Romanticism means for Jones is that, steeped as he was in German and British Romantic traditions, he could exhibit all of the internationalism and working-class solidarity I mentioned in the first paragraph. His writings include both individual subjectivity and collective identity; they use the aesthetic forms of a literary print culture and of popular ballad and song; they appeal to nature's inspiration while they urge mass political action. His use of Romantic lyrical forms for communitarian, class-conscious ends both deploys the voluntarist potential of self-definition implied in their individualism and unequivocally declares the speaker's choice to define self in terms of community and class without regard to nation or birth. By carefully looking at the vital role of literary forms and sensibilities in its cultivation, this chapter will endeavor to trace the importance of internationalism throughout Jones's writing. It builds on and deepens Janowitz's theories but differs from them by scrutinizing some of Jones's lesser-known poems and his novel *The Maid of Warsaw,* constellating them with his journalism and oratory of the 1850s, and arguing that within his work may be seen a microcosm of the changing "poetico-political" consciousness of Chartism as a whole. By teasing out the interplay of poetic traditions in his political development and the correspondence between shifts in political consciousness and the imagery Jones uses across genres, this chapter begins the exercise to which all of the subsequent chapters contribute in their own ways. Collectively they demonstrate the dual nature of art in general and literature in particular, as not only a uniquely sensitive and revealing register of political consciousness but also a surprisingly active agent in its formation and development.

Internationalist and Romantic Traditions

Jones should be briefly situated within a tradition of internationalism among radicals and working-class activists. Certainly he is representative of Chartism's recognition of ties among workers in all countries, evident in the leading roles Chartists played in the People's International League and the Society of Fraternal Democrats, as well as their active opposition to England's colonial domination of Ireland. Chartism inherited its solidarity with other nations from the radical tradition stretching back to the Jacobins of the 1790s. The radical and working-class presses featured reports on republican struggles in Ireland, Poland, Italy, and other Continental countries.[3] In 1833 the Owenite movement issued a "Manifesto" addressed to "the Governments and People of the Continents of Europe and of North and South America" and opening with the words "Men of the Great Family of Mankind" (Thompson, *English Working Class,* 829). In the same year the trades unions of Britain, France, and Germany discussed the formation of alliances among their respective groups (ibid.). Thus, though the persistence of Jones's solidarity through periods in which other activists lurched backward toward patriotism was unusual,[4] among radicals and Chartists his internationalism itself was not.

Jones's interest in and commitment to international causes abundantly manifests itself in his large corpus of published work, which includes nine different newspapers and periodicals he edited and many speeches and pamphlets with such titles as *Foreign Affairs* and *Our Colonies* (1856–7), *The Slaveholder's War* (1863), and *The Danish War: Non-Intervention Meeting at Manchester* (1864). He also published numerous volumes of poetry in the decade between 1846 and 1857, and four novels: *The Wood-Spirit* (1841), *The Lass and the Lady; or, Love's Ladder* (1855), *The Maid of Warsaw, or the Tyrant Czar: A Tale of the Last Polish Insurrection* (1854), and *Woman's Wrongs: A Series of Tales* (1855). Significantly, the titles of his novels reveal his concern with the plight of women as well as of oppressed nationalities.

Two poems Jones published in 1847 in *The Labourer,* the journal he co-edited with Feargus O'Connor, appeal to a sublime nature reminiscent of Romanticism: "The Factory Town" and "A Song for May." In "The Factory

---

3. When George Julian Harney was editor of the Chartist newspaper *Northern Star* in 1845, he included in its columns various reports of international struggles. Reflecting later on that period and editorial policy, he wrote that "pains [were] taken to make the English democrat aware of the part that was being played by his brethren on the different stages of the political world" (Charlton, 56).

4. Violently pro-English nationalism surged during the Sepoy Rebellion, for example.

Town," "wild-winds" blow through a night both "bleak and cheerless," "cleaving clouds, and splitting seas" (lines 2–3, 86). A "solemn heaven" portends divine anger (line 81), and in the coming war between workers and masters, "God and Nature" are arrayed as mighty combatants on the side of labor (line 103). Though this is not the only version of nature presented in "The Factory Town," it is in these lines a formidable, frightening, powerful force that should be feared and invoked. By contrast, "A Song for May" presents a different, but no less Romantic, version of nature, one that is integrally connected to humanity, in fact setting the example to which people should aspire. Earth here is "kindly," "generous," and "like a mother" nursing its young (lines 29–31), and it summons the "hearts of men" to cast off their cold slavery and become "worthy of [their] God" by cultivating the "fruit of Freedom's hour" (lines 11–12, 20). This is nature as instructor and nurturer of humankind, and its aggressive movement from "slavish" winter to "gallant" spring (it "dashes," "bursts," "teems," and "clasps") is intended to inaugurate and mirror laborers' shedding the shackles of exploitation. The "correspondent breeze" inevitably comes to mind.

The Dialectic of the Self and the Social: "A Song for May" (1847)

In addition to its Romantic depiction of nature and its idealization of rural scenes of "cottages more bright" with proud "fireside[s]," all situated in the "wood-embosomed village" (lines 63, 68, 71), "A Song for May" exploits the expressive potential of individuals in its scenes. The poem is worth some examination here because it effectively demonstrates the double perspective of public and private, which Jones so deftly exploits elsewhere for the purpose of fostering internationalism. Narrowing its focus from more general views of nature and harvest, "A Song for May" concentrates for a time on a particular cottage where, in "the hour of harvest— / Little mouths shall ask for bread" but receive none (lines 37–38). Instead, the produce of the agricultural laborer's effort goes "To the farmer's rich home-stead" (line 39), showing capitalism at work in an agrarian setting. Jones provides details of the worker's home which are full of pathos: "Dies away the children's laughter— / Hungry hearts are tame and still" (lines 41–42). These unnaturally subdued, lethargic children belong to one who "toil[s] on with brow of anguish, / From the cradle to [his/her] grave" (lines 49–50). Representative as they are, these figures nevertheless receive attention as one family, a particular person expending all of life's energy and joy in a struggle for subsistence, burdened with the knowledge of inability to feed these particular children, to make them laugh, to enliven and stimulate their minds and their hearts. In moving, as it were, from the macrocosmic sphere of nature to the microcosmic sphere of the home, Jones evinces a grasp of the criticisms made by his contemporary Elizabeth Barrett Browning, whose Aurora Leigh critiques too-generalized philanthropy by saying,

> I hold you will not compass your poor ends
> Of barley-feeding and material ease,
> Without a poet's individualism
> To work your universal. It takes a soul,
> To move a body: it takes a high-souled man,
> To move the masses . . . .
> (*Aurora Leigh*, bk. 2, lines 476–81)

In art as in life, one cannot deal only in universals and generalities, so Jones includes this moving family vignette in the middle of his poem to crystallize the themes which bracket it: nature itself calls on laboring humanity to assume its true dignity, to throw off its abject slavery to masters, kings, and priests, and to appropriate for itself the products of its labor. It is a class-based summons that relies partly on the poem's appeal to individual sympathies and self-recognitions.

In addition, throughout "A Song for May" the speaker directly addresses an unnamed "thee," demanding reflection as well as action. Just who the interpellated subject is seems to shift in the course of the poem from any thinking person to the specific struggling laborer described above to a plural "we the people" in the conclusion. Of note is the poem's repeated command to "thee" that s/he "*think!*" (line 8) The initial, italicized command ends the opening stanza and inaugurates reflection on spring's salutary example to humankind. Its double reiteration occurs just at the moment when the poem turns to the particularized example of the agrarian laborer, as if to stress that the case of a specific individual demands the special attention and contemplation of another individual: one calls to the other across the lines of this poem. While addressing and describing the impoverished agricultural toiler, the speaker dares that person to ventriloquize the empty formulas of patriotism and religion:

> Then, amid the desolation,
>   Stand—a helpless human thing;
>   Cry: 'We are a glorious nation!
>   Love the church! and serve the king!'
>   ("A Song for May," lines 45–48)

The absurdity of repeating those final clauses is thrown into relief by the preceding scene of spirit-numbing injustice done to the cottager's family, and by the pitiful portrait here of "a helpless human thing" simply standing—as if too shocked to do anything else—amid "desolation." That the individual has been alienated and dehumanized by exploitation is painfully clear in the designation of him or her as a human "thing" (line 46). In evoking the individual, the poem foregrounds precisely how personhood is submerged by capitalism, thus contributing to the poem's broad agitational impact.

Moreover, the hollow rhetoric of government propaganda ("'We are a glorious nation! / Love the church! and serve the king!'") represents an effort to erase individual circumstances and personal realities in favor of a transcendent national identity. The poem's forceful inclusion of poignant scenes from one family's cottage—that is, its insistence on the plight of individuals—resists that erasure and mandates that there be no contest between personal suffering and the veneer of membership in some glorious national identity. Jones thus undercuts nationalism through his emphasis on individualism, thereby opening the door to internationalism. Once one rejects a false national identity of prosperity, security, and superiority based on the chasm between that image and lived personal experience, one can begin to recognize a common interest with other people who share that experience, regardless of nationhood. Though the final stage of this process is not explicit in this particular poem, this is how internationalism is born, and its midwife is individualism.

Interestingly, though, Jones calls this poem a "Song" for May. Of course a song is a popular style of lyric which, whether set to music or not, implies public use and group consumption rather than private reading by a closeted, solitary being. And undoubtedly this song's publication in a monthly journal signaled that its audience was broadly conceived. Other norms of this subgenre include a relative brevity of composition, simplicity and directness of content, and strength and clarity of rhythm. Though a total length of 84 lines probably makes this poem too long to be sung, Jones's subject and descriptions (the new life of spring, abundance of harvest, suffering of workers, and calls to emulate nature) are suitably conventional for song, as is his use of the familiar stanza form of quatrains. Also appropriate to song is his choice of rhyme scheme: the poem opens and closes with four pairs of couplets, and its quatrains very often comprise *abab* end rhymes, convenient devices which aid memory and singing (no tune or music is specified, however). Its emphasis on summoning others to action also colors the poem as an outward-oriented, interventionist one designed not simply for personal education and private reflection. Its direction at a community *as* a community is commensurate with song.

"A Song for May" is nevertheless not especially easy to classify. It certainly is songlike in the ways previously mentioned, and given the title's self-designation as a song and its openly agitational intent this is important. But there are features of its form that make the poem complex and serve to illustrate the dialectical paradigm, which I contend is so crucial to Jones's internationalism. For example, the first and last stanzas stand out from the rest of the poem by virtue of being octaves rather than quatrains, something not likely to be detected except visually, by reading. The opening octave sets the scene and prepares, by directly addressing, the thinking person to think; the closing octave seeks to rouse people to action through its crescendo of commands to "rise," "wield" the arms of courage and hope, and "strive" to win social change (lines 77–84). The octaves also slightly deviate from the norm of the quatrains in their metrical pattern: the entire poem is trochaic, but in the octaves, all eight lines are catalectic (missing the final, unstressed syllable). Only the second and fourth lines of each quatrain are catalectic, with lines one and three having their full complement of four trochees. Again this might be slightly easier to perceive and track visually than aurally. Traditionally, poets use catalexis to maintain the serious tone of a poem and keep it from sounding like light verse. This might explain not only its alternating use in the quatrains but also its dominant use in the arresting first and final octaves. The use of catalexis here might suggest that, though this is a song of spring, the song carries a heavier burden than that lyrical form usually does. Jones's metrical choices mute the celebratory feel of song and of May, reminding readers to ponder the human bondage of relentless, unrewarding toil.

Jones's choice of the trochee as the basic foot for his song is somewhat startling because in English verse, trochaic feet occur most often as substitutions in prevailingly iambic lines; they are unusual as the basic metrical pattern of a poem. For this "song," one might expect a rising rhythm to match the uplifting feel of the arrival of spring, when "Lighter beats each human heart" (line 2). But the trochee is a falling foot with a more somber, if insistent, tone. Perhaps that is one reason that, on those infrequent occasions when poets do use a trochaic rhythm as the basis of a poem, they almost always use it catalectically, so that the line ends on an upbeat rather than with the unstressed feminine ending. Jones, though, rigorously includes the final beat in every other line of "A Song for May," an alternation most easily perceived when the poem is read rather than heard. Indeed, much of the metrical and stanzaic variation, and its contribution to the maintenance of a serious tone, can best be seen and seems intended for the eye as much as for the ear. Jones makes full use of his print medium, which, though by no means exclusively a private one, is predominantly a medium of the solitary individual.

The stanza variations visible chiefly to the eye, the serious tone contradicting the feel of spring and of song, the alternation of complete and catalectic trochaic lines, and the surprising choice of basic metrical foot for a work bearing the appellation of "song," all create some tension in this poem over its status as public or private. Is it a song, intended for a communal audience and aimed squarely at intervention in public affairs? Or is it a sober, metrically complex lyric best appreciated by the private reader examining its graphic, printed incarnation? Or could it be both? Its form, like its topic, straddles a position in between communal and individual. Perhaps the form of the poem follows a rationale somewhat similar to that of its theme: it makes use of and orders its material in ways that presuppose the private reading of a printed work but does not permit itself to halt at the purely aesthetic and solitary, disarticulated from social engagement; rather it moves up and out from those materials to the creation of the sort of community and class solidarity often present in popular chants and songs. Though vital to the existence of the poem as well as the liberation of the individual, solitude serves solidarity.

This same dialectical paradigm is at work in Jones's poem "The March of Freedom" (1848), which blends popular and literary forms in an explicitly internationalist narrative. This work personifies Freedom, whose march through southern and northern Europe allows for a survey of various popular struggles against political tyranny, ending with an admonition to English workers to break the yoke of servitude and unite with their Irish counterparts against monopoly. The vision of Freedom as the moving force and inspiration for each of these struggles also unifies them through a common genesis, appropriate since unity is a major theme of the poem. Its length of fifty stanzas, along with its lines' being basically iambic trimeter (rather than alternating tetrameter and trimeter), in some measure disqualifies it from being a ballad, a distinctly popular genre. But its rhyme scheme, narrative progress, and quatrains suggest the common ballad form. The poem's orientation is also toward a broadly conceived populace: the speaker seeks to stir English imaginations and motivate cross-national unity "To fight in Freedom's wars" (line 156) and "To conquer or to fall" (line 28). This emphasis on agitation, unity, and action places the work firmly in the tradition of radical poetry and public oratory.

The tone is hopeful and inspiring as well as agitational, signifying its connection to a thriving movement with the aim of increasing its gathering momentum. This is not the poetry of decline or retreat, poetry aimed more at educating a private individual who lacks a viable public forum for action. Instead it takes for granted the existence and strength of such a forum and intervenes in the struggle by instilling courage and confidence in its participants. The poem's opening lines announce this assumption of vibrant community identity:

> The nations are all calling,
>   To and fro, from strand to strand;
> Uniting in one army
>   The slaves of every land.
>
> Lopsided thrones are creaking,
>   For "loyalty" is dead;
> [. . . . .]
>
> And coming Freedom whispers,
>   'Mid the rushing of her wings,
> Of loyalty to nature,
>   Not loyalty to kings.
>   ("The March of Freedom," lines 1–6, 9–12)

This is "one army" and it consists of one class of people: the "slaves" (toilers) of every nation. Members of this army have discarded traditional "loyalty" to thrones and their respective monarchies and nations in favor of a new collectivity: class. It is their common relationship to the means of production that defines this throne-threatening international camaraderie; their lack of ownership of anything but their labor power is what makes them "slaves" (not in the historic sense, of course, for under chattel slavery the slaves did not own even their labor power). This definition of self transcends national boundaries and, indeed, transcends the individual. Since most people do not have the power to choose their position *vis á vis* the necessities of survival, class can be said to be a customary identity, something over which one has little power, a position assigned to rather than selected by each person. Thus the poem at once lifts atomized Britons out of seclusion and thrusts them into a transpersonal selfhood.

On the other hand, those who share this community have replaced their erstwhile "loyalty to kings" with "loyalty to nature" (lines 11–12), a signal that, for all its communitarianism, the poem still relies on a Romantic conception of nature as the "correspondent breeze" of humankind. The poem's personified Freedom comes "from mountains" and is likened to "the avalanche" and "the thunder-cloud" (lines 33–36), suggesting that it is an element of nature, sublime in its overwhelming vastness and might. Under its influence, xenophobic bigotry is "swept as white as snow" (lines 39–40), and a "heart-quake" of the people precedes their deposing of a tyrant (line 89). Nature here cleanses the masses, preparing and enabling them to take power by breaking down the barriers of national prejudice. When they do rise, the stirrings of their collective heart resemble an earthquake with the power to crumble a tyrant's foundations and erect democracy instead. Finally, with the winning of the Charter, the people become "scythemen" who are urged "to the harvest!" There, the final line commands, "Reap! you who sowed the seed," an image indicative of the notion of personal responsibility and reward (lines 197–200). The intensity of the connection between nature and human beings recalls the tropes of Romanticism and its emphasis on the solitary person's imaginative engagement with nature.

The "scythemen" of the final stanza are, however, explicitly identified as hailing from Ireland and Scotland as well as England ("Shannon, Thames, and Tweed"), reminding readers of the urgency of international unity in taking the prescribed actions. One might be personally responsible for sowing and reaping, but s/he does so in an inescapably social context. A subtle transformation has occurred here in the conversion of a natural force from the primary actor and surveyor of the piece into that which is cultivated and harvested by British Chartists. Both images utilize nature, but the shift from nature as actor to nature as object hinges on the intervention of a person or people; in effect there are two versions of nature, linked by human agency. The poem includes not only individualism and nature but also action and international coalition.

The logic of the poem reveals that what permits the international coalition is disentangling oneself from the biases inherited along with national identity, opting instead for a new definition of self in terms of class: this "army" drawn from "every land" is an army of "slaves," unmistakably a class designation (lines 3–4). These soldiers share none of the contamination of "gold . . . coined with blood of childhood" or "bank notes . . . That 'justice' buy and sell," for they do not belong to the class whose "heritage [is] in hell" (lines 13–15, 17–20). The speaker goes to some lengths here to specify the class oppositions at work in the world and the poem. Jones thus adds an important layer to the politics of internationalism: it is not enough simply to embrace the self-fashioning of individualism and reject inherited nationality (an expatriate could, for example, simply substitute Turkish chauvinism for German and make no progress toward internationalism). He contends that recognition of membership in the body of "slaves," or exploited laborers, is the key to a principled internationalism that can mount an organized and effective opposition to political tyranny. At its most succinct, the formula of Jones's internationalism now reads: utilize personal volition to eschew inherited nationality, and instead embrace membership in the collective identity of the international working class.

Jones's Oratory and Journalism as a Microcosm of Chartist Poetics

Ernest Jones entered the Chartist movement during the latter half of its history, beginning in 1846, and though his internationalism in that year was already fully fledged, there is a discernible development in his notions of class polarization, agency, and strategy, a progression perhaps easiest to trace in his speeches and journalism. The pattern of Jones's change resembles a trend in Chartist poetry, which Mike Sanders has mapped and analyzed.[5] By examining the use of metonymy and metaphor in Chartist poems from the beginning to the end of the movement, Sanders demonstrates that "changes in poetic strategy are symptomatic of changes in political understanding" (Sanders, "Poetic Agency," 111). Early Chartist poems feature abstract goals (such as "liberty" and "justice") and no concrete agents who can effect their achievement, reflecting the limitations of early Chartism's political analysis: it had not yet appreciated the distinctiveness of its demands from traditional radicalism, or formulated a class analysis adequate to address the specific obstacles and opponents to its success, or identified the social force potentially capable of winning the Charter. Later poets' shift from the use of metonymy to metaphors of nature indicates a political alteration as well: now there is a clearer understanding of class opposition and an appeal to a force capable of greater things. However, though such metaphors offer more concrete instances of political activity, they pose some dangers insofar as they liken the movement to nature. If Chartism is a force of nature, either its victory is inevitable and that fact obviates the need for activism, or the impressive technical advances of the bourgeoisie over natural forces would render Chartism just another phenomenon to be subdued. Thus the metaphors must—and do in late Chartist poetry—shift away from more passive images of inevitable processes (winter giving way to spring) to ones of overwhelming and catastrophic power (fires, earthquakes, volcanoes). These forces cannot be subdued, but the emphasis on destruction of the existing order suggests a new problem for Chartist political strategy. Sanders sees the menacing tone of such metaphors as symptomatic of "frustration at the absence of any concrete agency capable

5. See "Poetic Agency: Metonymy and Metaphor in Chartist Poetry, 1838–1852," *Victorian Poetry* 39:2 (2001): 111–35.

of performing the task" (ibid., 119). The class polarization is clearer; the necessity of replacing the existing social order seems clearer; but after 1848 the mass organization of the working class has dissipated, leaving Chartism without the necessary agents of change.

There is an alternative Chartist poetic that develops alongside the ones already outlined. According to Sanders, this tradition avoids rhetorical abstractions and defines the movement in terms of class polarities, as well as emphasizing the agency of the working class. This poetic thus gives expression to the clearest political insights and strategies of Chartism. Interestingly, for Sanders the exemplar of this most sophisticated strain of poetics and politics is Ernest Jones's "The Song of the Low" (1852). Yet on the evidence of his speeches and newspaper articles, from 1846 through the 1850s, Jones himself underwent a learning curve that approximates that of the Chartist movement as a whole, only his curve was steeper and benefitted from the prior history of the Chartist movement and its poetry.

From the very beginning of his involvement with Chartism, Jones showed himself a capable orator and journalist as well as a poet. Some of his finest and sharpest statements urging internationalism occur in these writings, but even here it is possible to perceive a marked development in the clarity of his thought. His experiences inside a vibrant activist movement of working people taught him many of the same political lessons that find expression in the poetry Sanders has examined, even though he came on the scene later. From 1846 to 1848, the new convert to Chartism advocates internationalism in clear and convincing terms, but the rhetoric of his writing includes a greater number of abstractions about the agents and strategies for change. For example, in his speech to the French Democratic Society published in the *Northern Star* in 1846 ("The Fraternity of Nations"), Jones vigorously opposes the "battles of tyranny" kings have waged with the blood of "the people" and predicts that with the growth of international solidarity "we" will no longer take up arms in their causes (Jones, "Fraternity," 87). However, the imagery he uses in his vision of progress is largely abstract and metonymic: "Can [tyrants] stop the progress of enlightenment? Arrest the invisible mind? or place barriers across the road before the march of intellect?" (ibid.). The "democrats" of all nations are represented here only by the mind, and it is an "invisible" one at that! This fragment of the people, plus the abstraction of "enlightenment," are to carry forward the unity of nations. There is little sense of just who the "apostles of liberty" thus represented are or what they have in common to help them overcome national biases in their effort to destroy "despotism" (ibid., 88).

Jones's use of religious language ("apostles of liberty") in that speech is echoed in his address to the German Democratic Society for the Education of the Working Classes in 1847. Here he blames "kingcraft" and national "prejudices" for such "shame[s] of humanity" as Waterloo ("Speech" 92), calling for a "fair distribution of earth's wealth for all" (ibid., 93). Then he poses the sharp and critical question of "what power we possess of obtaining" that goal of global sharing (ibid.). However, the speech actually offers very little answer to that excellent question, turning instead to religious language he clearly intended as an encouragement to the zeal of his listeners: "you take with you a sacred mission, you are the apostles of the holiest religion, the religion of humanity; become the prophets of a millenium [sic]—the millenium of liberty" (ibid.). This group of standard-bearers he urges to remain in readiness to march at the sound of some unspecified "trumpets of liberty," another image whose lack of concreteness indicates that Jones, like most of the early Chartist poets, did not enter activism with a fully formed, clear analysis of political goals and forces, or with their later awareness of how important was the defining of specific goals in agitational work.

Yet in 1848 this son of an army officer published an open letter criticizing the class nature and abuses of the British military. "Soldier and Citizen. To the Oppressed of Either Class" reveals a much clearer class consciousness than the earlier speeches, indicting the class interest of government and arguing that economic deprivation forces large numbers of working men to enlist in the "voluntary" army. That "economic draft" makes the working class the majority of those who suffer and die in Britain's imperialist wars and gives working people a vital interest in avoiding those wars and in reforming the military. Jones's language and proposals in this letter are notably more concrete than in earlier speeches. His contentions that "The essence of class-government is exclusiveness" and that his readers must "show to all sections of the community, how their just interests are identical with those of the working classes" show a movement towards a sharper sense of class polarization and working-class agency ("Soldier," 99–100). Other reformists must tie their fortunes to those of the working class, and not the other way around.

Just months after publishing that letter in the *Northern Star*, Jones was arrested and imprisoned for a period of two years, during which his journalism and speechmaking necessarily halted. However, he resumed those and his other literary tasks upon his release in 1850, and the tenor of his 1850s writings differs from the works of his first years as a Chartist. Britain's 1854 war in the Crimea provided a new arena for concrete criticism and a class analysis of wars and militaries. Jones's belief that the allegiance of ordinary people in all countries should be to each other and not to their respective rulers is crystal clear. In a famous speech on internationalism, he declared that "the nation I belong to is [. . .] the nation of the oppressed. I acknowl-

edge but two nationalities in existence [. . .]: the rich and the poor—and in
the latter I am a soldier" ("On Internationalism," 215). The language of these
formulations reveals a well-defined sense of class antagonism—the existence
of an "oppressed" implies an oppressor, and "soldiers" are required only in
sharp conflict—and it communicates an assumption of the power to redefine
nationhood in terms of one's role in production rather than situation within
arbitrary geographical boundaries.

The thoroughly radical potential of defining nationality through class
rather than geography is evident in an editorial on the Crimean War published in Jones's *People's Paper* in 1854.[6] Recognizing that the interests of
the princes and rulers of Europe (including Britain), despite their having
"declared" war on Russia, do not seriously diverge from the Czar's except
insofar as they clash over mutually coveted spoils, the article suggests that
the war's real political divisions are between rulers and ruled, not nation-
state and nation-state. In fact, he asks rhetorically whether "the Allies" (Britain and France) "represent anything different" from the "despotism" of Czar
Nicholas and the rulers of the German powers ("The German Powers," 213).
And interestingly, the question is formulated even more precisely than the
names of countries would imply: it is their rulers he names (Aberdeen, Louis
Bonaparte, Franz Joseph, Frederick Wilhelm), and each one's crimes he enumerates, stressing that the people are distinct from their leaders. In order for
the war to stop the spread of Russian tyranny and reaction as Jones wished, it
would have to be a class war waged by the oppressed against their oppressors,
regardless of citizenship or any false national loyalties. Perhaps England and
France will wage such a principled war against oppression, "but not the England of Aberdeen—not the France of Louis Bonaparte. A serious war against
Russia would be a war of principles—a war of revolution—*a war that is only
possible after the overthrow of the French and English governments . . .*" (ibid.,
214, emphasis added). Far from being a shrill cry for the destruction of Russia
as somehow incurably and inherently marauding or evil, this editorial calls
for the overthrow of Britain's own expansionist and oppressive leaders on the
way to stopping Russian imperialism. Jones reasons that rulers who share the
same class interests with their national "enemies" cannot wage a genuine war
against the economic interests that drive their repressive domestic policies
and groping foreign policies, since at bottom they are indistinct from their
own. As a result, neither can they destroy the basis of international conflict,

---

6. John Saville wrote of this editorial that its authorship is not certainly Jones's, though
it does represent Jones's views expressed in many similar writings about the Crimean War and
it might be his writing. Saville also noted that the views articulated in this piece accord with
those of many groups within the working class at the time (*Ernest Jones: Chartist*, 213).

no matter what their rhetoric about democracy, freedom, and the like. The termination of wars abroad and injustices at home will, according to this article, require the overthrow of capitalism and the ruling class it creates. The real "allies" are the oppressed of Russia, France, Britain, and all other nations, and their enemies are their own heads of state. The Crimean War thus occasioned a demonstration of the highest level of class consciousness and internationalism that Chartism ever achieved.

Britain's disastrous handling of the Crimean War prompted many domestic criticisms and attacks, including one by Jones in 1855, which focused on "Britain's Duty to Her Soldiers." Here he reaffirms his class analysis of the military, contending that "War, though made by the rich, and for the rich, falls in its entire burden on the poor" because it is they who supply the soldiers as well as the money necessary for its prosecution ("Britain's Duty," 177). Jones here calls for a "Soldier's Charter" and enumerates both six grievances and six demands for their remedy. He urges working people to agitate for a petition on behalf of the soldiers, and he is specific in his recommendations about the formation of committees, the drafting of petitions, publicity for the meetings, slogans, and the class leadership of the proposed movement (ibid., 180). Not only has Jones's grasp of class antagonism and power significantly matured since the mid-1840s when he joined the Chartists, but his rhetoric and recommendations have grown dramatically more concrete. Since the soldiers are from the laboring class, laborers must also lead the movement on their behalf, though all who agree with their program may lend their aid. He says there is "one additional advice I would emphatically give you: *keep the movement in the hands of the working classes* . . . soldiers are working men, and therefore working men have a right to look after the interests of soldiers" (ibid., emphasis his). Jones not only outlines a clear, tangible program but also leaves no room for doubt about who the agents of change are and must be. His notions of social conflict and change, as articulated in his nonfiction prose writings, thus follow a similar, if later, trajectory to that along which many other Chartist writers moved.

The Maid of Warsaw (1847–48, 1854)

Jones also wrote a novel that directs reader attention to the international dimensions of revolution and the importance of maintaining ties between workers in all countries. *The Maid of Warsaw* has an interesting and complex publication history, but it is important to note that it began (and almost completed) publication in the pages of the monthly journal *The Labourer* in

1847–48. Its title at that time was *The Romance of a People. An Historical Tale, of the Nineteenth Century*. Fictionally recounting the events of the Polish revolution against Russia in 1830–31, the serialized novel simply breaks off after the successful insurrection in suburbs near Warsaw, even though the journal continued publication for some months afterward and the last instalment of the tale promises that it is "To be continued" (Jones, *Romance*, III: 183). Possibly the disruption occurred because Jones was arrested on June 6, 1848, and was detained in prison—with limited writing privileges—for two years thereafter.[7] He did eventually complete the novel and bring it out in book form, but this was not until four years after his release from prison, timing its completed publication to coincide with the Crimean War of 1854.

It would have been timely in 1854 as a contribution to the working class's long tradition of opposition to the Russian Czar as the most reactionary and the most formidable enemy of "progress and democracy throughout Europe" (Morton, *A People's History of England*, 410). The Russian Czar sought to capitalize on his country's new, unrivaled power in Central Europe by extending its domination into the weakening Turkish Empire. To stop this and to protect its own imperialist interests in India and the Eastern Mediterranean, Britain (with France) waged the Crimean War against Russia. The British populace bitterly opposed the march of the Czar and would have welcomed a novel such as *The Maid of Warsaw*—but not so much because they cared about maintaining British merchants' hold on foreign ports and markets. Rather, the memory of Russia's destruction of revolutionary movements like those in Hungary and Poland was fresh in their minds.[8] It was this prodemocracy sentiment on behalf of all of Europe that such a novel was suited for tapping into. Its publication should not be mistaken, therefore, as simple anti-Russian propaganda or as support for the British government's policy in the war. Jones was a thoroughgoing internationalist who supported the oppressed people of every nation, including Russia.

It is important to talk about Jones's internationalism, particularly as it finds expression in *The Maid of Warsaw*, where it forms an indispensable plank in revolutionary strategy. While the oppressed of Poland fought to overthrow Russian domination, advancing the cause of "European liberty, what did Europe for Poland?" the narrator asks (Jones, *Maid*, 59). The answer showcases some of the novel's fiercest—and most witty—sarcasm. Liberals in England and France formed committees, gave fancy balls, attended Polish ballets,

---

7. Miles Taylor contends that, contrary to Jones's own dramatic accounts of writing under duress while in prison, he did indeed have access to pen and paper at certain periods of his incarceration. See *Ernest Jones*, 133–36.

8. See Morton, *A People's History of England*, 409–412.

wore Polish fashions, ate Polish foods, and draped over cabaret doors banners ablaze with exciting slogans—what more could be asked of them? "But they actually did even more than this!" the narrator excitedly and sarcastically declares. "A secretary of state told an under-secretary who told a private secretary to tell a secretary of a Polish Association, to inform the Polish envoy, that, if Poland really rose, and if it maintained a suitable policy, and formed a suitable government, the English people would, in that case, act towards Poland in a suitable manner" (ibid., 61). Those accustomed to "bureaucratese" will appreciate the painfully familiar joke.

Jones does more in this novel than scoff at the empty gestures and insincere rhetoric of the European elite, though; he analyzes the basis of French and British rulers' resistance in the 1830s to aiding Poland in meaningful ways. It is important to note that the novel distinguishes between the perspectives of the prosperous minority and the laboring majority of those nations. One of the novel's protagonists, the Palatine, writes a letter in which he explains that "the feeling of either people [French and British] is strongly with us . . . [b]ut their governments will not stir" because they fear their own populations. The rulers assume that revolution is contagious and that a successful Polish revolution would inspire the ordinary people of France and Britain to rise up against their own undemocratic governments (ibid., 63). The narrator explains that, though perfectly willing to interfere in "the internal polity of weak states" (ibid., 60), Britain and France refuse to meddle in that of the strong mainly for two reasons: (1) like Russia, they dominate other peoples (such as India and Ireland) through their own imperialism and wish neither to have their hypocrisy exposed nor to abridge their power to "tyrannise" (ibid., 61), and (2) like Poland's feudal lords, the bourgeoisies of France and England might support an uprising that rids a country of foreign competitors for economic dominance, but will scramble to suppress a movement that surpasses nationalist ends and "contemplate[s] the emancipation of the servile class" (ibid., 20).

In *The Maid of Warsaw*, the Palatine and the son of Count Tyssen differ from their fellow aristocrats precisely because they recognize that it is not enough simply to rid Poland of the Russian troops which enforce the right of plunder of Russia's wealthy. That would merely re-establish the right of plunder of Poland's elite, leaving the serfs in the same exploited and unequal positions they occupied under the Russians. Just moments before he dies, Tyssen makes an impassioned plea to his fellow revolutionaries to "give freedom and equal rights to all: array the great body of the people for their country, not for *yourselves;* let them be freemen before they are soldiers, and there is a chance of victory" (ibid., 78, emphasis in original). This pushing the fight for national independence to its logical conclusion in social equality is exactly what governments in Britain and France fear from their own "servile class." Support the Polish peasants in their battle against the Russians, and you might later find yourself in the embarrassing position of having to withdraw that support from an emboldened population challenging the right to rule of oligarchies and monarchies.

The novel presents their fear as not unfounded. In a letter to a friend, the Palatine urges Polish insurrection because "France will rise . . . the people of England will . . . overturn an oligarchy; the German will reject a despotism; the Hungarian, the Italian, and the Sclave, a conqueror; and Spain, an inquisition and a Jesuit" (ibid., 63). It is clear that Polish revolutionaries expected popular, democratic uprisings to spread to other European countries, and though the narrator informs us that the various movements and revolts were mostly defeated, there is hope for the future because "the people of the earth had for once spoken to each other in the same great language" (ibid., 64). This "same great language" is perhaps best clarified in the famous speech Jones made the same year he published *The Maid of Warsaw* and quoted above: "My country is the world [. . .] The language I speak, the men of every country understand [. . .] It is the language of liberty" ("On Internationalism," 215). More specifically, it is the language of internationalism, of alliances between the working people of all countries regardless, or even in defiance of alliances made by their rulers.

Less fully articulated in the novel are two fascinating references to alliances between the people of Poland and of Russia. Such sympathies between the citizens even of warring countries should not be overlooked, though, especially given this novel's publication during the Crimean War. Moreover, their presence in the novel constitutes internal evidence to corroborate Jones's careful distinction between the people of Russia and the hated Czar, as evidenced by his speeches and journalism. Early in the novel the narrator mentions the failed Russian insurrection under Pestel and Ryleyeff which aimed to free Russia and all of the countries under its domination, making possible the establishment of "one vast, free, northern republic of independent states" (Jones, *Maid*, 26). Significantly, the planned revolution involved a conspiracy between Russians and Poles: "Secret meetings were appointed and held, and an invisible thread spun between the betrayed of Poland and the oppressed of Russia" (ibid.). It would seem that the Polish insurrection that forms the subject of this novel actually grew out of that international connection and conspiracy. The other indication of sympathies between ordinary Russians and Poles comes late in the novel, during one of the decisive battles between their respective armies. The Polish revolutionaries march out to meet the forces serving the Russian Czar, hoisting aloft banners that read "*For our liberty and yours*" (ibid, 84). It is an expression of solidarity highly complicated by circumstances, but it remains an important statement of workers' internationalism nevertheless.

When Jones began publishing this novel serially in 1847–48, he did so under the title *The Romance of a People. An Historical Tale, of the Nineteenth Century.* Some explanation for this choice comes roughly mid-way through the novel when the narrator comments on the successful insurrection in Warsaw: "The time for the second romance of our century had arrived—the romance of a *people,* as Napoleon's had been that of a *man*" (*Romance,* I: 81). Jones wants to use the romantic mode and capture as wide an audience as that term's implications of high adventure, formidable quests, and unlikely triumphs can do. Yet he transmogrifies the hero of the adventures and victories from an exalted individual to a collective of semi-enslaved people: the serfs of Poland. Already the writer exploits a generic label while adapting the material it describes to more nearly approximate his own proletarian commitments. But by the time he completed and reissued the novel in 1854, domestic and world politics had changed, so Jones exercised further authorial prerogative by dropping the romantic reference and altering the title to *The Maid of Warsaw; or, the Tyrant Czar. A Tale of the Last Polish Revolution.* The references to Poland, Warsaw, and the "Tyrant Czar" signify his intention to relate the novel to the contemporary Crimean War and to secure readers on the basis of their opposition to the Russian bastion of reaction. This title is much more specific than the original one, specifying the original "people" now as "Polish" people, and narrowing the temporal reference from a rather shaggy "nineteenth century" to the more vividly memorable "last Polish revolution," just a couple of decades ago and well within the lifetimes of many of his potential audience. As evident in his aesthetic choices discussed above, Jones thus shows a decided turn towards greater specificity and concreteness.

Interestingly, this was not the only modification he made to his novel. Very near the place in the narrative where he reveals the reasoning for his original choice of title, Jones deletes a paragraph of dialogue in the 1854 version. In a letter to a friend describing the international balance of forces in the wake of Poland's insurrection, the Palatine originally says, "Centuries may have passed in slavery, and nations may appear to be dissolved under the inscrutable dispensations of Providence; but nothing wholly perishes; the march of creation is progressive, and what does not perish must *improve.* Thus *kingdoms* may fall, but *nations* never die, and thus our nationality survives our throne" (ibid., I:81–82, emphasis in original). This paragraph, which appears intended to encourage revolutionaries despite a feeling of isolation on the international stage, disappears from the later edition of the novel. One can only speculate about the reasons for the deletion, but it is tempting to view the artistic revision as an effort to downplay any nationalist sensibilities in revolutionary characters. Instead a maturer Jones might prefer cohesion and identity based more firmly on class (an internationally transcendent category) than on some notion of inherent national character. Generally speaking, this pair of modifications Jones made (the title change and the paragraph deletion) demonstrates how informative it can be to study the revisions of aesthetic texts. More particularly, they reveal how larger and smaller artistic changes can alert readers to political content.

Though his principled internationalism is a dominant motif in all of Jones's writing, what guided the selection of his diction, metaphors, and metonyms were his political convictions and his assessment of the status of the Chartist movement at the time of writing. These formal details are the subtle but unmistakable registers of the nuances of his social outlook. One might even say that his later tendency toward the genres of fiction and analytical prose resulted from his perception of the political scene. Indeed his protean generic adaptability says something about his political suppleness as well as his literary skill. His class-conscious revolutionary politics were near-unique in the context of Victorian literature and his recasting of the novel and the epic poem (discussed in chapter 2) for revolutionary and utopian ends extended Victorian uses of these genres, anticipating twentieth-century anti-imperialist fiction.

· 2 ·

Epic Agency

For all the corrective texturing of our apprehension of Romanticism and later nineteenth-century poetry that it performs, Janowitz's influential *Lyric and Labour in the Romantic Tradition* has also had the effect of reinforcing the longstanding, prevalent belief that the chief poetic ancestor of Victorian working-class writers was Romanticism.[1] The belief has substance and utility, not least because it places self-taught writers within the same literary heritage and sphere of influence as their canonical contemporaries, encouraging readers now to regard working-class poetry not as a thing apart from but as a fellow participant in the same broader cultural life as Tennyson and the Brownings in the early years of Victoria's reign.[2] Nevertheless, the aesthetic genealogy of such writers as the Chartists is more varied—ideologically, formally, and chronologically—than such critical commonplaces would suggest. This chapter will demonstrate that claim in order to show how Chartist poetry's wide-ranging intellectual and artistic eclecticism played a role in the movement's democratic and increasingly multifarious range of economic, social, and political demands.[3]

---

1. For an example of such belief, see Vicinus's *Industrial Muse,* which especially emphasizes Byron and Shelley in its discussion of Chartist literature.

2. Stephanie Kuduk Weiner contends for the benefit of seeing such continuities among Romantic and Victorian, elite and popular poetry, within the English Republican tradition in her Introduction to *Republican Politics and English Poetry, 1789–1874* (Houndmills: Palgrave Macmillan, 2005).

3. In a characteristically vivid metaphor, Herbert Tucker describes how "the meal that epic made of pastoral, georgic, ode, ballad, soliloquy, oratory, epistle, *et cetera* was a standing

More specifically, three Chartist epics—Linton's *Bob Thin,* Cooper's *Purgatory of Suicides,* and Jones's *New World*—engaged with Renaissance and eighteenth-century precedents, contemporary religious and architectural strains, medieval grotesque, and satiric and pastoral conventions, as well as the epic tradition itself, and in their effort to articulate political critiques and demands, they simultaneously exhibited their potential to effect qualitative changes in the Chartist movement itself. Like the rest of the book, this chapter argues for the political agency of aesthetic choices, in this case through Chartist epic's handling of the diverse topics of Poor Law reform, insidious religious practices, and the necessity for internationalism. Yet my analysis is not limited to the *what* of these directly political topics; it also includes the *how* of their handling and the possible cognitive and organizational impacts of using the condensed, historically hypertextual medium of epic poetry.

As distinct from the sort of utilitarian language leveled at them in workplaces, shops, and courts of law, aesthetic language made beauty or pleasure or emotional engagement part of lived experience for its readers. In this way it stood opposed to the "Gradgrind school" of bare, unadorned, strictly functional interaction with the world enjoined on laborers through laissez-faire philosophy and political economy. Using poetic language, then, constituted a form of resistance to merely skeletal existence on a survivalist plane. More than that, literature coaxed people out of or beyond the world as they knew it (by becoming the "I" who tours Purgatory in Cooper's poem, for example, or by ranging over the globe—and especially India—to witness political events there, in Jones's). Cultivating such imaginative reach potentially enabled a similar operation at home, for if (in these poems) it is possible to conceive of such radically foreign locales and practices and systems of thought, it might also be possible to imagine one's own city or country (retrospectively or prospectively) as other than what it currently is. The disjuncture potentiates the cognitive dissonance that drives action to resolve the mismatch. The aesthetic encounter generates a cognitive flexibility that—while its tendency or outcomes are not predictable—makes possible the political.[4] This is the Chartist imaginary at work.

All three of these writers garner discussion elsewhere in this book, but it is arguably here in these poems that they are writing at the top of their abilities, revising the epic tradition in complex ways that have (Linton excepted)

---

narratological demonstration of its definitive roominess—a generic amplitude [. . .]" (*Epic,* 18).

4. With some differences, Christopher Caudwell ("plasticity" of consciousness), Isobel Armstrong ("mediation" as an activity of thought and feeling), and Mike Sanders ("psychic structuring" and "the Chartist imaginary"), among others, have described this effect of the aesthetic for qualitative transformation. I also discuss this quality in the Introduction.

invited a range of sophisticated and theoretically informed interpretations, noted below. What the following argument adds to the conversation—beyond its constellating the standard choices of the *Purgatory* and *New World* with the underanalyzed *Bob Thin*—is a detailed consideration of how their formal properties perform a sweeping cultural literacy in a politically enabling manner.

Grotesque Epic: Linton's *Bob Thin* (1845)

Few have been the references to, much less discussions of, William James Linton's epic poem *Bob Thin, or the Poorhouse Fugitive* (1845). The poem's bouncy tone, together with its composition in what Linton himself calls "doggrel rhyme" (2), would seem to mark its ambitions as decidedly modest rather than epic. However, the long historical view of its narrative and the coupling of one man's fate to the whole previous trajectory of British economic and social development reveal its larger aims. Additionally, if "genre-absorption" was a key means by which to attain "epic aggrandizement" (Tucker, *Epic*, 17), Linton here at least nominally attempted it, denominating *Bob Thin* in his parodically descriptive subtitle "A Political—Philosophical—Historical—Biographical—Anecdotal—Allegorical—Parenthetical—Pathetical—Prophetical—Poetical—Logical—Metrical—And Moral New Poor-Law Tale" (3). The poem bears resemblance to Byronic mock-epic (Tucker, *Epic*, 223), since it not only flouts epic's generic norms but also unfavorably compares modern practices with some of the norms and values the epic tradition itself valorized.

As its title suggests, Linton's grand historic survey carries a sustained attack on the Poor Laws, particularly as amended in 1834 when "outdoor" relief was abolished and new strictures and humiliations imposed in an effort to render workhouses as repellent as possible. The opening sections of this 40-page work survey the treatment of the economically distressed from feudal times through Elizabethan Poor Laws and up to the Poor Law Amendment Act of 1834. Then the jocular narrator introduces to us Bob Thin, a very un-Malthusian weaver whose tireless industry nevertheless enables him to support his many children. When the demand for weaving slumps, though, Bob and his family must resort to the workhouse. In accordance with the new regulations, they are obliged to travel to his birth-parish to do so—despite its being far from London, where he might actually be able to get work when demand resumes—and there the family is split up, badly fed, and hastened toward death through depression and neglect. After some years, Bob "escapes" the workhouse (probably through death) and enters an idyllic future world where he is treated as an equal and attends a festival commemorating humanity's "deliverance" from trade, selfishness, economic insecurity, and useless work (Linton, *Bob Thin*, 36).

Though this latter section of *Bob Thin* has its place as being the site of an imaginative effort to create a postrevolutionary world towards which Chartist activists might strive, its celebration of vague utopian concepts and its extended descriptions of pastoral delights pale considerably in comparison with the earlier section of the poem. However, its allusion to the long tradition of pastoral in English poetry serves to highlight the degraded conditions in which the modern poor subsist.[5] The contrast serves an obvious purpose by reminding readers that current conditions are historically contingent and therefore susceptible to change, if people change them. More subtly, the utopian scene's invitation to readers to imagine a world that is other than the one they currently inhabit can effect a change in consciousness, an apprehension of the world as becoming or in process. Such an invitation represents an appeal to the creative, generative inclinations that Marx and others have identified as integral to humanity's "species being."[6] To that extent the aesthetic object—in this case the poem—accesses something fundamentally human and humanizing, both recognizing and conferring the imaginative and agential qualities essential to those wanting to make social change. The poem does not itself make the social change but could be said to make the person who makes the change.[7] Despite the diminution of intrinsic interest in this latter portion of the poem, in its day the work "became part of the repertoire of radical reciters," according to Linton's biographer (Smith, *Radical Artisan, William James Linton*, 64).

The most immediately striking feature of the pamphlet edition of *Bob Thin* is its copious illustration with woodblock engravings executed by Linton, T. Sibson, W. B. Scott, and E. Duncan. A number of the illustrated capital letters beginning each stanza of *Bob Thin* also appeared in Linton's later books of

---

5. Pamela K. Gilbert provides a more comprehensive discussion of the juxtaposition of different historical times and spaces in the utopian, epic, and religious discourses at work in Jones's and Cooper's poems discussed in this chapter, but her analysis would apply as well to Linton's *Bob Thin*. See "History and Its Ends in Chartist Epic," *Victorian Literature and Culture* 37 (2009): 27–42.

6. See for example Christopher Caudwell's *Illusion and Reality* (London: Lawrence & Wishart, 1973 [1937]); Isobel Armstrong's *The Radical Aesthetic* (Oxford: Blackwell, 2000); J. Ranciere's *The Politics of Aesthetics* (London: Continuum, 2004); Mike Sanders's *The Poetry of Chartism* (Cambridge: Cambridge University Press, 2009).

7. For better or worse. As Ranciere and Sanders have pointed out, the change made by a changed consciousness can be either reactionary or progressive.

Figure 1. The Letter W.
(Harry Ransom Center. The
University of Texas at Austin.)

illustrated alphabets for children (sometimes accompanied by strongly acerbic political verse), books to whose making Linton often turned for a fairly
reliable source of income. These sinuous capitals—reaching backwards to
Blake and forwards to Aubrey Beardsley and Walter Crane—provide a run-
ning commentary on the text and are integral to its total vision and meaning. In addition they highlight Linton's desire to appeal to a popular audience
comprising the full spectrum of literacy, from those who would recognize
the eighteenth-century precedent for his mostly iambic tetrameter couplets
to those whose literacy did not surpass a visual one derived from political
and union banners, broadsides, the theater, and illustrated copies of the Bible
or Bunyan. This broad democratic appeal signals the inclusive scope of its
imagined readers, who cohere into a single political movement; in that respect
the poem—its form and its illustrated presentation—serves to unite people
around a shared complaint that suffrage would give them the collective power
to change.

The image in Figure 1, for example, physically unites the "extra-reverend
thicker- / Bodied and crowned bench of pastors, / Who, cheek by jowl with
our lay-masters, / Make Poor-laws for us working folk" (Linton, *Bob Thin*, 7),
thus literalizing the poet's phrasing and powerfully conveying the mutually
constitutive symbiosis of clerical and legislative power. This representation
of the creepy relationship between a mitered ecclesiastic and a crowned law-
maker so blends the two figures that the robed, legless priest seems to rely on
the government figure for his lower limbs (i.e., agency), while the black-faced,
skeletal legislator sports hooves and possesses a sinister length of devilish tail.
The incestuous feel of this wedding, figured in the almost congenital conjunction of powers twinned in social effect as well as body, conveys visually what
Linton does verbally in his attack on the new Poor Laws. The poem doubles
its representational power by appealing not only to textual literacy but also to

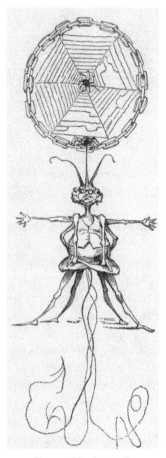

Figure 2. The Letter O.
(Harry Ransom Center. The
University of Texas at Austin.)

that visual and cultural literacy that properly reads the images of crown, miter, hooves, and pointed tail and the meaning of their ugly union.

Many of the poem's illustrations deploy the grotesque to disturbing, and politically suggestive, effect, as does the letter O in Figure 2, showing "the Solons of the nation" who "Out of their bag of legislation / (The bag o' the spider, not o' the bee) / Have spun a web, a twist of three, / Of such a monstrous complication— / [. . .] It threats the poor with worse starvation / Than when bluff Harry kick'd the monks out" (ibid.). Here the hybrid human/insect form united to winding vines produces a weird, flylike humanoid with three pairs of legs, multiple (four or five) sets of arms, antennae, and a webbed connection to the spider above that makes the figure seem to be of the arachnid's spinning. The figure also seems to be wearing glasses, though how that adds

to its freakishness might be lost on (or unappreciated by) modern bespectacled readers.

Linton's choice of grotesque figuration in this section of the poem seems
important, in part because of the illicit potential of the grotesque famously
described by Bakhtin. More recent critics have usefully revised and extended
his formulations beyond the rituals of carnival to their deep structures of vio-
lation of rigid conceptual oppositions such as between rulers and ruled. For
instance, the binary structure of transgression described by Stallybrass and
White is useful with respect to Linton, inasmuch as it concentrates on the
political power generated by the grotesque's incorporation of the oppositional
term whose exclusion is so necessary to bourgeois identity formation.[8] The
merger of high and low (whether art or class, etc.) at work in transgressive
cultural and aesthetic practices undermines the exclusionary "Othering" by
which a dominant ideology constructs itself, revealing the degree to which
bourgeois selfhood, for example, depends on the working class psychically
and symbolically as well as in literal economic terms (laborers confer status
as servants and as beneficiaries of middle-class charity, in addition to creating wealth). Implicitly acknowledging the frequent dismissal of workers as
subhuman or animal, Linton's grotesque turns the tables on the upper classes
by collapsing the distance between them and animals and insects.[9] In this
manner he problematizes one of the binary distinctions used to justify the
power and privilege of one class over against another. Linton's self-conscious
inclusion of grotesque figures amplifies the verbal satire of which it is, in a
literal orthographic sense, an essential part. The engravings elicit a visceral
repugnance that exceeds as well as comments on the poetic indictment of
ruling-class machinations for maintaining the clear division between themselves and the poor.

Before any twentieth-century critics, though, Ruskin too recognized the
satiric potential of the grotesque and particularly associated such uses with
class conflict when he wrote that "nothing is so refreshing to the vulgar mind
as some exercise of this [satiric] faculty, more especially on the failings of their
superiors; and that, wherever the lower orders are allowed to express themselves freely, we shall find humour, more or less caustic, becoming a principal feature in their work" (Rosenberg, *The Genius of John Ruskin,* 212). This

---

8. *The Politics and Poetics of Transgression* usefully revises the oversimplified celebration
of Bakhtinian carnival. For example, "If we treat the carnivalesque as an instance of a wider
phenomenon of transgression we move beyond Bakhtin's troublesome *folkloric* approach to
a political anthropology of *binary extremism* in class society" (Stallybrass and White, *The
Politics and Poetics of Transgression,* 26).

9. In this respect there is a species hierarchy inscribed in the grotesque, which potentially
undermines its liberatory capacity and complicates its use by an otherwise progressive movement. I am grateful to Jennifer McDonell for pointing this out to me.

strikes me as important for two reasons: in the first place, it points to how the satirical humor of Linton's grotesque illustrations and doggerel verse in some measure trivializes or deflates those large political topics of whose competent handling working people were supposed incapable. Linton models a collo- quial, familiar handling of civic concerns that would habituate his readers to their own fitness for addressing broad public questions. In the second place, Ruskin's remark shows that at least some of Linton's contemporaries recog- nized and even theorized the transgressive gesture latent in grotesque rep- resentations, however much the trends of their thinking might have tended toward different ends than Linton's (as the discussion of Ruskin later in this chapter shows). Of course Ruskin's treatment of the grotesque formed part of his famous analyses of painting and Gothic architecture, analyses which took as their model and ideal many medieval artistic principles and prac- tices.[10] That he had so much to say about the grotesque, then, resulted from his broader celebration of the medieval period, a characteristic feature of the mid-Victorian period to which I will return in a moment.

In Linton's grotesque image in Figure 2, whether the humanoid figure is one of the legislating "Solons" or one of the threatened "poor" is somewhat ambiguous, but rather than detracting from a transgressive reading, that uncertainty feeds it. I am inclined to see the figure as a Solon. The bizarre form invites irreverent laughter and provokes revulsion; it reduces high and mighty persons to bespectacled cousins of spiders; it shows the dealers in lofty abstractions to be intensely, even absurdly, corporeal. In this straightforward sense the grotesque image is parodic and subversive, but in conjunction with the verse with which the image necessarily interacts to produce meaning, the attack goes further. The narrator points out that these Solons operate from the "bag o' the spider, not o' the bee" (Linton, *Bob Thin*, 7), a distinction that high- lights the predatory, rather than industrious, activity they undertake, clearly subordinating them to the productive workers so often represented by the bee (and represented here by the skill bestowed on this poem by four work- ing craftsmen) and overturning neat distinctions between higher and lower orders of being. Moreover, the laws they create are "monstrous," a verbal echo of the hybrid figure that attracts and repels our gaze. Furthermore, one ironic couplet effectively consigns them to that lowest place of the low: hell ("Good meanings it is said pave hell: / There's not a doubt but they meant well—" [ibid.]). Linton's verse performs a series of inversions not unlike those per-

---

10. See *Modern Painters* part 4, chapter 8 ("Of the True Ideal:—Thirdly, Grotesque") and *The Stones of Venice* vol. 2, chapter 6 ("The Nature of Gothic") and vol. 3, chapter 3 ("Grotesque Renaissance").

formed in the suggestively grotesque illustrations with which it powerfully collaborates. The urbane, light tone of this section of the poem itself withers bourgeois pretensions and, by treating them as mere trifles to be dallied with in "doggrel rhyme" (ibid., 3), asserts the self-confidence, centrality, and power of the abject and marginalized. Such verbal and visual deconstruction does not of itself shake economic and political structures of power, but it can do important cultural work in deflating the mystique of power and privilege and in constructing the consciousness which grasps both the basis of protest and the entitlement to do so. That is, it foments the Chartist imaginary with which this book is centrally concerned.

Linton's simultaneous selection of epic form and doggerel idiom packs a formidable ideological punch. To appreciate why this is so, compare his adoption of an unassuming, popular voice (through doggerel) to a similar adoption by bourgeois poets (through balladry). The mid-Victorian rehabilitation of the ballad represented a formal, rather than thematic, instance of 1840s medievalism. Associated as the ballad was with a romanticized medieval period for which some Victorians famously yearned, it should come as no surprise that this decade saw a revival of interest in the form.[11] Such nostalgia served particular discursive ends, idealizing the period insofar as its values of duty, Christian belief, chivalric manliness, desexualized love, and fixed social relations validated the prevailing (but contested) cultural ideologies of nineteenth-century Britain.

However, as Herbert Tucker has shown, there were also immediate political exigencies motivating the renewed middle-class zeal for balladry: "it was to the freshly threatened stability of an unresolved national constitution that the 1840s ballad revival spoke its vernacular word of reassurance—in the people's voice and therefore, so the implicit logic ran, in the people's name" (*Epic*, 314). Forced to acknowledge the emerging democratic ideal, but loath to extend it so far as working-class activists demanded, the middle class sought to protect static class relations partly by reconfiguring themselves as "the people" and their own rise to power as the triumph and end of democracy. In the 1840s writers articulating bourgeois values resuscitated a poetic form long associated with folkloric traditions and the voice of "the people," appropriating it to their causes and infusing it with their voices in a poetic sleight

---

11. Tucker compiles a convincing compendium of evidence of the decade's interest in both balladry and the medieval ideals it elicited, including the Eglinton Tournament (1839), Pugin's *Contrasts* (1836, 1841) and Parliamentary architecture, Barham's 1840 *Ingoldsby Legends*, W. E. Aytoun's *Book of Ballads* (1845) and *Lays of the Scottish Cavaliers* (1849), and the sudden enthusiasm for Bishop Percy's *Reliques of Ancient English Poetry*, which was republished almost every year between 1839 and 1850 (*Epic*, 311–12).

of hand akin to the political one whereby they represented the 1832 Reform Act as having given "the people" a voice in Parliament. Their valorizing and appropriation of the ballad form itself was as much an ideological gesture as that performed by writers with working-class commitments who commandeered high cultural genres such as epic for their own ends.

Linton's *Bob Thin* counters the bourgeoisie's aesthetic/political move to wrest popular authority away from the working class by speaking with its own, quite different proletarian voice: doggerel. Announcing by its very first, very approximate rhyme that this poem harbors no pretensions to high seriousness, *Bob Thin* also playfully declares in its opening couplet that "Men like not prosy tales: we'll try / How doggrel rhyme fits history" (3). The lines almost shrug, so casual and experimental is their tone; nevertheless they assert both their popular aim (to be what "Men like") and how natural and unsurprising it is that an ordinary person should survey national history, even if the voice in which one speaks of it is a disparaged one such as doggerel (or, alternatively, a Lancashire dialect). Linton ostentatiously utilizes a vernacular "voice of the people" to denounce the laws made by the very middle class then seeking to paint its own speech and acts as "the people's." These examples provide compelling evidence for the claim that, on issues of paramount importance to midcentury Victorians, poetry represented not only a battlefield but also a weapon, for combatants on both sides.

Spenserian Epic: Cooper's *Purgatory of Suicides* (1845)

Also epic, also published in 1845, Thomas Cooper's *Purgatory of Suicides* could hardly differ more radically from *Bob Thin* in its form and ambitions. Cooper (1805–1892) represents not only one of the most extraordinary autodidacts to emerge from the British working class in the 19th century but also one of the most literary of Chartists. Today his *The Life of Thomas Cooper* (1872) probably commands more readers than any of his fiction or poetry, but his imaginative writing (notably the two-volume collection of short stories *Wise Saws and Modern Instances* and *The Purgatory of Suicides*, both published in 1845) is also making its way into modern anthologies and scholarly articles. *The Purgatory of Suicides*, written in the unusual Spenserian stanza format, is a blistering critique of religion that has still garnered too little sustained critical attention.[12] It should be acknowledged that Cooper's stridently anti-

---

12. Cooper later wrote a second epic in Spenserian stanzas—a sort of retraction or companion to *The Purgatory*—called *The Paradise of Martyrs* (1873), which expressed his faith in Christianity rather than his skepticism of it. The 1850s saw him publish several novels, one

religious secularism, acquired largely during his imprisonment in 1843–45 for sedition, was sandwiched between his stints as a Wesleyan minister (when young) and as a Baptist preacher (when old). But in the prison years, during which he wrote *The Purgatory of Suicides,* Cooper was a skeptic and penned scathing attacks on Christianity. His changes of faith point to not only a pattern of alternations in Cooper's personal life but also to some of the paradoxes and ambiguities within the Chartist movement itself. Though primarily a secular movement, the Chartist ranks included religious believers (mainly Methodists, for whom that sect's rejection of rank in both church and society resonated) as well as free thinkers. Especially during the years of downturn from 1842 to 1848, some members of the latter category moved toward dissenting belief, so that mobility among the shades of belief and nonbelief was not peculiar to Cooper.

The most recent and comprehensive endeavor to untangle a "Chartist theology" occurs in Mike Sanders's essay about what might be the only extant copy of any Chartist hymnal: the *National Chartist Hymn Book,* the image patterns in which differ markedly from contemporary, traditional Victorian hymnody.[13] Taking the *National Chartist Hymn Book* as his evidence, Sanders outlines Chartist beliefs that, since God created free people in a world of abundance, deprivation and political oppression are not only the result of economic and social mismanagement but are actually anti-Christian. Sanders shows that while Chartists affirmed their belief in God's activity on their behalf, they also insisted on their own knowledge and agency in achieving the social transformation ("resurrection") they sought. Most importantly, Sanders highlights the differences between "Chartism's religious attitudes and its attitudes to religious institutions" in ways that are useful here ("'God is our guide! Our cause is just!' The *National Chartist Hymn Book* and Victorian

---

of which (*Captain Cobbler, or the Lincolnshire Insurrection: a Story of the Reign of Henry VIII*) appeared serially in connection with his own periodical *Cooper's Journal.* In addition, he published the novels *Alderman Ralph* in 1853 and *The Family Feud* in 1855.

13. Earlier discussions include Eileen Yeo's "Christianity in Chartist Struggle, 1838–42" in *Past & Present* 91 (May 1981): 109–39, and her "Chartist Religious Belief and the Theology of Liberation" in *Disciplines of Faith: Studies in Religion, Politics and Patriarchy,* edited by J. Obelkevich, L. Roper, and R. Samuel (London: Routledge, 1987), 410–14. See also Eileen Groth Lyon's *Politicians in the Pulpit: Christian Radicalism in Britain from the Fall of the Bastille to the Disintegration of Chartism* (Aldershot: Ashgate, 1999). Miles Taylor (cited elsewhere) and Roy Vickers focus on modulations in Ernest Jones's use of Christian religious language in "the creation and representation of individual and collective Chartist identities" (Vickers, "Christian Election, Holy Communion and Psalmic Language in Ernest Jones's Chartist Poetry," 60). For a detailed history of the British secular movement prior to and beyond the Chartist years, see Edward Royle's *Victorian Infidels: the Origins of the British Secularist Movement, 1791–1866* (Manchester: University of Manchester Press, 1974).

Hymnody," 686). While Sanders demonstrates, as I do, Chartism's hostility to
organized religion, he also details how the movement's secular images simultaneously carried religious meanings (ibid., 695–96). This seeming paradox
can help elucidate how a poem as fiercely antireligious as the *Purgatory* can
also rely on Christian figures of bondage, transformation, and God's favor.
Sanders concludes that "Chartist theology therefore acts as a deep generative structure informing Chartist consciousness—and, hence, wider symbolic praxis—not just at the level of specific ideas, but more fundamentally
in terms of ethos and attitude" (ibid., 696). While attacking the clergy and
their allies, Cooper predicates his whole poem on a Christian notion of an
afterlife, regards such figures as Luther as forbears in related struggle, and
anticipates a day when "Knowledge" and "Truth" will regenerate the world,
language distinctly reminiscent of the Christian New Testament. The double
consciousness of theological inspiration and ecclesiastical condemnation produces intriguing tensions in the *Purgatory,* but to allow for a careful reading of
the poem's aesthetics as well as its themes, the argument below concentrates
mainly on the half of that binary aimed at clerical debunking.

The spiritual fluctuations in Cooper's own life serve to reveal how vital to
his politics was a critique of religion. During his most intimate, active engagement with Chartism and labor, he questioned his earlier beliefs and boldly
exposed the harmful secular utility of cynical divine mysticism. His most
complete statement of religious skepticism is *The Purgatory of Suicides,* which
despite its relative critical neglect is a major work giving extended expression
to a significant strand of Chartist politics. In it he leveled a sustained and earnest, though sometimes witty, denunciation of the baneful uses to which religion has been put, with particular reference to its effects on the class to which
Cooper belonged. As a counter to the personal and political damage done by
churches and creeds, the spread of knowledge and reason stands out as the
key to a utopian future towards which the poem yearns. The basic pattern of
the work is its division into ten books, each beginning with Cooper himself
meditating on various topics from his jail cell. These opening exordia give
way to the poet's dreams of a Purgatory in which many historical and mythi-
cal figures (each a suicide) genuinely debate themes of importance to Chartist
thinkers.

It is worth noting the very particular poetic form he adopted for the
Purgatory's contribution to Chartist politics: an epic in Spenserian stanzas.
Spenserian stanzas were rare in the nineteenth century,[14] but they had a his-

14. Byron used them in *Childe Harold's Pilgrimage,* Keats in "The Eve of St. Agnus," and
Tennyson wrote a handful of Spenserian stanzas at the beginning of "The Lotos-Eaters." Only a

tory of being the vehicle for poetic narrative. The more common epic form was Milton's, a less challenging blank verse which, because it lacked a regular rhyme scheme, would in some ways have been more difficult for Cooper under his circumstances: a prison environment without access to pen and paper (at least when he began composing), so that he had to memorize the first stanzas before later committing them to paper. The rigid rhyme scheme of Spenser's nine-line stanza would be an aid to recalling his verses. It also afforded Cooper the chance to make a cultural assertion of political ability: since members of the working class can negotiate the most stringently challenging literary forms, they are by implication equally qualified to acquit themselves in the less arduous task of voting.

A more important dimension of Cooper's (and Linton's and Jones's) choice of epic form was the political gesture it implied. By definition, epic poems treat some historic quest, event, or achievement of heroic proportions and central to the beliefs or identity of a nation. Yet rather than recounting some war-time conquest (the *Iliad*), the founding of a nation (*The Aeneid*), or the superiority of a country's church and monarchy (as Spenser's own *The Faerie Queene*), Cooper's epic makes the claims and cause of Chartism the great heroic center of Britain's modern history. As Stephanie Kuduk puts it, the "epic form enables Cooper to assert that Chartism is the contemporary instantiation of a centuries-old struggle for British liberty" ("Sedition, Criticism, and Epic Poetry in Thomas Cooper's *The Purgatory of Suicides*," 166). For all three of these poets the choice of poetic form, then, was itself not only an assertion of working-class pride but also a daring political statement of Chartism's rightful place in the annals of Britain. Through poetic form as well as by its inherent claims to justice, Chartism assumed the mantle of modern myth, a central element in the forging of a nation.

Cooper's principal spokesperson in parts of the poem is a figure named Lycurgus. This character appears early in book one as the voice which challenges social inequality and the rule of kings, and he is the champion of the dignity of human understanding. He appears again in book ten, where his earlier arguments are vindicated and others congratulate him on the correctness of his views. It is interesting to ask why Cooper chose Lycurgus as the prophet of the spread of knowledge and the demise of monarchy, and why the Spartan enjoys such prominence early and late in the book.

The answer lies in the ancient history of the Spartan leader Lycurgus (*circa* 800 BCE), who first gained the admiration of his people by *setting aside* his

---

few others in the 19th century experimented with the form, including the "sempstress" E. L. E. (discussed in chapter 5) in her poem "The Fate of Diffidence. An Allegory."

chance at supreme power. Later when he did return to lead Sparta, Lycurgus instituted sweeping reforms of its constitution and society, the appeal
of which to a Chartist one can immediately perceive. His reforms included
eliminating inequalities of wealth (and hence robbery and bribery), creating
a senate to check the absolute power of royalty, undertaking a radically new
education system for boys and girls, and de-emphasizing luxury by legislating
simple houses for all and common tables in public eating halls.

Though Plutarch's account (in *Lives*) of Lycurgus includes policies Cooper surely would have considered harsh and wrong (the merciless oppression
of slaves, the prohibition against foreigners and foreign travel, the severity
and authoritarianism of military training, for example), the most celebrated
and memorable portions of Lycurgus's history make it fairly easy to see why
Cooper might have elected him as a speaker. In that role, he eloquently and
calmly resists belief based on the denigration of clear thought and sane evaluation, favoring instead the spirit of "Truth" and "Freedom" which will inspire
humanity to shake off civil and religious servility and acquire its rightful dignity through learning and mental clarity. Unquestionably the Lycurgus of the
Purgatory gives voice to Cooper's own fervent desire for social change, which
cannot be realized without uprooting religion's valorizing of blind faith.[15]

The eclecticism evident in Cooper's selection of Spenserian epic form and
an ancient Greek spokesperson could not fail to garner his readers' notice,
and his recourse to ancient history could not do other than signal the value
of historical knowledge to a movement for political reform and set forth to
other Chartists some of the qualities possessed by effective leaders. Activists
who needed any emboldening for their intellectual independence (whether
challenging established religion or received doctrines of proper government)
would find it in the figure of a democratic spokesman with all the authority of
Greek antiquity. In these respects Cooper's formal choices, over and above the
explicit content of his poem, serve to confer on the Chartist cause authority,
confidence, and respect for historical knowledge—essential equipment for a
national movement.

---

15. That Cooper had in mind the Spartan Lycurgus is unmistakable both because of his
frequent designation as "the Spartan" and because that figure committed suicide by not eating
(hence his presence in the Purgatory of Suicides). An intriguing coincidence, however, is the
existence of a second Lycurgus, king of Thrace, who would also make an outstanding spokesperson for a rational, antireligious viewpoint. Mythic accounts detail this Lycurgus's opposition
to the worship of Dionysus, whose cult was one of ecstatic, wild, and savage belief and practice.
His sole fame seems to derive from his driving Dionysus into the sea with an ox-goad, so vehe-
mently did he oppose the new god's inspiration of disorder, irrationality, and religious madness.
Whether mythic or historical, the name *Lycurgus* is a powerful shorthand expression of many
values articulated in Cooper's latter-day epic.

Religion as a Mystical Veil on Reason

Cooper's critique of religion falls roughly under four headings which I will examine in turn: that it mystifies the world and clouds people's reason, provides a cloak for war, suppresses knowledge, and colludes with the state to justify its existence and subdue civic rebellion. The Chartist poet begins his epic by showing how institutional religion, through its teachings and even its very architecture, steeps people's minds in darkness and mystery. Book one casts a glance toward the contemporary discussions of Gothic architecture by A. W. N. Pugin and John Ruskin that I mentioned earlier. Cooper's audacity in intervening in debates among the foremost aesthetic theorists of his time is admirable and an important instance of working-class self-assertion. Perhaps unsurprisingly, Cooper's view departs from those of both the Catholic Pugin, for whom Gothic is the organic expression of the medieval Catholic values he advocated, and the Anglican Ruskin, for whom the Gothic represents the freedom granted to individual workers in its construction. In contrast, Cooper indicts Gothic architecture as itself one of the tools traditionally used by institutional religion to bewilder people's minds and ready them for deception and bondage.

Though the height of British enthusiasm for Gothic architecture was not until the decades following the 1850s, it was already coming into high regard in the 1840s when Cooper penned his *Purgatory*. In his 1841 work *The True Principles of Pointed or Christian Architecture*, the architect Pugin had said "An old English [i.e., Catholic] parish church, as originally used for the ancient worship, was one of the most beautiful and appropriate buildings that the mind of man could conceive; every portion of it answered both a useful and a mystical purpose" (42).

Just four years after Cooper's poem was published, John Ruskin's *The Seven Lamps of Architecture* appeared (1849), followed two years later by the first volume of *The Stones of Venice* (1851). In these works Ruskin famously developed his theories of architecture in general and Gothic architecture in particular. What is most interesting and innovative about his advocacy of the Gothic is his claim that its irregularities and incongruities express the freedom and humanity—with all its flaws—of workers not reduced to the mechanical reproduction of prescribed, premeasured, monotonous perfection. Yet his interpretation of its "savage" and "grotesque" ornaments could not differ more starkly from Cooper's, the latter of whom thinks less about its creators and more about its uses and effects on its beholders (Cooper also clearly differs from Linton, whose subversive use of the grotesque matches neither his nor Ruskin's formula). For Ruskin, "Gothic is not only the best, but the *only rational* architecture" (Rosenberg, *Genius,* 189, emphasis his), and its "ugly goblins, and formless monsters, and stern statues . . . are signs of the life and liberty of every workman who struck the stone" (ibid., 179). Cooper contends to the contrary that those wild forms are signs of religion's *irrationality* and its *fettering* of people's minds.

In the *Purgatory* Cooper opines that Gothic architecture's blending of fantastic and wildly contrary shapes prepared simple worshippers to accept notions that would otherwise confuse and offend their reason. Through cathedrals, the spirit of "Phantasy" aimed "all contraries to blend and wed / Until with hybrids she had filled the mind, / And with wild wonderment its powers misled, / So that, its grasp grown loose and undefined, / The shaven and shorn enchanters might its freedom bind" (book 1: stanza XXX: lines 5–9). On his argument, one's continual confrontation with "imp, saint, angel, knight with battle-blade, / Griffin, bat, [and] owlet" lit by "'dim religious' shade" and bathed in overpowering incense habituated him or her to the acceptance of the vaguely perceived and half understood. If things physical are a token of things spiritual, the architectural imposition figures the imperative to grow similarly accustomed to a suspension of logic in belief (1: XXX: lines 4, 8–10). This "gloomy" and "grotesque" setting served as a stage on which the "conjuror[s]" performed, exercising a species of paralyzing magic over human minds. The beneficiaries of the diffused light, altered colors, gloomy heights, and incongruous—and vaguely threatening—figures were the monks and priests who practiced their mystical craft there.

Cooper was responding not only to buildings but also to their apologists' tone of rarefied adoration for their impact on religious feeling and their ability to deflate any human sense of innate self-worth. The briefest of quotations from Pugin will illustrate the gulf that separates his views from Cooper's. Conceiving that churches are erected for God and not for humanity (*True Principles,* 38), Pugin celebrates precisely those features of "pointed" architecture that render it remote and intimidating to the human mind. His enumeration of the features of an idealized medieval church is so breathless that ordinary sentence structure breaks down in favor of an accumulation of phrases with no ultimate predicate:

> the oaken canopy carved with images of the heavenly host, and painted with quaint and appropriate devices,—the impressive doom or judgment pictured over the great chancel arch,—the fretted screen and rood loft,— the mystical separation between the sacrifice and the people, with the emblem of redemption carried on high and surrounded with glory,—the great altar, rich in hangings, placed far from irreverent gaze . . . . (ibid., 42)

Notice the pervasiveness of diction implying distance, severity, and subdued awe. There is nothing approachable in religious architecture so "impressive," "great," "mystical," and "rich," nor anything reassuring in an atmosphere of "doom" and "judgment." Its very virtue lies in its emblems' being "on high" and so "heavenly" that they enforce a "mystical separation" between the people and God, whose altar must be distanced and protected from the "irreverent gaze" of mortals. The absoluteness of division between worshipper and worshipped might also model an immutable social hierarchy, tampering with which would amount to sacrilege.

Nothing could be further from Cooper's ideas, and it is significant that the Chartist squarely rebukes a religious, artistic practice for its enshrinement of concrete political and social injustices. The debate over Gothic architecture illustrates why it is vital to consider not only the literature of the Chartists but also the politics of their literature. Cooper's explicit intervention, like Linton's implicit one in *Bob Thin*, in a discussion which appears to be purely aesthetic demonstrates how thoroughly convinced many Chartists were that art, and more especially epic, is an arena for social and political debate.

Cooper also addressed the standard religious claim that "humanity is too finite to understand the Infinite." To Cooper, one of religion's most offensive practices is its resort to a claim of the incomprehensibility of the Infinite to the merely finite minds of humanity. In essence, when reason scrutinizes the claims and doctrines of the church, raises their improbabilities and contradictions, and confronts their absurdities, religious teachers and devotees evade the difficulties by dismissing the human mind as too limited to comprehend the "mysterious ways" of God, and anyway arrogant for attempting to. Tennyson provides a sharp contrast in the anti-intellectual mystification of his *In Memoriam A. H. H.* (1850). Though not published until some five years after Cooper's poem, Tennyson's elegy to Hallam was seventeen years in the making (1833–1850) and represents a strong strain of cultural response to religious skepticism.

Since both Tennyson's and Cooper's poems were simultaneously composed, recalling some of *In Memoriam* shows just how radically Cooper's poem differed from prevailing ideologies. The speaker in Tennyson's poem urges us to follow the example of Lazarus's sister Mary, who found comfort and hope in her ignorance of the details of her brother's resurrection by Jesus. Her devotion to Jesus supersedes any natural curiosity and probing she might direct at the miraculous event: "All subtle thought, all curious fears, / Borne down by gladness so complete, / She bows . . . . // Thrice blessed" (lyric 32: lines 9–13). Curiously, it is when she bows down, not only physically but also intellectually, when curiosity and thought are "borne down," that she is "thrice blessed." If she inquires into the details of Lazarus's four-day absence, she receives "no reply" and is simply forbidden either to know more ("The rest remaineth unrevealed" [31: line 14]) or think more ("Nor other thought her mind admits / But, he was dead, and there he sits" [32: lines 2–3]). She is better off just gratefully accepting what Jesus and his disciples present to her, experiencing the paucity of detail and dim understanding as consolatory and a purer form of faith.

Repeatedly Tennyson's speaker seeks to emulate a type of blind trust akin to Mary's, though in places he struggles to find any comfort in mystification. In frustration at trying to sort out why individuals one loves perish, the speaker's faith falters as he labors "through the darkness up to God, / I stretch lame hands of faith, and grope, / And gather dust and chaff, and call / To what I feel is Lord of all, / And faintly trust the larger hope" (55: 16–20). He seems to sag here in the middle of the poem, as groping through darkness on the strength of nothing more than faint trust is not especially reassuring. Neither does confidence suffuse his declaration that "Behold, we know not anything; / I can but trust that good shall fall / At last—far off—at last, to all, // So runs my dream; but what am I? / An infant crying in the night; / An infant crying for the light" (54: lines 13–19). The syntax of line 15 ("At last—far off—at last, to all"), with its triple caesuras, repetition of "at last," and distancing of fulfilment "far off," strongly intimates the uncertainty of his unknowing trust. Furthermore, as if to underscore the shakiness of belief without knowledge, he follows up and undermines the declaration by likening himself to the ultimate incarnation of blank, unreasoning humanity: a benighted infant (ibid., lines 17–19). It is not enough to be simply an infant, without experience, instruction, and the simple biological development of the brain that allows for complex thought; this infant exists "in the night" and without benefit of light (ibid., lines 18–19). It is hard to think of a more complete metaphor for helpless ignorance.

This profound lack of understanding drives the speaker not to reject teachings that contradict reason and require such vague and unfounded hope, but to ask forgiveness for even questioning God and to glorify God's supremacy over finite humanity. The very impossibility of making sense of religious teachings leads the speaker to rely on them even more, believing the fault to lie in himself rather than the teachings. This is just the sort of capitulation of the human power to examine and evaluate that Cooper cannot tolerate, and which he sees as religion's final defense against a thinking person's inconvenient probing of illogical doctrines. The entire poem ends by being itself a mystification, an effort to find consolation precisely by being low on the ladder of understanding. That is what makes it the ultimate Victorian expression of the sort of mind-numbing belief enjoined by traditional religion and damned by Cooper's *Purgatory of Suicides*.

Of course, Tennyson merely gave contemporary expression to a long-entrenched religious dogma. One has only to think of the Hebrew Bible's Holy of Holies, where any overweening curiosity resulted in death, or the New Testament Paul's assurances that, though "now we see through a glass, darkly" and only "know in part, and we prophesy in part," in some unspecified future people will see "face to face" and then "shall I know even as also I am known" (1 Corinthians 13:9, 12). Though one must be content with thinking and understanding "as a child" in this world (1 Cor. 13:11), what is now clouded in mystery will be revealed at some distant time in eternity. It appears that any impatience to reconcile religious claims with experience and logic amounts to an impertinent lack of faith, a failure to wait on God's timing for the clarification of implausibilities. Insistence on understanding is an intellectually arrogant denial of human "childishness" and a defiant attempt to leapfrog the divine plan. Old Testament priest, New Testament evangelist, or Victorian poet laureate: Cooper takes on a religious tenet that has stood citadel for millennia against the natural human demands for reason and knowledge. No wonder he took up the largest cudgel poetry had to offer: the epic.

RELIGION AS A DIVINE COVER FOR WAR

Though he does not develop it extensively, another arrow in Cooper's quiver of antireligious critique is his claim that religion provides a cloak for war. In book seven he aims his barbs at the old alliances between the priesthood and military against independent thinkers. The narrator mourns not only the thousands whom war has killed but also the real heroes of Britain in the arts and sciences—those whom Church and military sweep aside as cowards and traitors because they have the temerity to value Thought and Philanthropy, not slaughter. Cooper intimates that, to the extent that heroes of the mind foster critical thinking and "mental freedom" (8: IX: 6) in society, they threaten the security of priests and generals who rely on people's automatic support. The church has a strong self-interest in preserving unchallenged the institutions of society such as the military:

Perchance the Priest forbodes his end is near,—
Unless he come less lazily with aid
To stem the torrent in whose strong career
Thrones, altars, may be whirled! Shall they be stayed—

Thought's whelming waves?—Can Priestcraft's joint crusade
With Carnage, against Mind,—arrest its course?—
      (7: XXIII: lines 1–6)

The same tide which threatens to upset the public's knee-jerk rallying behind martial exploits and exploiters could overwhelm "altars" too. For that reason "Fraud must to Force, its twin, be true:— / Mind must be bann'd" (7: XII: lines 8–9). It seems that priests and armies are the two arms of anti-intellectualism.

That the Church has long fulfilled its obligatory loyalty to the military is evident, Cooper says, in its affording honored places of burial to and continual supplications on behalf of dead state and military leaders, relegating the bodies of painters, writers, and scientists to small numbers and less honored places (though he does not name it, his case in point is Westminster Abbey). "Old comates in rule," priests and warriors seek to tear out from places of honor any but those whose work has been in the "Butcher line" of warmongering and legalized murder (7: XXIV: lines 1, 5). In a voice loaded with irony, he demands that the bodies of "Heroes of the Mind"—those "mean" "churls"—be cast out of the cathedral so as not to distract from the pomp and glory "rightly" belonging to "the great / And grand in murder" (7: XIX: lines 6–7).

Those who have waged war in the name of religion Cooper places in a region of Purgatory roughly akin to the lowest region of Dante's mountain of Purgatory, where climbers are purged of the sin of pride.[16] Cooper's climbers, too, exhibit pride, but it is a very particular species of this most base of the seven deadly sins: religious arrogance and an accompanying martial zeal to extirpate other faiths. The introduction of specifically religious pride and its issue in war is the Chartist poet's innovation. His speaker sees wild crowds uttering such words as "cross," "crescent," "heaven," "hell," "Tartarus," and "Elysium," religious symbols that "Have filled [the earth] with strife until the feverous throb / Issued in darkest, deadliest deeds of crime— / Each deed still hallowed by the things of slime— / The vermin priests" (2: XLVI: lines 3–6). This region includes Christians, Buddhists, Muslims, Hindus, and Jews—representatives of the world's major religions, who in the names of their respective gods "coined / A cursing tempest from their cursing tongues combined" (2: XLIX: lines 8–9). More than simply cursing each other, they have warred on each other, as references to "deadliest deeds of crime" and "earth's strife" and the armor of war make clear.

---

16. See cantos X–XII of Dante's *Purgatory*, which is of course Cooper's inspiration. The sins of which climbers of the mountain of Purgatory are purged are Pride, Envy, Wrath, Sloth, Avarice, Gluttony, and Lust.

Cooper includes multiple references to the Crusades, including the Knights Templar, a religious *and military* order formed by the Crusaders in Jerusalem between the twelfth and fourteenth centuries. Virulently anti-Muslim, this was a band which, even here in Purgatory, "signs of antique war / Displayed,—their zeal and guise alike bizarre,— / Shirted in steel and visored" (2: XLVIII: lines 4–6). The speaker expresses surprise both at their religious zeal and their military armor, "bizarre" outward markers of the very arrogance of which they are supposed to be purging themselves. However, instead of that intended purification, all of these zealots retain their thirst for war as well as their religious motives and justifications for armed conflict. Ironically, the spiritual leaders who should promote purification instead sanctify this continued combativeness, "each deed still hallowed by the things of slime— / The vermin priests." Our parting view of these bellicose religionists is almost humorous in its depiction of people so blindly intent on destroying others for God that they fail to notice their shared malady and doom:

Anathemas and hells eternal waged
They next against each other,—losing sense
Of their strange afterstate,—so madly raged
Each bigot at his fellow's difference
Of madness.
      (2: LI: lines 1–5)

This glimpse of the persistence of religion's instigation and sanctification of war plays a key role in Cooper's condemnation of supernatural faith.

Religion as an Antagonist to Learning

Arguably the major theme of Cooper's epic is the importance of knowledge in regenerating the world, and in this he represents the beliefs of vast numbers of the working class in general and of Chartists in particular.[17] Educational initiatives such as reading rooms, Sunday schools, and discussion groups formed part of Chartist culture from the beginning, but gradations of opinion on the

---

17. See Gregory Vargo's "A Life in Fragments: Thomas Cooper's Chartist *Bildungsroman*," *Victorian Literature and Culture* 39 (2011): 167–81. Vargo compellingly reads Cooper's short story collection *Wise Saws and Modern Instances*—written simultaneously with the *Purgatory*—as "the formal and thematic negation of his epic" (168). Rather than aping bourgeois self-help axioms that promise personal and social transformation through individual effort, education, and self-fulfillment, Cooper's stories, Vargo argues, revise the *Bildungsroman* tradition to show the frustrations and alienation of the poor in the absence of more than personal enlightenment.

priority of education naturally existed within the movement. Most notably, the cabinetmaker William Lovett, who as secretary of the London Working Men's Association wrote *The People's Charter* in 1838, published a further treatise in 1840 entitled *Chartism; A New Organization of the People.* Here Lovett surveyed various educational methods and proposed his own detailed system for all levels of instruction from "infant" to adult. Though the book also urged passage of the Charter, its talk of working people's "regenerating" themselves socially and politically invited attack from Feargus O'Connor. O'Connor successfully if somewhat unfairly portrayed Lovett's book as placing education ahead of enfranchisement,[18] dubbing it "Knowledge Chartism" and lumping it together with the "Teetotal," "Church," and "Household" Chartisms he rejected as distractions and delays to the passage of the clear, unifying Charter. Defenders of both positions took to the pages of the *Northern Star,* providing perhaps the most prominent debate about education to occur within the Chartist movement.

Cooper's vision in the *Purgatory* is far less specific than those earlier debates over education within Chartism. In book 3 the Indian philosopher Calanus[19] speaks of "Knowledge,—the new-born world's great heroine" (3: LXX: line 4) and prophesies about the brightness of a future under its influence. He also describes the unfurling of a banner whose message strikes mortal fear into the hearts of kings and priests. That banner, which might as well serve as the epigraph to Cooper's book, reads "'Knowledge is Power!'" (3: LXXIII: line 9) Knowledge serves as the harbinger of truth, brotherhood, freedom, and other democratic ideals espoused by proletarian activists of the time.

Such exaltations of knowledge occur throughout the *Purgatory,* and very often they are coupled with condemnations of the religious suppression of knowledge. The theme of these condemnations represents a third primary strand of Cooper's overall critique of religion. In book 6 his favorite spokesperson Lycurgus eloquently contends that priests have long endeavored to combat popular acquisition of knowledge:

> Say ye, Right's triumph, like a dream, shall fade,
> 'Neath swift rewaking vigour of throned Power?—

---

18. See Chase's *Chartism: A New History,* 168–78 for an explanation of and challenge to O'Connor's characterization of Lovett's aims.

19. Calanus (fourth century BCE) was an Indian sage who accompanied Alexander the Great. He fell ill and, considering that it would be better to relinquish life voluntarily than to undergo treatment and die slowly, he killed himself by mounting a funeral pyre. He was admired for his bravery.

> Monarchs, be not deceived! Right, now, hath aid
> From Knowledge—hid by priests in secret bower,
> And when thence 'scaped, caught, and to dungeon-tower
> By them condemned—yea, to the fiery flame!—
> They knew not of her high immortal dower,
> The veritable Phœnix—whom to tame,
> Or to destroy, will ever mock old priestly aim!
> (6: CXXV)

It is the priests, he says, who have fruitlessly endeavored to stamp out the spread of knowledge, who have tried to hoard it and protect it by means as drastic as imprisonment and destruction. The "fiery flame" to which religious officials have consigned knowledge applies both to the burning of radical books and pamphlets, and even sacred texts in vernacular languages, and to the grisly execution of people themselves who held "heretical" or anti-establishment views. For rhetorical and illustrative purposes, Cooper here chose the most extreme examples of priestly anti-intellectualism. Yet even such apparently effective methods—the physical annihilation of books and people—clearly failed in their purpose. Cooper perfected his metaphor of knowledge as Phoenix by saying that knowledge too arises out of the fire intended to destroy it. In book 8 Cooper extols great "Saxon" thinkers from the Reformation martyrs "who dared the flame" (8: IX: line 8) to Paine, Godwin, Owen, and many others in between. It might be surprising in a critique of religion that some religious figures (Huss, Wickliffe, Luther, e.g.) make it into this catalogue of honor, but he esteems them as "stalwart pioneer[s] / Of mental freedom" (8: IX: lines 5–6) who, even if they did not possess all of the truth, still fought for it against "the bondage of the Priest of Rome" (8: VIII: line 2). Likewise did "philanthropists" battle "Old Superstition" of other varieties and creeds, superstition which the poem depicts as snakelike in its opposition to the progress of "Young Knowledge." Cooper writes that "forth from his snaky coil / Old Superstition springs," but the wily opponent is conquered and counted a spoil of war by triumphant Knowledge (2: LXXII: lines 4–5). In a minor coup, Cooper inverts the usual religious metaphor of sin, temptation, or Satan as a snake. Instead, it is irrational belief itself that equates with the serpent and becomes the foe of all that is just, ennobling, and freeing.

Often the form of knowledge at which dogmatic religionists took aim was secular literature, and they attempted to restrict the scope of their adherents' reading to the Bible and other religious texts. Shakespeare, Pope, Byron, and many others appealed to working-class readers, but such reading brought parishioners into direct conflict with leaders of the congregations to which

they belonged. According to Jonathan Rose, denominations "with predominantly working-class congregations, such as the Baptists and Primitive Methodists, tended to be the most hostile" to secular literature, though opposition
"ran wide and deep" among Nonconformist and Anglican evangelicals generally up through the 1850s (31). His surmise is borne out by the evidence
provided in working-class autobiographies of the period,[20] many of which
"highlight[] the threat to religious belief and practice which was inherent in
the readers' commitment to pursuing knowledge to whatever destination it
led them" (Vincent, *Bread, Knowledge, and Freedom: A Study of Nineteenth-
Century Working Class Autobiography*, 181). Catholics, Anglicans, and Non-
conformists all had a stake in suppressing such knowledge and therefore all
fell under the sweep of Cooper's condemnation.

Some of these religious attitudes changed later in the nineteenth century,
particularly after the 1870 Education Act and the wide teaching of British literature in nondenominational Board schools. But during the Chartist period,
religious antagonism to working-class education in particular made spiritual
institutions a frequent target of criticism. Many Chartists viewed religious
anti-intellectualism as colluding with institutions of state power to bar working people from their rights as human beings and Englishmen.[21]

For working-class autodidacts and political activists such as Cooper, educational gains could only be hopeful and empowering. It is true that he, like
factory poet Ellen Johnston, encountered some suspicion from neighbors
and co-workers for his educational ambitions,[22] but given that intellect had
traditionally been the domain of their oppressors, proletarians could be for-
given for fearing that seeking mental improvement signaled a class betrayal
or an aping of middle-class manners. Such apprehensions could be over-

---

20. See Vincent's *Bread, Knowledge, and Freedom: A Study of Nineteenth-Century Working Class Autobiography*. The life narratives of Cooper himself (who was criticized for not
attending church so that he could read), Christopher Thomson (told to choose between books
and his soul's salvation), and Thomas Oliver (censured by his congregation for expressing
doubts raised by his secular reading), for example, demonstrate the clash between Methodist
orthodoxy and workers' intellectual freedom. The Methodists were not alone in fearing the
free-ranging and critical mental habits reading cultivated, and neither were those apprehensions unfounded. Joseph Gutteridge, whose secular reading coupled with material hardship
led to unbelief, and Joseph Sketchley, whose personal study resulted in a split from Catholi-
cism, provide more evidence of the threat to various religious sects.

21. As explained earlier, unanimity about education did not exist among Chartists, however. Some arguably saw it as an end in itself, a goal that replaced the attainment of the Charter's demands, while others saw it as a means to an end, an important aid in the analytical and
organizational tasks faced by women and men engaged in the struggle for the Charter.

22. See Johnston's "Autobiography of Ellen Johnston, the 'Factory Girl'" reprinted in Zlotnick's *Women, Writing, and the Industrial Revolution* (Baltimore: Johns Hopkins University
Press, 1998), especially page 261. See also Cooper's *The Life of Thomas Cooper*, 56–57.

come, but more implacable and better-founded were the fears of their socio-economic superiors, some of whom regarded overeducation of workers as a Pandora's box. Increasing self-confidence and ability to analyze and articulate social injustices, erasure of some previous bars to enfranchisement, and general insubordination all lurked. Those fears were evidently correct, if one judges by such examples as Cooper's and artisan Christopher Thomson's. In railing against the employer class's prohibition of thought among laborers, Thomson explained in his *Autobiography of an Artisan* that a worker was "forbidden to think" because such thinking "would have taught him to scan the war-debt . . . to assert his right of citizenship—his duty to control the law-makers—. . . would have taught him self-dependence and moral elevation, instead of serfish cringing crumb-picking" (qtd in Rose, 23). Certainly the concurrent emergence of working-class education, trades unionism, and Chartism could be placed in the evidence column for anti-intellectual polemicists.

One formidable obstacle to the popular acquisition of wide learning was dogmatic belief, and about this Cooper was nothing if not specific. What became Cooper's especial antipathy was the religious entombment of people's natural mental abilities. In a crescendo of excitement over the spread of knowledge to Europe, Africa, and Asia, Lycurgus concludes book one of the *Purgatory* by exclaiming that Africans and Asians will soon "disenthral / Their new-born spirits from Faith's mystical / Degrading chains, and shake their ancient slough / Of sottish ignorance off: no more to crawl / In abjectness 'fore hideous gods, nor throw / Their slavish frames 'fore kings" (1: CXXX-VII: lines 4–9).[23] The Spartan spokesperson firmly couples faith and mysticism with ignorance and the degradation of bondage to gods and kings. Political liberation accompanies spiritual liberation, and both are predicated on escaping the straitjacket of ignorance in which religion would constrain people. It is important to note that the chains that enslave people politically originate specifically in nonrational belief. Hence Cooper's critique of religion and his confidence that knowledge dispels both of the "twin theurgies" of political and spiritual power (2: LXXIV: line 2).

In *The Purgatory of Suicides,* Knowledge represents more than the abstract concept proclaimed in Calanus's banner "Knowledge is Power!" More than a vague, intangible moral possession, for Cooper knowledge represents the

---

23. Though there is some British chauvinism here, Cooper does include Europe, too, as only just beginning to hear the voice of Truth (see, e.g., 1: CXXXVI: lines 5–6). Elsewhere in the poem he admires ancient Asian thinkers murdered by "Falsehood" (9: XXXIII), sympathizes with Mexican and Irish condemnations of colonialism (10: LII–LX), and empowers a Jewish woman to indict the violent history of Christian anti-Semitism (9: XLII–XLVI).

seizure of one's democratic rights in the most immediate, concrete way. Calanus goes on to proclaim that "Knowledge, the great Enfranchiser, is near!"
(2: LXXIV: line 3) The grammar of this short sentence is suggestive, since the
appositional conjunction of learning and the vote permits not even a verb
to separate them. They are so firmly, so tightly linked that they brook not so
much as a grammatical division. The omitted verb, of course, is the verb of
being (*is*), but its insertion would subtly detract from the absolutely concurrent acquisition of learning and the demands of the Charter. Undoubtedly, in
Cooper's mind William Lovett's formula of "self-improvement before political rights" abandoned the majority of Britain to prolonged poverty and denial
of civil rights. The abridgement effected by the poet's choice of apposition
here revises that formula to lend greater energy and force to the poetic line
and greater urgency to the working-class demands for education and political
power. Therefore, to the extent that religion seeks to block people's endeavors
to learn, it denies access to basic democratic rights. In Cooper's cosmos, it is
doubly damned.

    More central to my consideration of the Chartist imaginary than broad
notions of education is the question of what happens when one confronts
not only knowledge but aesthetic knowledge. Marxists such as Herbert Mar-
cuse and Georg Lukacs have described how the aesthetic impresses people
with an awareness that the world can be other than it is, and this ability to
imagine beyond the already received is a precondition of political activism.
As Mike Sanders has persuasively argued, Cooper's (and other Chartists')
own first encounter with poetry unleashed "an almost insatiable desire for
more poetry," a "psychic structure [. . .] (the need to find out more)" that was
"instrumental in securing his conversion to Chartism" later in life (*Poetry*, 10).
Aware of the critical role poetry had played in his own intellectual and political development, perhaps Cooper went on to write the *Purgatory* in the belief
that poetry possesses a unique cognitive power, not just in its paraphrasable
content but in its aesthetic form, to induce the mental thirst and imaginative
distance from the given so essential to a worker's adopting and advocating for
the Chartist vision. This is why I contend for the unique political agency of
poetry (and other literature) within the Chartist movement.

RELIGION AS AN ALLY OF STATE REPRESSION

To conclude my consideration of the *Purgatory*, I will analyze a key scene that
opens book six, in which the speaker witnesses the procession of a convicted
man towards the scaffold. Leading the way to the "legal butchery" (Cooper's

footnote 1, 225) is a member of the priesthood, and this opens the door for a strong denunciation of religion's complicity in upholding the power of unjust laws and kings. The second stanza reads thus:

> It is the death-toll: there! they bear him on!
> I climb to read the lesson through my bars.—
> Hah! curse upon thee, priest!—is it well done,
> That thou, a peace-robed herald pattering prayers,
> Dost head the dead-march? Trow'st thou not it jars
> With that sky-message which proclaimed, thou say'st,
> 'Peace and Goodwill to Man'?—aye, that it mars
> The face of mercy to behold thee placed
> There, in grim state, 'tween spears with crape, in mockery, graced?
>   (6: II)

For this fourth of his critiques of religion, Cooper skillfully exploits the full expressive potential of his poetic form, manipulating rhythms and sounds to underline the content of his argument about religion and the state. For example, he deviates from the poem's prevailing iambic feet by substituting both spondees and trochaic inversions which deftly draw attention to such contrasts as that between the "dead-march" (II: line 5) sanctioned by the priest's leadership and the "sky-message" of "Peace" (II: lines 6, 7) which he proclaims on God's behalf. The disordering of the rhythmic norm faintly trips up attentive readers and invites a moment's pause over the irony of the ministers of mercy presiding at its obliteration.

To insist on the reader's further pausing, Cooper breaks up his stanza's concluding alexandrine with *four* caesuras. This deviates from the single caesura that more usually bisects the Spenserian stanza's final line. The result is that one halts and stumbles through a line whose theme as well should startle readers with incongruity and hesitation: a priest appears "There, in grim state, 'tween spears with crape, in mockery, graced?" (II: line 9) The absence of any smooth progression in the line imitates the Chartist's own disbelief in the Church's open participation in the most barbaric expression of state power. Also, Cooper here capitalizes on the power of emphasis inherent in the alexandrine. In a stanza of eight pentameter lines, a final hexameter line cannot but stand out, calling attention to its content even more than the rest of the lines do. In this case, the exceptional line rings with repeated vowel sounds that firmly interlock secular and spiritual power. The assonance of the long *a* in "state," "crape," and "graced" forms a thread through three decreasingly-distinct concepts: coercive government power, death, and religion. Admittedly "state" in this instance denotes condition rather than ruling body, but in the context of Cooper's critique, the double meaning is inescapable. So if "state" conjures up notions of legal oppression and "graced" suggests that religious institution which proclaims, if it does not practice, grace, then the medium of their imbrication—their literal fulcrum in this line—is execution, symbolized by the "crape" on either side of the priest in the death-march. Cooper masterfully links the three through the sounds of the stanza's concluding, longest, most pronounced line.

Religion's consistent association with the ability of the ruling class to subdue social rebellion earns its further censure in stanza eight. Again, the form as well as the content of the verse bears the burden of its message. Addressing priests, the speaker says

> . . . ye preach
> To slaves: Christ's precepts are for them! . . .
> [and ye are]
> Dark ambidexters in the guilty game
> Of human subjugation!—how to tame
> Man's spirit ye, and only ye, have skill:
> Kings need your help to hold their thrones,—while claim
> Of sanctity enables ye, at will,
> To wield o'er prostrate Reason subtler empire still!
>   (VIII: lines 1–9)

Skillful poets establish metric patterns partly in order to deviate from them expressively, and Cooper here departs from the prevailing iambic feet of his lines precisely in those places where the key phrases occur. As I hear the lines, spondaic substitutions occur in (and only in) each of the four phrases "Christ's precepts," "Dark ambidexters," "Man's spirit," and "Kings need" (VIII: lines 2, 4, 6, 7), phrases which can be strung together almost without addition to form the damning sentence "Kings need dark ambidexters [in] Christ's precepts ["to tame"] man's spirit." While one of the priest's hands claims sanctity and preaches Christ's precepts of peace and forgiveness, the other hand subdues humanity's "Reason," and so subtly muddles people's minds with superstitious fear that they abdicate their power to question and challenge clerical and monarchical authority.

The final line's contention that priests wield over humanity's mind a more insidious "empire" than kings do over its body nevertheless couples a political relationship of dominance and exploitation (imperialism) with religion. Unlike both Spenser's bisected alexandrine and Cooper's own choppy alexandrine referred to above, this stanza's final line contains no internal pauses at all, as if to imitate the smooth veneer religion provides to the sway of kings. To give occasion for pause or reflection on the church's "subtle empire" might defeat its very subtlety, opening it to questions such as those posed by this poem. The line even hastens through one of its words by eliding a letter and syllable; perhaps significantly, the truncated word is the preposition that describes the spatial position of the fearsome ecclesiastical conquerors *vis-à-vis* humanity's "prostrate Reason": *over*. Again, calling attention to this mental dominion could have a dangerously destabilizing effect on hierarchical social relations—dangerous at least in the eyes of those priests and kings who would prefer to have the whole line swallowed up in a cough or a throat-clearing anyway. The absence of the caesura is a small departure from the Spenserian norm, but the deviation—along with the elision—nevertheless draws attention to itself.

One of the unique features of the Spenserian stanza form Cooper uses is its rhyme scheme (*ababbcbcc*), which unifies the logic and sense of the stanza and pulls together the thematic content of its two quatrains. As well as carrying over the *b* rhyme well into the second quatrain, the stanza tightens its coherence by means of the central couplet, which in *The Purgatory* is almost always open[24] so as not to suggest, by drawing a false enclosure around itself, that its idea is complete and independent of the lines before and after. The couplet, in other words, has a foot in each quatrain and grows organically out of the merger of the two. The central couplet therefore has about it something slightly special, a prominence deriving from its functionality as the stanza's fulcrum and its status as the semantic synthesis of the two quatrains. To look at two examples from stanzas II and VIII, which I have been discussing, one should consider how the words are rhymed, which words Cooper places at the line termini for rhyming, and what themes the paired lines seem to select and lift forth from the quatrains.

In the second stanza describing a priest's presence at a state-sponsored execution, the speaker apostrophizes him thus:

> . . . is it well done,
> That thou, a peace-robed herald pattering prayers,
> Dost head the dead-march? Trow'st thou not it jars
> With that sky-message . . . [of peace]?
>   (6: II: lines 3–6)

---

24. Paul Fussell explains that "couplets in which the second line is stopped or retarded by strong punctuation at the end, and in which the first line exhibits a high degree of syntactical integrity, are called closed couplets. . . . When enjambed, on the other hand, couplets are called open" (*Poetic Meter and Poetic Form*, 129).

The most interesting fact about this couplet is that its rhyme, unlike the vast majority of the others in the poem, is slant. The *b* words in this stanza include "bars," "jars," "mars," . . . and "prayers," which is as noticeably discordant with its mates as the priest's pronouncing peace and good will from the pulpit while sanctioning death and damnation from the scaffold. The sound literally "jars," as the themes of the stanza's two quatrains—execution in the first and mercy in the second—jar when united in this couplet and in practice. There is a necessary relationship between the form and the sense of the stanza, a structural and semantic inseparability that marks the successful poem.

In contrast to stanza II, the rhyme of the central couplet in stanza VIII is a perfect rhyme, accusing priests of being

> Dark ambidexters in the guilty game
> Of human subjugation!—how to tame
> Man's spirit ye, and only ye, have skill:
> > (6: VIII: lines 4–6).

In this case, the semantic concerns of each quatrain that the couplet joins and foregrounds are preaching meekness and peace (VIII: line 1), and subduing civic rebellion (VIII: line 7). In these twinned tasks the church is equally skilled with both hands—"ambidextr[ous]" at enforcing, on the one hand, precisely those personal virtues which breed a timid recoiling from the combative tendency of Chartists to inquire into matters considered above their comprehension and, on the other hand, exploiting people's belief in priestly integrity to provide divine cover for corrupt and merely human power.

Also of interest in this couplet are the two words Cooper opts to place in that all-important slot at the ends of the lines: "game" and "tame." That the church would take part at all in "human subjugation" is damning enough, but that such a grave participation should take on the air of a mere dalliance or "game" consigns it to even lower levels of human guilt. Moreover "game" implies a distance between the players and the consequences of their play: if the majority of society remains disenfranchised, overworked, and hungry, that reality has an aura of trifling unreality as long as political and social relations remain diversionary abstractions and pursuits. One favorite diversion of the nineteenth century's leisured classes, though priests less frequently participated, was the hunting of small animals, an amusement perhaps lurking in Cooper's choice of "game" and reinforced by its rhyming word "tame," something one typically does with animals. Yet in this case, what priests tame is "Man's spirit" (VIII: line 6), which would otherwise naturally rebel at oppression and deprivation. There is more than a whiff of brutalizing condescension in the priest's imputed assumption that laboring humanity is some sub-species that requires the firm hand of moral and penal authority to become domesticated. Both the tightness and the prominence of the couplet enhance the poem's ability to conjure up the specters of these unflattering truths.

Ultimately, Cooper's censure of religion for its role as defender and supporter of an unjust state folds into itself the other criticisms discussed in this chapter. One might even consider the opening of book six a *mise en abyme* for the whole poem's anti-religious peroration. For to what end does it tend if people's power of critical analysis is blunted? Or if the organizational skills and self-assurance education affords are limited or withheld? Does it not preserve the *status quo*, Cooper would ask? Does it not maintain the subservience of the majority under a state whose power to punish them and send them to war is fundamental to the rule of the minority? It was Cooper's conviction that the answer was "yes," and in putting forward that answer through the well-wrought execution scene opening book six he reached his highest poetic achievement.

Poetry was the vehicle of choice not only for Cooper's critique of religion but also for his proffered alternative too. Of course he versified the arguments for Chartist reform, as hundreds of other working-class men and women did, but even more than that he extolled its benefits in a poetic form explicitly counterposed to traditional religion: a Chartist hymnal. Such a collection of Chartist verse, to be sung to traditional church tunes, in a public meeting hall and on Sundays, effectively filled the old skins with new wine: it adopted the old sacred forms but infused them with new secular content which expressed the best and most immediate aspirations of their working-class singers.

While this gesture openly offered itself as an alternative to established religion, at the same time it acknowledged the values of community and inclusion implied by the religious practice of hymn-singing. Chanting familiar words and tunes on a weekly basis meant illiterate parishioners could participate equally with literate ones in worshipping God, or in this case, in claiming the right to equal participation in politics. Moreover, each individual could feel the satisfaction of contributing to something larger and more beautiful than any one person alone could produce. There was a democratic strain in the practice, however thoroughly other church rules and teachings militated against that underlying impulse. This partly accounts for why Owenites, Chartists, and socialists later in the nineteenth century all used songs as part of their propaganda work, and why Cooper's hymnal stands as part of a tradition of music by and for the producing class.[25]

---

25. For a treatment of late nineteenth-century socialist songs, see Christopher Waters's

Recognizing the democratic potential and value of regular group singing, in 1842 Cooper initiated the composition and publication of a Chartist
hymnal for the Leicester Chartists who gathered in the Shaksperean Room[26]
several times a week to hear Cooper and others lecture on politics and a host
of educational themes.[27] With varying degrees of reference to God, the hymns
express common democratic themes of equality, class injustice, and the righteousness and eventual triumph of the Chartist cause. What is distinctive is
their collection *as hymns* to be sung in public gatherings on the ordinary
church day of Sunday—a self-conscious substitution of secular, Chartist ritual
for religious ritual. Though Cooper delivered an incisive critique of religion
in *The Purgatory* and elsewhere, he distinguished himself from merely negative critics by additionally offering a positive alternative. He was not alone in
appreciating the value of hymn singing, though, since there seem to have been
at least three Chartist hymnals in existence. Just one of those books is known
to exist, and its contents, as discussed by Mike Sanders, resonate with what is
known of Cooper's hymnal.[28]

Heroic Epic: Jones's *New World* (1851)

In drawing some conclusions to her study of the creation of a British national
identity in the years leading up to Victoria's accession, Linda Colley general-
izes that the three forces most responsible for defining what it meant to be
British were religion, war, and economics (especially imperialism).[29] It seems
logical, then, that an internationalist such as Ernest Jones (as demonstrated
in chapter 1) would take on all of these topics in their relation to nationalism

"Morris's 'Chants' and the Problems of Socialist Culture" in *Socialism and the Literary Artistry
of William Morris,* edited by Florence S. Boos and Carole G. Silver (Columbia: University of
Missouri Press, 1990), 127–46.

26. This was Cooper's consistent spelling of the name. Historians such as Martha Vicinus
(*The Industrial Muse,* 109) and G. D. H. Cole (*Chartist Portraits,* 198) utilize the more usual
spelling of Shakespeare.

27. By his own account, he contributed only two songs, while local working-class poets John Bramwich and William Jones wrote the other thirty. Though the sixpence volume
"achieved a wide popularity" (Cole, *Chartist Portraits,* 198), unfortunately *The Shaksperean
Chartist Hymn Book* itself seems to be lost. But Cooper printed the hymns in his weekly paper
Extinguisher, and in his autobiography he reprinted one hymn by each contributor, also men-
tioning the tunes to which each was sung.

28. See Sanders, "'God is our guide! Our cause is just!' The *National Chartist Hymn Book*
and Victorian Hymnody," *Victorian Studies* 54.4 (2012): 679–705.

29. See, for example, *Britons: Forging the Nation, 1707–1837* (New Haven, CT: Yale University Press, 1992), 367–71.

and class exploitation in his epic poem *The New World, A Democratic Poem* (1851). With its lengthy preface and dedication, this work took pride of place on the very first page of the very first issue of Jones's new journal *Notes to the People,* which continued publication throughout 1851 and 1852. As Jones describes it, the epic traces the "successive phases through which the nations of the earth have passed, to shew how the working classes have been made the leverage by which one privileged order has subverted another" (*The New World: A Democratic Poem,* 3). Royalty cedes power to the feudal nobility, which eventually succumbs to the wealthy middle class, and now "we stand" at a point of decision between the forces of "democracy" and "reaction" (ibid., 4). As a contribution to the forces he sees as contending for democracy, with this poem Jones hurls a violent attack at colonialism and its base financial aims, as well as indicting the role religion plays in papering over economic aggression with pretenses to civilization and salvation. Furthermore, he seeks to persuade working people that they have nothing whatever to gain from warring with each other on behalf of their rulers. In an effort to foster inter-nationalism, he devotes considerable attention to all three of the major factors Colley identifies as primary contributors to British nationalism.

The poem's length means that modern readers have convenient access to short excerpts at most, and therefore it might be useful to provide some summary and a sense of the texture of the work. *The New World* lays out the vision of a war between British forces in India and various regional militaries, with colonial Britain in retreat before a victorious Hindu army. Against this background, the narrative launches into an ambitious political and historical survey of civilization and the ways in which its governance has varied over the centuries, but with a wry satire of the slogans and pretenses of contemporary Britain. For example, perceiving its own precarious position, the nobility seeks to take power from the tottering monarchy by recruiting working-class sympathies thus: "*'If burdens crush ye, and if bread is high, / It is the King—the King's to blame!'* they cry, / *If famine threats, work lacks, and wages fall, / The King, the King alone, is cause of all!'*" (ibid., 8, all italics are in the original). These were precisely the arguments used in Jones's time by middle-class Corn Law repealers who hoped to shake the power of the aristocracy.

In the poem, once the nobility has transferred power to its own hands, they bid the masses to disarm, go home, and for "the future wait, / And hope the best, for—*they'll deliberate*" (ibid.). But nothing of general use happens, the people continue in misery, and eventually the nobility face their own challenge for power from the middle class. Now the traders rally the masses by saying "*'If burdens crush ye, and if bread is high, / The landlords—landlords are to blame!'* they cry" (ibid., 10). Though it is becoming a familiar refrain, it works because ordinary people are so desperate, and the middle class acquires legislative ascendency over the nobles. That done, they quiet the unrest they had fomented by commanding the populace to "'Disarm!—go home!—and wait—*while we reform!*'" (ibid.) Jones captures the formulaic nature of the rhetoric used to urge on and then pacify the majority, the promises sworn and forgotten.

When time passes and the plight of the people fails to improve, "*they wake to find, once more betrayed, / 'Tis but a change of tyrant they have made*" (ibid.). The lack of any real change and the absence of middle-class urgency about making change have serious consequences, as evidenced by one of the best and most powerful lines in the entire epic: "And 'give us time!'—and 'give us time!' [the traders] cried: / Another generation starved and died" (ibid.). The latter line's brisk pace and unadorned statement of fact are reminiscent of the business world in which traders have made their fortunes, while the rhyme juxtaposes their whining pleas for procrastination with the stark and massive consequences of their delay. Inescapably memorable, it is a supremely effective couplet. Here the poem pauses to note the role of state and religious institutions as tools of the ruling class. The narrator shows that they are not neutral arbiters of unbiased laws and customs, above and independent of social conflicts, but they exist to protect the interests of those in power.

Yet at last the people themselves have had enough of merely "changing tyrants" and "the nations" thoughtfully and peacefully rise, overthrowing with ease those old, oppressive institutions. The uprising is not limited to Europe alone, but sees the "swarthy" peoples of Africa smashing slavery, South Americans throwing off colonialism, Jews gaining a homeland,[30] and women sharing equal rights with men (ibid., 12–13).[31] Throughout the poem, Jones maintains a sweeping global vision that reaches beyond not only Britain but also Europe, always reminding readers that internationalism is essential

---

30. If indeed he had any particular region—not just *some* place of rest and refuge—in mind, Jones must have been unaware of the millions of people inhabiting Palestine. He envisions the Jewish people's entry to "Jerusalem" as a peaceful, uncontested march into a place with "no prior owners" and where it would not be necessary to commit the "crimes revolting" of conquerors (*The New World,* 13). Quite possibly he had no specific locale in mind, since later Zionists themselves discussed a handful of possible places to settle, scattered all around the world. Regardless, Jones's admirable championing of a persecuted people is consistent with his political vision in this poem.

31. Gilbert makes an interesting point about how Jones here (and to a lesser extent Cooper, in book 9 of the *Purgatory*) couples Jews and women as somehow set apart: "The irreducible particularity represented at this historical moment by women and by Jews troubles the possibility of a homogenous and universal public and the elimination of all geographical boundaries" ("History and Its Ends in Chartist Epic," 36).

to freedom. Concluding the epic is a celebratory, futuristic vision of scientific achievement ("aeronauts," public health, weather control, "cars of steam," "rays of light" which can transmit messages—perhaps even images—over vast distances, etc.), of international peace, and of the abolition of property ownership and class distinctions (ibid., 14).

The preface to *The New World* scathingly exposes the cynicism of the great empire in which Britons are supposed to take pride, revealing the justice of resistance to it and enlisting Britons to oppose it as well. Instead of portraying imperialism as the extension of the British customs of alleged fairness and the code of law, as the spiritual rescuer of perishing souls, and as the bringer of enlightened education and technological progress, Jones condemns it as a marauding bid to extend the economic power of Britain's ruling class. While admitting the customary boast that on Britain's colonies "the sun never sets," he caustically adds "but the blood never dries" (ibid., 1). His poet's ear serves him well in this terse formulation, which exactly follows the rhythm of the boast and thus twines itself like a clinging vine around an unwilling host, making it difficult any longer to say the one clause without hearing the other. He acknowledges that Britain's "commerce touches every shore, but their ports have been opened by artillery, and are held by murder" (ibid.). Jones makes explicit the necessity of military conflict to capitalist economic expansion, simultaneously exploding the notion that "private enterprise" is private; in his observation, the state's military might serves as a crowbar for entrepreneurial encroachment. It is significant that this preface appeals not only to Britons to withdraw support for "their" nation's conquest of others but also addresses itself to the working people of the United States in a gesture of international fraternity.

The poem itself includes numerous metaphors that similarly point to the imbrication of economic and military means in imperial expansion. Describing how "Nations, like men, too oft are given to roam, / And seek abroad what they could find at home," one extended metaphor uses the terms of commerce to characterize military campaigns (ibid., 7). Speaking of nations who deploy "their armies" abroad, Jones calls them

> Destruction's traders! who, to start their trade,
> Steal, for the bayonet, metal from the spade.
> The interest's—blood; the capital is—life;
> The debt—is vengeance; the instalment—strife;
> The payment's—death; and wounds are the receipt;
> The market's—battle; and the whole—a cheat.
> (*The New World: A Democratic Poem*, 7)

In these lines warfare is a thoroughly financial concern overseen by "traders," the identical appellation given to middle-class rulers elsewhere in the
poem. While their trade might appear to be in wine, tea, sugar, or textiles, it
is at bottom a trade in "destruction" of human lives for the plunder of foreign
markets, materials, and labor. The metaphor is slightly strained but succeeds
in impressing on readers the point that, for capitalists, war is a matter of business. It also suggests that "cheat[ing]" is every bit as routine a characteristic
of business as are receipts, payments, interest, markets, etc. War is stripped
of its ideological justification by being equated with what most Victorians
regarded as filthy and corrupting (hence the necessity for women to be the
moral guardians of and restoratives for those men who engaged in "the public
sphere"). And it is condemned by the concluding declaration that both war
and business amount to nothing more distinguished than "a cheat."

The predication in these six lines is also of interest, since the couplets are
overwhelmingly dominated by forms of "to be" (eight times) and include only
two transitive verbs ("start" and "steal"). The implied or stated "to be" verbs
signify the equation of war and commerce, casting military exploits entirely
in terms of financial transaction and calculation and giving the lie to claims
that invasions serve to "'civilise, reform, redeem!'" (ibid., 5). In light of this
poem's republication during the Sepoy Rebellion, it is worth noting that Jones
includes the vengeance of the conquered against their conquerors as a natural
and predictable part of imperialist expansion, not some unaccountable craze
brought on in the "natives" by the heat or their inherited disregard for human
life. In fact, their violent resistance to conquest is a "debt" which is by definition *owed* to the "traders" in destruction (ibid., 7).

By implication, it is a debt the workers of England should help the conquered pay, for the metal in the conqueror's bayonets is filched from much-
needed spades at home. Here is where the two transitive verbs in these lines
occur, showing the ruling class at its most energetic: the traders "start" warfare internationally by "steal[ing]" spades domestically. The agricultural
implement stands in not only for the potential jobs and incomes earned by
those who would ply it but also for the all-important yield of a life-sustaining
harvest. This fact, along with the reality that working people are the ones who
must wield the bayonets and suffer the "wounds" and "death" of battle, illustrates in part how imperialism abroad costs poor people at home. This is a
portion of the economic transaction which rulers would prefer to conceal or
sanitize, but which Jones's use of metaphor reveals (an instance of the epistemological power of metaphor). So too do his careful choice and arrangement
of verbs which, while indicting by equating finance and war, also draw our
attention to the two moments of *active* bourgeois initiative: domestic theft to
sustain the prosecution of international theft.

As mentioned, Jones cast his broad historical survey against an Indian background, a choice he would later regard as prophetic. For although originally published in 1851, *The New World* appeared again in 1857 under the new title *The Revolt of Hindostan or The New World*. Its republication came in direct response to the domestic British reaction to the Indian Uprising of 1857. Periodicals of the time overwhelmingly reflect a sentiment for revenge on the sepoy army and other rebels,[32] with calls for retribution growing increasingly vitriolic as news of Hindu excesses was revealed. After the British began to regain control of India, they carried out a ruthless suppression which included the killing in one city of over six thousand people regardless of age or sex, as well as the gloating vigilantism of volunteer execution parties and hangmen (Morton, *A People's History of England*, 467–68; Bates, *Subalterns and Raj: South Asia since 1600*, 65–92). In his writings about these events, Jones did not deny the atrocities committed by some mutineers but counterposed to them the slaughters perpetrated there by Britain and contextualized them within the disastrous impact of British rule over several decades. He also did not let pass the opportunity to draw some parallels with English rule in Ireland, describing what he called English "sepoyism" (atrocities) and calling for the independence of both colonies from England.[33] His arguments on behalf of decency and Indian independence sharply distinguished him from his contemporaries then and still earn him respect now. Perhaps too his views on this matter partly explain the prominence of *The New World* in modern critical discussions of Jones.[34]

Jones wrote *The New World* during his inhumane imprisonment from 1848–50, a time when he would have been keenly aware of whose class interests were served by state institutions such as the army and police. In the poem he imagines the defeat of British forces in Hindostan, and though he respects the strength of ordinary soldiers and can appreciate their "misused courage," he recognizes the "centuries of wrong" which prompt rebellion on the Indian subcontinent and cries, "God, hope, and history take the Hindhu side!" (*The New World*, 6) His analysis of the dilemma of British soldiers sent to "murder[] millions to enrich the few" (ibid., 5) reveals his view that the soldiers themselves fight in a cause not their own and from which they gain nothing,

---

32. Modern historical accounts make clear the range of motives (reinstatement of kingdoms and chiefdoms, military grievances, anger at taxation and moneylenders, etc.) and participants in the insurrection—from rural elites to peasants to nomadic communities to soldiers. Crispin Bates provides a thorough account of the multifarious nature of the rebellion in chapter 4 of *Subalterns and Raj: South Asia since 1600*.

33. See, for example, Jones's articles in the *People's Paper* for September 5 and October 31, 1857.

34. See, for instance, Ronald Paul's "'In Louring Hindostan': Chartism and Empire in Ernest Jones's *The New World, a Democratic Poem*," *Victorian Poetry* 39:2 (2001): 189–204.

not even a living wage. At home they "leave starving families to beg bread," indicating the insufficiency of their pay. And he makes the point still more forcefully when the poet asks British rulers, "Think ye that men will still the patriot play, / Bleed, starve, and murder for four pence per day[?]" (ibid., 6) Whether in uniform or out, working men face severe exploitation for which the language of patriotism cannot compensate; since the men and their "starving families" cannot eat glory or medals and they are no better off as soldiers than they were as weavers, they are right to question where the profits of war, like the profits of cotton, go. Such questioning is part of Jones's project, for if soldiers will no longer "the patriot play," they evaporate the capacities of their nations to wage war.

This section of the poem depicts British soldiers as victims of their own rulers, not of their Indian counterparts. They are "Marched against men, God never made their foes," and thinking of this and of their starving families back home, they "strike unwilling blows" (6). They glimpse the fact that they actually have no quarrel with people in other countries who seek independence, and though for the time they go through the motions of war, their sense of righteousness and resolution erodes and they fight half-heartedly. Their awareness that those who stand to gain from the mutual murder of poor Indian and poor Englishman are corrupt feudal princes and avaricious British merchants will, Jones believes, lead to a cessation of armed conflict:

> What gain they, save they, by the deathful strife?
> What meed have they to balance risk of life?
> They conquer empires: not a single rood
> Is their's—not even the ground whereon they stood,
> When victory drenched it with their gallant blood!
> Think ye, that men will . . .
> [. . . . .]
> Go forth for others vile designs to fight[?]
>   (*The New World*, 6)

In the poem's vision of the future, these warring workers will have recognized their own interests, put down their arms, and united the world in friendship (ibid., 14). It is significant that this realization of international peace follows from a distinct consciousness of shared class interest. Jones posits that membership in a community defined by class has the power to negate national identities and boundaries, "for nigh the day has come, / When country signifies a larger home" (ibid., 13). Apparently, class consciousness also contributes to the eradication of artificial barriers for women, as Jones tantalizingly suggests in the lines "And when the strong the weak no more o'erbears, / But equal rights with Man sweet Woman shares" (ibid.). It is a sweeping conception of a future transformation, but what emerges unmistakably from this and Jones's other writings is that it cannot be achieved without the solidarity of the international working class.

That Jones wrote this epic after the defeats and setbacks of 1848 and during his own imprisonment might go some way to explaining some formal features of the poem that distinguish it from his earlier writing. Of course its length is striking—fifteen pages of tiny, double-columned print with few breaks—meaning that its reading requires a degree of sustained effort and the sort of literary patience one gains by some practice and leisure. Its many hundreds of iambic pentameter couplets also might make it less accessible than much of his own previous writing and of Chartist song, for example. So too would its grand scope—a survey of civilization and systems of government, along with a good deal of historical and literary allusiveness. Though it includes some cautions directed to the "democrats" of the United States, the poem is noticeably less immediate and agitational in its tone than his earlier poems. All of this suggests a more aesthetic and educational orientation to the poem, an orientation that might have resulted partly from his isolation in prison and partly from the symptoms of decline in Chartism in the last two years of the 1840s. Nevertheless, Jones's epic poem—like his fiction, speeches, and journalism discussed in chapter 1—showed his unwavering commitment to internationalism and expressed his continued hope for a better future.

It might seem peculiar that Jones incarnates this hortatory vision of a future world in the anachronistic medium of heroic couplets. The use of neo-classical poetic modes in the first half of the nineteenth century was not uncommon among working-class writers (Linton also used couplets—though not heroic—in *Bob Thin*), even though poetic norms among educated writers had dramatically shifted toward a more expressive, personal idiom under the influence of the Romantic poets. This might well be attributable to the fact that poor readers had much cheaper access to older rather than modern poetry, so that their models had about them a rather musty air in more than physical ways. But like Cooper's Spenserian stanzas, Augustan couplets must also have represented a level of cultural attainment that worker-writers sought as a kind of surety to their poetic bonds, a formal backing that lent authority and gravity to their efforts and voices. In Jones's case, though, these explanations seem inadequate because, though rendered economically unstable (he was disinherited) and socially marginal by his commitment to Chartism, he hailed from a well-to-do family and enjoyed a sound education in Germany prior to his move to England. He undoubtedly knew that the legacy of Romanticism had changed the field for contemporary poets; did he choose heroic couplets as a formal identification with or appeal to other working-class poets? If so, it is a striking instance of political solidarity *by specifically poetic means,* irreducible to theme or even ordinary language.

Probably Jones also knew how eighteenth-century poetic conventions lent themselves to satire, denunciation, and moral judgment as well as the expansive and detailed knowledge or analysis so characteristic of the age of essays, dictionaries, and biological classification schemes. Closed iambic pentameter couplets (with their hierarchy of pauses, balanced rhetoric, and tidy correspondence of syntax and line) represented detached empirical observation, logical demonstration, balance, and command—in other words they were the perfect choice for the expansive global epic Jones had in mind, one which offered and interpreted the stages of human history viewed synchronically. Personal awareness or individual self-expression is not the goal here, so open couplets or other lyric forms will not do. Instead Jones requires a form simultaneously empirical and morally denunciatory, as he desires to tip the balance of opinion and action towards finally liberating the working classes from their historical role of enabling others to grasp power. As for all the epic poets discussed in this chapter, the nature and history of his medium, as well as the burden of his expressed message, form part of the power of his work.

A node that my discussions of these three epics all touch is Victorian medievalism. As for other cultural barometric readings in this chapter, the preeminent exemplar of a traditionalist engagement with medievalism is none other than the poet laureate Tennyson, who composed Arthurian poems throughout his long career and, through them, represented contemporary conventional values and practices as natural and nonideological.[35] The transmission of those values is the ultimate end toward which his "Morte d'Arthur" (1842), for example, marshals its readers.[36] Framed by the poem Tennyson called "The Epic," "Morte d'Arthur" concludes with the paradox that the dying king and his famed sword Excalibur must physically part and depart in order that the legend and values they represent may be communicated down the ages in the form and power of myth. Tucker's important reading of the poem concludes that "the subject of 'Morte d'Arthur' is cultural transmission, the handing on or handing over of a communal ideal whose

---

35. For a convincing analysis of Tennyson in these terms, see Antony Harrison's *Victorian Poets and the Politics of Culture: Discourse and Ideology* (Charlottesville: University of Virginia Press, 1998), 17–43.

36. The following discussion of "Morte d'Arthur" draws on Herbert Tucker's reading of the poem in *Tennyson and the Doom of Romanticism* (Cambridge, MA: Harvard University Press, 1988), 317–45.

[. . .] essence is communication" (*Tennyson,* 318). If the epic ideal previously had consisted in transmitting a culture (epic serves as a conduit for the passing of a set of beliefs, values, practices across generations and places), here it consists in the notion that transmission *is* culture (the act of communication, without alteration, itself becomes the belief, value, or practice to be preserved). In other words, an epic attains to the status of culture only insofar as it performs a conservative, preservationist role—such a definition is inherently defensive and reactionary. If culture equals transmission, then it is precisely the *maintenance* of existing power relations—sexually, economically, domestically—that is culture.

Chartist epic's aesthetic and social challenge to dominant values represented the very antithesis or negation of culture so defined. [37] This is why Chartist appropriations of aesthetic cultural forms were potentially so powerful: the very practice of writing in high cultural forms such as epic while also challenging the conservative values embodied in Victorian medievalism created an ideological disruption, a cognitive dissonance, a destabilizing fissure in the lockstep association of epic with the transmission of culture which finally mutated into the notion that transmission *is* culture. To the extent that Chartist epic did not transmit or instantiate the values neo-medievalists represented as inevitable and absolute, it could not be "culture." Yet it was "culture," a pedigreed aesthetic practice and form with a lineage stretching further back than those favored middle ages. For these reasons the Chartist project of self-representation in epic forms—whether through heroic couplets or Spenserian stanzas or grotesquely illustrated doggerel verse—marked one of the most powerful and richly engaged cultural practices ever undertaken by the Chartist movement.

---

37. Arguably such poets as Arnold, the Rossettis, Morris, and Swinburne also demonstrate a counterhegemonic use of medievalism (Harrison, 17–43).

· 3 ·

REVOLUTIONARY STRATEGY
AND FORMAL HYBRIDITY IN
CHARTIST FICTION

When one thinks of Chartist literature, one generally imagines poetry, and for good reason. But as the re-publication of Chartist short stories and novels in recent years has shown, these writers also generated a considerable body of fictional self-representations. This chapter highlights three examples of Chartist fiction that bookend the ten years of greatest activity in the movement, with extended analysis of one important work. Thematically, the stories discussed here share a central preoccupation with revolution: its advisability, its prospects during the Chartist decade, and the mechanisms essential to its success or failure. Alexander Somerville's *Dissuasive Warnings to the People on Street Warfare* (1839), as its name suggests, seeks to convince Chartists not to resort to physical force and insurrection, while "Argus"'s serial story "The Revolutionist" (1840) promotes revolutionary activity by setting its tale in a triumphant Paris during the 1789 revolution. Finally, Thomas Martin Wheeler's novel *Sunshine and Shadow* (1849–50) mounts an extended case for the necessity of independent working-class leadership in the success of the revolution it envisions.

Of particular interest for this study is the fact that each of these fictional tales partakes of some hybridity of forms or genres or literary conventions, whether by mixing epistolary form with journalism and fiction, or allegory with history, or prose narrative with poetry. In these ways they register the state of flux in which literature more broadly found itself in the mid-Victorian period (think of Dickens's novelistic incorporation of farce or of his journalism/sentimental sketches in *Sketches by Boz*, Barrett Browning's verse novel *Aurora Leigh,* or Dante Rossetti's double works combining poetry and painting). Introducing a special issue of *Studies in English Literature* devoted to the topic of "Victorian Hybridities," U. C. Knoepflmacher briefly surveys how early human fears of "unnatural" mixing and mingling partly gave way by the eighteenth and nineteenth centuries, under the influence of botanists and physiologists who demonstrated that species routinely crossed, with results that were stable, fertile, and beneficial. Of course many people still recoiled from the conclusions suggested by these data, and even before Darwin, "the notion that seemingly arbitrary recombinations were not only far from erratic or capricious but could also result in the creation of enduring new structures posed a severe challenge for traditionalist believers in the fixity and authority of established forms" ("Editor's Preface: Hybrid Forms and Cultural Anxiety," 745–46). For writers such as Thomas Carlyle, George Eliot, and Arthur Hugh Clough, contradictions could yield to new forms of belief. For others such as Matthew Arnold and, later, John Ruskin, hybridity signaled a distinctly modern affliction characterized by a lack of wholeness and purity as well as by corruption, disease, and deformity.[1] How do working-class writers fit into our schematics of Victorian attitudes toward the blending of alternatives?

Rob Breton discusses a kind of hybridity in his essay on "Genre in the Chartist Periodical," arguing that Chartist intellectuals, far from perceiving as contradictory or problematic their inclusion of sentimental language or sensational fiction in their political writing, instead regarded it as continuous with a diverse working-class culture in existence since the late eighteenth century. "Conceding to the infusion of popular expressions and fiction," he says, "was a way to demonstrate that [the Chartist press] were joining a culture and not attempting to convert it" ("Genre in the Chartist Periodical," 117). There is merit in his broad historical argument, but I want to look in a more detailed, literary technical way at the specific effects generated by the blending of distinct genres, including the cognitive flexibility it engenders as part of the Chartist imaginary. Choosing examples focused on revolutionary themes not only showcases the oppositions and nuances of Chartist thinking on this topic but also reduces the number of variables in considering the particular impacts of certain generic choices.

It is significant that the concept of "hybridity" in the nineteenth century has been consistently connected with subversion. Post-colonial theorists have most often used the term, seeing its amalgamation of racial and cul-

---

1. For more extended demonstrations of this summary, see Jonathan Smith's "Domestic Hybrids: Ruskin, Victorian Fiction, and Darwin's Botany" and Knoepflmacher's "Hybrid Forms and Cultural Anxiety" in *Studies in English Literature, 1500–1900* 48.4 (Autumn 2008).

tural categories as potentially (albeit conflictedly) liberatory.[2] Dino Felluga's account of the Victorian verse novel, likewise, showcases the ways in which that hybrid form "resist[s]" not only the century's emerging profession of literary criticism but also the dual (and dueling) ideologies represented by Romantic lyric and the bourgeois novel ("Verse Novel," 174). Mikhail Bakhtin established the vocabulary for discussing hybridity as part of his argument for the novel's dialogic destabilizing of ideological discourse.[3] Yet despite this long literary critical association between resistance and hybridity, "in relation to the Victorian working-class writer, hybridity has just begun to enter critical discourse," as Kirstie Blair has observed ("'He Sings Alone': Hybrid Forms and the Victorian Working-Class Poet," 526). The tradition of examining working-class writing through thematic and political, rather than aesthetic, lenses largely accounts for this belatedness. Performing its own small "hybrid" of approaches, this chapter argues for the utility of approaching the semantic categories of these Chartist stories through their formal categories, and simultaneously points to important exceptions in the coupling of hybridity with subversion.

Somerville's *Dissuasive Warnings* (1839)

In the summer of 1839, Chartists presented their first mass petition to Parliament and awaited the result of their deliberations in July. Anticipating the rejection of their demands, the movement fitfully prepared for a month-long strike, or "sacred month," to begin in August, and as Malcolm Chase explains, the plan for that month was "not an action short of outright insurrection, it *was* insurrection" (*Chartism: A New History*, 80). In an effort to stem the tide in favor of such a confrontation, the "radical" rural laborer turned middle-class journalist Alexander Somerville[4] published a series of six one-penny letters weekly between May and July, clearly announcing his position in the debate among Chartists over preparedness and advisability in his title: *Dissuasive Warnings to the People on Street Warfare* (1839). Somerville's writings

---

2. See Homi Bhabha and Edward Said, for example.

3. See his *The Dialogic Imagination,* trans. Caryl Emerson and Michael Holquist (Austin: University of Texas Press, 1981).

4. Somerville published his *Autobiography of a Working Man* in 1848, and it has been reprinted numerous times. For an assessment of the many identities he fashions for himself there and in his other writings, see Julie F. Codell's "Alexander Somerville's Rise from Serfdom: Working-Class Self-Fashioning through Journalism, Autobiography, and Political Economy," in *The Working-Class Intellectual in Eighteenth- and Nineteenth-Century Britain,* ed. Aruna Krishnamurthy (Farnham [Surrey]: Ashgate, 2009), 195–218.

consistently represented him as the opponent of injustice and oppression, and he regularly directed his discourse to the working class from which he sprang, so his voice was not a new one in Chartist ears even if his politics would gradually come to appear mercenary and unprincipled (Thompson, *Chartists*, 305; Chase, 108; Codell, 202–5; and *passim*). For the purposes of *Dissuasive Warnings*, Somerville identifies not only as a working man but also as a Chartist (which he certainly was not), and he is at pains throughout the text not to denigrate as malicious or stupid his physical force opponents; instead he wishes to correct their mistakes.

Somerville begins his second letter by stating that his "purpose is to dissuade the Chartists from the use of physical force. The plan is to carry conviction by argument and demonstration, so far as demonstration can be carried in writing" (*Dissuasive Warnings to the People on Street Warfare*, 106). Especially intriguing here is his introduction of the idea that argument alone will not convince people the way "demonstration" in "writing" can, setting the stage for a presentation that is not only polemic but also something more. What that something is he hints in a subsequent paragraph. Referring to the popular *Defensive Instructions for the People on Street Warfare* (1832) by Macerone, Somerville says that those instructions "are now about to be tested by a sketch of street warfare supposed to be raging in the town of Birmingham" (ibid.). A suppositious sketch, or fictional story, will carry the burden of his polemic in a hybrid form that is itself framed in a third generic category: a series of epistles. He urges his readers to "ponder[] well" the story that follows, because in it one can "test the power of a military, against an insurgent enemy" (ibid.). It is a remarkable claim. Repeatedly using the language of scientific experiment ("demonstration," "test," "test"), Somerville posits that imagined scenarios are the testing grounds for political and military theory. His literary laboratory for social and martial trial follows a sound scientific protocol by creating the most favorable circumstances for the success of the hypothesis; he sets a scene of insurrection in Birmingham because, he says, that city has the *best* chance of success in such an event.

Few scientific tests are designed to make one laugh, though, and it is hard to know whether the patriotic ex-soldier Somerville had any such intention here, but the absurdity of how badly the rebel Chartists fare is almost funny, if it were not so awful. One of his main threads of dissuasive argument is that government forces completely outmatch the rocks and pikes and fowling pistols wielded by brave but outgunned Chartists. Progressively ratcheting up the firepower, the narrator moves us from the fixed bayonets and muskets of the infantry, to "a rocket troop" and the firing of shells, to "an eight-and-a-half-inch mortar" and a "Shrapnell shell" (ibid., 109–10). When the insurgents manage to capture some of the rockets, they do not know how to use them, so the shells fire backwards into their own people and wreak havoc and death (ibid., 111).

If the unequal firepower is not enough to discourage the physical force Chartists, Somerville deploys his second thread of dissuasive argument: the inequality between a disciplined army poised against men "moved by impulse and ruled by their measure of enthusiasm" (ibid., 114–15). He describes a tragicomic scene among the untrained rebels in which men who were assigned to the back of the lines move to the front, and some from the front move to the back, but those in the back whose sense of duty kept them in place shove the front men towards the front where they belong, making them bump and stumble against the backs of those in front, causing those in front to swear at the "blundering men" and the bunglers to swear back at the front men, etc. (ibid., 115). The confusion and mistakes continue and multiply until nearly all of the insurgents are killed by a charge of the cavalry (ibid., 116). Is this comedy or tragedy? Does he intend for this to be humorous, even while he repeatedly praises the bravery and the "strong right arms, and the stout hearts" of the insurgents (ibid.)? The skitlike foolery could be judged offensive, if it were not for the tone of pity and regret that occasionally creeps in. In other words, the very admixture of tragedy with the comedy is where Somerville places his faith that he will not completely alienate the audience to which he addresses himself in some earnest. He seems to rely on this generic mingling as the vehicle that will carry his arguments through.

Such a subtle, and perhaps even unintentional, combination of modes pales in comparison with the much more explicit concatenation of genres across the whole series of letters. Somerville's personal narrative voice frames everything else in its direct address to his readers in an epistolary mode, and this establishes an intimacy between author and audience, compelling our attention. Within that epistolary frame he includes what he marks as fictitious "letters" from a correspondent on the scene in Birmingham to some person in London. This enables him to create interest in his narrative by giving readers the immediacy, excitement, and uncertainty of an eyewitness account. He dates this person's letters by the hour of writing, breaks off one letter mid-sentence—as if events intervened—and resumes it some hours later, and even has his correspondent express uncertainty about surviving the events he describes until morning (ibid., 112). By this means Somerville briskly paces the events and helps readers briefly forget their didactic intent.

Letter IV moves from the personal correspondence of an eyewitness to the reportorial accounts of various London newspapers, including a macabre, bloodthirsty Tory newspaper (ibid., 118), an opposing newspaper that chastises the Tories for their political opportunism, and other newspapers. This gives way to a first-person account of related events in Glasgow, written by a participant in the insurrectionary activity there. Including this physical force sympathizer is undoubtedly part of a strategy to appear balanced in his presentation, much like including the opposing newspapers. Finally, the organizing, editorial voice returns to continue the narrative of events in Glasgow, and inserts the texts of conflicting "bills" or broadsides posted there by the insurrectionaries, on one hand, and the Magistrates, on the other, capturing the excitement, heightened rhetoric, and confusion of the moment.

Personal letters, newspaper accounts, a participant's narration, public address announcements, and an omniscient narrator join forces in this tragi-comic fictional polemic that uses imagination to test reality. *Dissuasive Warnings* is as generically hybrid as can be, but its orientation is firmly antirevolutionary, thus challenging the prevailing consensus that sees heteroglossia as by definition counterhegemonic. Of course being antirevolutionary does not necessarily preclude all possibility of unsettling linguistic, social, and literary norms. By juxtaposing (albeit faintly and unevenly) the voices of Chartist rebels with those of magistrates and official newspapers, Somerville does open up a discursive space that is at least contested. Perhaps with some desire to register that contest more forcefully than his multivocal but lopsided presentation does, he significantly ends his imaginative experiment *in medias res,* with plenty of "din and disaster" (ibid., 130) but also with decisive victory on neither side. As Haywood points out in his introduction to the tale, "the narrative is not resolved" and "the cities are left in partial rebel control" ("Introduction" to *Literature,* 16). In this respect his narrative closely resembles the other two—prorevolutionary—fictions in this chapter, again troubling any neat correlation between formal devices and ideological intentions.

Some months after *Dissuasive Warnings* and before "Argus"'s "The Revolutionist," discussed below, a profoundly important insurrection did occur in Newport, a port town of great importance to the collieries and ironworks in South Wales. Precise details are elusive, but the original plan was for workers to make pre-dawn seizures of power not only in Newport but also in Brecon and the significant market and communications center of Abergavenny, to show the Chartist muscle behind demands for passage of the Charter and secure the release of such jailed Chartist leaders as Henry Vincent.[5] At the same time, Chartists in West Yorkshire, Tyneside, and Carlisle would also

---

5. My account here follows the narrative provided by Chase (106–140). For a still more detailed version of these events, see D. J. V. Jones's *The Last Rising: The Newport Insurrection of 1839* (Oxford: Oxford University Press, 1985).

take insurgent action, though this part of the plan faltered early and never took any definite shape. Welsh plans ultimately focused on Newport alone (though disturbances aimed at industry, police, and civic authorities took place elsewhere in the region the same night), and in November 1839 about 9,000 men armed with rifles, pikes, and other weapons converged on Newport under the leadership of John Frost, Zephaniah Williams, and William Jones. Soldiers systematically fired on the Chartists, resulting in "the largest number of fatalities of any civil disturbance in modern British history" (Chase, 109–10). Leaders were swiftly arrested, tried, and sentenced to death, though their sentences were commuted to transportation for life. This was a confusing, frightening, dispiriting event in Chartist history, and certainly sharpened polarities within the movement over the use of (offensive and defensive) violence. Newport had a strong impact on Chartist literature as well as theory and practice, and might have seemed to bear out Somerville's predictions in *Dissausive Warnings*. Nevertheless, by the summer of 1840 it was possible for the writer "Argus" to imagine, and advocate in the Chartist press, a successful revolution.

"Argus"'s "The Revolutionist" (1840)

One year after Somerville's serial denunciation of revolution, the pseudonymous author "Argus" published a serial rebuttal in the summer issues of Glasgow's *Chartist Circular*. In what could serve as a direct reply to Somerville's "overwhelming force" argument, when the angry crowd in this story begins to stir against tyranny, the narrator cries with what seems to be heavy irony, "O no! it cannot be. They have no arms! What signifies a mere tumult? [. . .] and amid a host of soldiery!" ("The Revolutionist," 132). Set in the beginning period of France's 1789 revolution, this story shows how the crowd rushes in among the royal troops and divides them into separate parties, creating confusion among them (ibid.). The soldiers do fire into the crowd and kill some people, but the rebels capture their enemy, try him, and execute him.

As if to repeat Somerville's imaginative experiment, "Argus" constructs a series of events that "test[s]" both the firepower and discipline of rebels ranged against armies. When word comes of an impending military attack, the armed rebels immediately form themselves into detachments, and the unarmed are instructed to "gain positions at the windows and house-tops" and gather stones and other missiles with which to harass the soldiers (ibid., 135). Everyone is strictly enjoined to "act in small detached bodies, so as to confuse the 'regulars'" (ibid.), and this "injunction was obeyed willingly" (ibid.). In stark contrast to Somerville's troop (troupe?) of stooges, there is good planning and discipline here. Tension mounts when the government's "heavy guns" and foot soldiers and cavalry arrive (ibid.). But these rebels obviously have a concerted, and very disciplined, plan, because all those forces are met by . . . no one; the streets are silent and deserted, leading them to think they have triumphed unopposed. However, when the troops start to leave the city, they get trapped in a long, narrow street and find themselves barricaded in on both ends. They suffer massive casualties when the insurrectionists release two giant, cleverly modified wagons filled with stones and gathering deadly momentum. The people stationed in and on the houses then exacerbate the soldiers' confusion and panic by "shower[ing]" them with brick bats, stones, and other moveables, until they throw down their arms and try to flee (ibid., 137). The crowd then collects the abandoned weapons (presumably to aid in coming battles) and celebrates its victory.

This experiment, then, yields results directly opposed to Somerville's, though the generically hybrid test conditions correspond. Like Wheeler's novel some years later, "The Revolutionist" quite deliberately seeks to correct what it sees as a skewed historical record, claiming that "many of our readers have no means nor opportunity of ascertaining more" information about "republican France than what the pleasure or policy of a government paid 'historian' may condescend to grant" (ibid., 134). The story self-consciously casts itself as both fiction and history. What is odd, though, is trying to set "history" straight by means of a tale that is flagrantly fictionalized (an anonymous Napoleon shows up to aid the working man who leads Parisian laborers in defeating Louis XVI's army), and transparently anachronistic (the narrator makes reference to Macerone as being known and followed in 1789, when he would have been a year old in 1789 and did not publish his *Defensive Instructions* until 1832). It also freely tampers with its historical sources, corroborating the identity of the unnamed Napoleon by quoting a (fictitious) passage from the (genuine) *Memoirs of Emanuel Augustus Dieudonné, Count de Las Casas* (1818). "Argus'"s ostentatiously flexible definition of *history* as a compendium of fact and fiction complements, I would argue, his or her thinly veiled double vision: less an account of republican France than Chartist England, less interested in 1789 than 1839–40. The Chartist movement in the summer of 1840 badly needed a voice of confidence and hope, since the first six months of the year had seen John Frost transported and Feargus O'Connor imprisoned, among other leading Chartists punished for their connections to the previous year's disturbances. That it should be an openly revolutionary voice seems surprising, given the recoil from militancy and violence after the uprisings in Newport and Birmingham. This is where its hybrid status as a "history of republican France" provides it with political cover. Without risking government reprisals for advocating British insurrection, an historical fiction strategically flaunts its hybrid elasticity to galvanize militant Chartists after the setbacks of '39 and in the face of emerging challengers such as the "new move" Chartists.[6]

There are also allegorical dimensions to this story that superimpose on its narration of events a mystical or quasi-religious layer of meanings. It is striking that the story's celebrated protagonist is named only "the Operative," making him less an individual than a category of identity with whom all working people might identify.[7] After he leads the people to this first triumph over government power, a similarly symbolic, young unnamed maiden who stands for "Benevolence" crowns him with a wreath of flowers (ibid., 138–39). The story clearly invites readers to regard this strapping young artisan, whose shirt is "of a snowy whiteness" (ibid., 131), as a transcendent hero, and it is significant that "the Operative" and the unnamed Napoleon figure must temporarily leave France at story's end, promising that "we shall return to lead you on to victory or death!" (ibid., 139) The odd departure in the moment of victory and the promise to return in a crisis resonate with New Testament stories in which Jesus explains that though he must leave his disciples, he will return to aid them when the fullness of time demands it. "Who or what the leaders were, we cannot positively determine," says the narrator near the end of the story (ibid.), echoing the bewildered but faithful response of the apostles to the resurrected Jesus (or anticipating later bystanders to the elusive Lone Ranger).

The story's use of these allegorical tropes opens a number of interpretive possibilities, not the least of which is the nearly automatic connection between allegory and Bunyan's *Pilgrim's Progress* in the minds of most nineteenth century autodidacts. As Richard Altick demonstrated long ago, Bunyan's allegorical tale was as much a staple of "common readers" as the Bible itself. Any invocation of allegory therefore would surely elicit a reflexive connection to that work and the values it represented: democracy, faith in a utopian future, and the use of a comparatively accessible vernacular English which made it in some respects an early instance of the populist literary tradition in which many Chartist writers saw themselves as participating. By hybridizing his or her historical fiction with allegory, "Argus" thus uses genre as a literary short-

---

6. See Chase 169-ff for some description of "the new move."

7. For an extended example of Chartist allegory, see Thomas Doubleday's 1839 novel *The Political Pilgrim's Progress*, which advocates physical force Chartism. Haywood edited a modern edition of the novel, published by Ashgate in 1999.

hand for the literacy of a generation of proud autodidacts and for the democratic values typically associated with Bunyan's classic.

A more important interpretive possibility resulting from "The
Revolutionist"'s allegorical tropes is closely related to the story's prorevolutionary stance and its slightly ambiguous ending. The triumph in Paris as
described here is unequivocal, but "The Revolutionist" still has some dan-
gling threads to its conclusion. The reader knows the revolutionary struggle
is not over because the narrator says "Thus ended the *first* Parisian real trial
of strength" (ibid., emphasis added), implying a sequence of "trials" to follow. As already mentioned, the Operative promises to return for some future
conclusive struggle, but he also enjoins the rebels to act in small detachments
rather than to "act in large bodies" while he is gone, suggesting their continued involvement in conflict during his absence (ibid.). Even the Operative's promise of leadership on his return poses alternatives: he will lead them
to "victory" or he will lead them to "death" (ibid.). All of this means that
the story, like Somerville's before it and Wheeler's after it, has an open ending, with a futurity undetermined and dependent on human intervention.
In other words, the open ending interpellates its readers and asks them to
complete the narrative. Presenting a leader who is more allegory than indi-
viduated being, the story creates a discursive space that must and will be
occupied by others who are likewise "born to labour for [their] daily bread"
(ibid., 131). The Operative's apotheosis probably carries the allegorizing effort
too far, placing the role out of the reach of all but the most exceptional working people and thus collapsing the space it endeavors to make available to
future leaders. However, "Argus" emphasizes the role of leadership by stating
that the Parisian triumph proved successful "solely through the wisdom of
the leaders, and conveys a great moral lesson, both to the ruler and the ruled"
(ibid., 139). That "lesson" would, I believe, be clear without this assertion,
because the story's incorporation of allegory with respect to the Operative
draws our attention to precisely that empty space created by the stereotyped
language in which he is described, a vacuum that summons other worker-
leaders to fill its place.

Wheeler's *Sunshine and Shadow* (1849–50)

"The Revolutionist"'s stress on the role of leadership in revolutionary struggle gives it a particular similarity to Thomas Martin Wheeler's *Sunshine and
Shadow* (1849–50), which uses the serial novel form, blended with historical narrative and political treatise, to give sustained attention to questions of

revolutionary strategy. What follows is among the first sustained readings of this Chartist classic.[8]

Wheeler's[9] novel represents a dramatic alternative to the mainstream social problem novel and thus has an important claim on the attention of literary scholars. Among its more overlooked qualities are the book's revolutionary politics, yet to miss Wheeler's political innovation entails an incomplete understanding of his fictional innovation. The novel's form and interests, plot devices and authorial choices derived from a conscious desire (shared by Somerville and "Argus") to use fiction as a medium for debating the real issues at stake in deciding the future path of the workers' movement. For Wheeler, the desirability of revolution is the point of departure—not a regrettable illusion to be corrected by the hero's acquisition of wisdom—for a plot which then goes on to a frontal assault on the problem of how. The novel is not only a retrospective of a dead movement but also a fictional interpretation of history for the purpose of advancing a living movement that must seek out new theories and methods of organizing, namely on the basis of working-class independence and a centralized leadership. Here is a working-class man reaching conclusions similar to those of his contemporary Marx, independently of the philosopher and at least 50 years in advance of Lenin, with

---

8. Gustav Klaus, in chapter 3 of *The Literature of Labour: Two Hundred Years of Working-Class Writing* (Brighton: Harvester Press, 1985), briefly discusses this novel as part of his lucid argument about the tendency of Chartist fiction to concentrate on history. The ways in which the novel "proletarianizes" the hero of the *Bildungsroman* and disturbs the orthodoxies of middle-class morality form the substance of Ian Haywood's remarks on it (*Working-Class Fiction,* chapter 1). Chapter 3 of Martha Vicinus's *The Industrial Muse* draws attention to the novel's mixed generic tendencies, asking whether "it is possible to write revolutionary fiction using a traditional form" (133). See also Jack B. Mitchell's "Aesthetic Problems of the Development of the Proletarian-Revolutionary Novel in Nineteenth-Century Britain," in *Marxists on Literature,* ed. David Craig (London: Penguin, 1975); and P. Mary Ashraf's *Introduction to Working-Class Literature in Britain,* Part 2, *Prose* (East Berlin: Ministerium für Volksbildung, 1979). More recently, Rob Breton has published essays including commentary on Wheeler's novel. See for example "Ghosts in the Machina: Plotting in Chartist and Working Class Fiction," *Victorian Studies* 47 (Summer 2005): 557–75 and "Genre in the Chartist Periodical," in *The Working-Class Intellectual in Eighteenth- and Nineteenth-Century Britain,* ed. Aruna Krishnamurthy (Farnham: Ashgate, 2009), 109–28. Chris R. Vanden Bossche does include a full chapter devoted to working-class agency in this novel in his book *Reform Acts: Chartism, Social Agency, and the Victorian Novel 1832–1867* (Baltimore: Johns Hopkins University Press, 2014), 113–25.

9. Wheeler (1811–1862) held posts as a baker, gardener, woolcomber, and schoolteacher, as well as various positions (between 1840 and the mid-1850s) in the National Charter Association. As an industrial correspondent for *The Northern Star,* he had been known to its readers for some years before beginning publication of his novel, which was not issued in book form until Ian Haywood's 1999 edition *Chartist Fiction* (including both Wheeler's novel and Thomas Doubleday's *The Political Pilgrim's Progress*). The most complete account of his life is Stevens's *A Memoir of Thomas Martin Wheeler* (London: J. B. Leno, 1862). Wheeler did not publish any other novels.

whom the notion of a democratic and centralized party is chiefly associated.[10] In this respect his novel is truly original, and from this it derives its energy and urgency.

Unlike fictional portrayals of industrial Britain by Disraeli, Gaskell, Charles Kingsley, Dickens, and Eliot, *Sunshine and Shadow* does not gloss over the real dilemmas[11] facing England's employed classes by offering the salvation of emigration, heaven, sudden revelations of aristocratic birth or inherited fortune, or an all-conquering goodwill. Such endings can betray a fear of working-class agency and a pessimism about the immediate prospects of significant change. They evade the central debates the characters face, thus distancing readers from the reflective workers the novels portray and preventing a serious examination of the problems facing the movements in which they participate. Even the barest recollection of the working-class protagonists in *Mary Barton* (1848), *Felix Holt* (1866), *Alton Locke* (1850), and *Hard Times* (1854), for example, reveals a pattern of anti-heroes. John Barton is dominated by bitterness and despair, resulting in his guilty assassination of an employer's son and his banishment from the plot; both Felix Holt and Alton Locke become involved in frightful mob violence as if that must be the result of active, reform-minded agitation; and Stephen Blackpool's patient, passive, fog-headed suffering ("it's aw a muddle") poses what readers are to regard as a positive alternative to the collective efforts of his coworkers to better their conditions through their union.

Sunshine and Shadow directly confronts the debates and problems that so centrally occupy the mind of its worker hero. Its outlook is ever hopeful of the efficacy of workers' collective activity, examining various conflicts and modes of organizing with an expectant, rather than frightened, eye. The book does not assume that revolutionary change in the 1840s is impossible and ill-advised, and therefore its tone *vis-à-vis* the failure of revolution is tragic rather than congratulatory. The reader is presented with a character who identifies with the great struggles of the nineteenth century, who does hope for a dramatic reconstitution of society, and who consequently proceeds from those premises to a grappling with the organizational "machinery" necessary to achieve it. Unique among social problem novels, Wheeler's serialized tale confronts from within Chartism, based on current events and conditions, the possibility of an imminent English revolution.

---

10. Marx and Lenin elaborated their later ideas much more thoroughly and systematically than did Wheeler, but they were not writing fiction or trying to balance the demands of narrative with political theory.

11. Their novels forcefully represent the hardships and handicaps imposed by grinding poverty, but in my view they then fail to address adequately the dilemma of what exactly to do about those conditions.

The aim of my analysis, then, is to highlight the political theory that results from the novelistic treatment of some notable points in Chartist history. While Wheeler hangs his interpretations on the frame of Chartism's historical trajectory, allowing that chronology to impose a certain structure on the novel, he also exerts narrative control by inserting his hero's exile to the West Indies and United States. If one follows the analogy of scientific experiment articulated in Somerville's *Dissuasive Warnings* and practiced in "Argus"'s "The Revolutionist," *Sunshine and Shadow* takes history as its data but uses fictional plotting to postulate about other, concurrent experiments (slave and "free" labor, immigration schemes, and attempts at capitalist democracy) and to hypothesize about the ingredients and outcomes of future trials in the UK itself. From these plot elements the novel derives the political conclusions which set it apart both from other social problem novels and from earlier notions of how to carry on liberation struggles: its contention that laboring men and women must break from reliance on the middle class, seek revolution and not simply reform, and organize themselves in a tightly cohesive party for the greatest effectiveness in achieving that aim. The remainder of this chapter will take up the novel's presentation of each of those political conclusions in turn.

GENERIC DOUBLENESS: THE NOVEL AS HISTORY AND FICTION

It is difficult to extricate the accounts of historians from the novel's account of Chartist history, since Wheeler is quite consciously and deliberately interpreting history through his fiction. The narrator tells us that much of the novel's plot is formed from "history, but of history that has to be rewritten, to clear it of prejudice and calumny" (*Sunshine and Shadow*, 96). Apparently, the "prejudice and calumny" to which his novel stands as a correction occurred not only in press and historical accounts but also in creative writing as well. The narrator disparages fashionable novelists who either neglect working-class characters altogether or else portray "democrats" only in "warpaint" because they do not know any of the actors in these historic struggles (ibid., 99). By contrast, the aim of his explicitly hybrid book is to combine "a History of Chartism, with the details of our story" precisely by "depict[ing] one of yourselves," that is, by depicting a working-class hero in a more complex and interesting way than had mainstream novelists (ibid., 192). Though Wheeler makes his hero Arthur Morton a "Type [. . .] of his class" (ibid., 99) and an "ideal representative[] of known realities" (ibid., 129), at times even seeming to forget his character in order to make the most explicit possible commentary on the events and political issues under scrutiny, what is striking about this hero is his moral ambiguity (by middle-class standards). Notwithstanding that he is the novel's mouthpiece of Chartist propaganda, Arthur engages in a semi-adulterous relationship, later undergoing a desperate period in which he turns to alcohol, and even robs another man on the street. When his circumstances improve, he nevertheless maintains distance from his wife and home, devoting himself more fully to politics than to personal relations and eliciting the narrator's verdict that "if he was a better citizen, he was no longer so affectionate an husband" (ibid., 176), a remarkable negative judgment in a novel advocating devotion to Chartism and justifying working-class politics. Never could Dickens, for example, have permitted Oliver Twist such weaknesses and flaws.

However, besides verisimilitude, why would Wheeler make his hero complex in these ways? Audience is part of the answer. His tale aims at working-class readers whose experience has taught them how profoundly history and circumstance shape character and behavior, and who might be less wedded to the platitudes of bourgeois morality than are those whose children (unlike Arthur's) have not perished due to malnutrition and inadequate health care. Arthur's "character" flaws thus become an occasion for Wheeler to make a point about literary conventions and moral philosophy: good is not always rewarded, nor evil punished; and far from being a set of fixed, abstract principles, ethical standards and behaviors are heavily determined by material circumstances. The narrator contends that the "true source" of evil is "the unequal distribution of wealth," and that despite its ugliness and the desirability of its elimination, crime "is an effort of nature to restore a due balance amongst the varied members of her giant body" (ibid., 166–67). The novel's formal structure also suggests an important reason for allowing Arthur to sink temporarily into crime and drunkenness: the chapter whose substance those acts form follows immediately on a chapter that concludes with Arthur's humiliating resort to parish assistance (ibid., chap. XXX). Defeated and degraded in his own and others' eyes, Arthur submits to pauperism's extermination of self-respect out of desperate concern for his ailing wife. The experience permanently mortifies him, and the narrator draws attention to this fact by commenting on the "apathetic dullness," stupefaction, and semi-animate despair that often submerge a person who has sunk so low as to lose all self-respect (ibid., 162–63).

Arthur's character, however, is subsidiary to his participation in making the history with which the novel concerns itself. More than once the narrator defends his orientation to recent events at the expense of the usual novelistic fare: "We might have made our tale more interesting to many, by drawing more largely from the regions of romance, [. . .] We might have made it more piquant, by delineating the portraits of the active minds in the movement," but the true subject and hero of the book is Chartist history (ibid., 192). Not a romance, not a hagiography or exposé; Wheeler carefully distinguishes which genres his literary experiment will comprise. The result is a work of fiction with an unusually high degree of historical content and commentary, a blend that has understandably prompted some commentators to find fault with the literary style. Wheeler also recognized the pitfalls of such a project, correcting himself more than once with such statements as "But we digress from our tale" (ibid., 151) and "But we are not writing a political essay, and therefore must discontinue this theme" (ibid., 91). Still, while sometimes backing off from more extensive historical reference and analysis, Wheeler freely admits his conscious choice to make the history of Chartism the subject of his novel.

That said, the book is not merely a history but fictionalized history, recognizing the unique potential of artistic expression to win sympathy, stir the imagination, and inspire action. In his dedication of the novel, Wheeler laments the fact that "The fiction department of literature has hitherto been neglected" by Chartists and he acknowledges its power over minds, particularly those of youth (ibid., 72). It is, he says, a political tool too little wielded by partisans of their cause, and he hopes his efforts in *Sunshine and Shadow* will prompt others to write fiction as well. That Wheeler was concerned with the relation between fiction and history is evident from the very beginning of his novel, not only in his dedication but also—perhaps ironically—in the poetic epigraphs to each of his first two chapters. He selects two complementary passages from John Richard Beste's *Cuma, The Warrior-Bard of Erin, and Other Poems*. The apparently opposite epigraphs carefully balance fact and fancy, truth and imagination, and quite effectively introduce the twin concerns of *Sunshine and Shadow*. Above chapter I is placed a passage beginning "Fair truth shall be my theme" and ending "For, in sooth, / Fiction's best dress is still the garb of truth" (ibid.), announcing from the very first line that Wheeler's fiction, too, will focus primarily on real events. Following this, and inaugurating chapter II, is another quotation from Beste in which the charms and music of literature hold a character in a "spell," waking "Imagination" and moving him to call on "fancy" both to make and to console his sorrows (ibid., 73). Clearly there is an enchantment, an almost magical power in stories that Wheeler will seek to use for political ends. Thus the novel declares its historico-fictional double vision from the outset, and it does so in yet another genre: poetry.

The practice of using poetic epigraphs was commonplace in nineteenth-century novels, and for many novelists it undoubtedly marked a desire to graft onto their "degraded" narratives the more elevated, serious cachet historically attached to poetry. Almost every one of Wheeler's very many chapters (each weekly installment was short) features one or several poetic epigraphs from a wide range of writers, including German and Romantic poets, working-class contemporaries such as Eliza Cook and Thomas Cooper, Renaissance and eighteenth-century dramatists, and others. Although Wheeler's dedication declares his intention to champion fiction for its appeal to "the youth of our party," he cannot seem to resist the urge to incorporate large chunks of poetry (ibid., 72). The explanation for this might be equal parts literary norm, self-legitimating display, acknowledgement of Chartist cultural history, and a sort of character reference for fiction's quotidian subjects. However, if one thinks specifically through the lens of hybridity, which this chapter proposes, Wheeler's grafting of this range of canonical and noncanonical poets onto his own fictive voice expresses his complicated position as one whose writing marks both his belonging in and his exclusion from the traditions of authorship. He speaks in his own voice, the voices of literary elites, and the voices of minor and working-class writers, and while his intention in doing so might not be subversive, his praxis permits him to underscore what Blair would call his "'hybrid' status as working-class writer[]" ("He Sings," 527).

In *Sunshine and Shadow,* Wheeler traces the history of the Chartist movement through the ups and downs of a fictional orphaned working-class hero patriotically named Arthur Morton, beginning with his student days at a second-rate boarding school where his uncle had sent him, more to be rid of him than from any concern that his young relative strengthen his mind or make lasting friendships. Physically the young Arthur was small and pale, though bright-eyed and intense in keeping with his predilection for the books that constituted the early companions of his lonely boyhood. Perhaps because the characters in those books were his only society, his attachment to them was tender and strong, and "many a hot tear did he shed over the woes of the Madelines, and Rosinas, the Algernons and the Aubreys" about whom he read (*Sunshine and Shadow,* 74). A timid and dreamy lad whose favorite subject at school was poetry, Arthur suffered "the jokes and taunts of the wild urchins around him" (ibid.) until one day, when he reached his limit and pummeled two classmates, he gained the notice and respect of the school's most popular and rugged boy Walter North. Arthur transferred his loyalties and affection to the older Walter, regarding him as an elder brother even though Arthur was more intelligent, trusting, courteous, and loyal than his new idol. Nevertheless, Walter did impart to Arthur some of his self-confidence, and the friendship represented the first time in Arthur's life that he experienced real affection and kindness, the warmth of which called forth from him a new patience and love for his temperamentally opposite class-mates. Indeed, this first taste of genuine fondness permanently colored his human relations and transformed him from a shy and moody boy to a more generous and open man. Unfortunately this is the last time in the novel that anything positive can be said about Walter, who reappears later in the story after the two friends drift apart, the result of distance and Walter's neglect.[12]

Wheeler skillfully introduces Arthur through this vignette of his adoles-cence, capturing readers' sympathy and interest from the outset by demon-strating the hero's unassuming, faithful nature alongside his capacity to be passionate and even fierce when conditions warrant it (his ferocity also seems rather defensively designed to assert his masculinity against the contaminat-ing femininity of his poetic proclivities). The narrator cultivates our fond-ness for an imaginative child whose compassion for others can extend even to literary creations (in this respect he models the very sort of identifica-tion with narrative creations which *Sunshine and Shadow* itself here solicits for Arthur). Since Arthur will later espouse quite radical ideas and become the novel's mouthpiece for a polemic on politics and working-class organiza-tion, his early presentation as a vulnerable and virtuous boy goes a long way towards disarming any suspicious readers. The narrative presentation renders him less threatening than if he had sprung fully-formed from the head of, say, Feargus O'Connor.

Revolution, Not Reform

One of Arthur's convictions that informs the entire novel is that revolution-ary change—in explicit contrast to reform alone—represents the hope of the future. For example, during a period of exile in the United States, Arthur sadly observes that "There, as in Britain, the mass of the population was at the bot-tom of the wheel—the many dependent upon the capital of the few" (ibid., 139), and expresses an earnest hope that Americans will "renovate themselves, ere the curse of wealth and distinction shall have penetrated so deep into the vitals of their social system as to render them unable to reform themselves, unless through the purifying power of a world-shaking revolution" (ibid., 140). Here he makes a distinction between a society susceptible of reform, a society whose economic and social relations do not require a total overhaul

---

12. Arthur's friendship with Walter resembles the relationship between Steerforth and David in Dickens's *David Copperfield,* also published serially in 1849–1850. Wheeler's boy-hood friends began their public life some months prior to Dickens's (Wheeler introduces them in March 1849, and Dickens in the numbers for July and August 1849).

for justice and humanity to be served, and a society corrupt enough to require the complete transformation effected by social revolution. He further clarifies his view by remarking that the usual mechanisms and foci of reform—extended suffrage and "Liberal Institutions"—are not enough to remedy the inhumanities of capitalism. Arthur muses that "political liberty was only valuable as a means to an end, that in itself it was powerless against the spirit of competition; that the slavery of poverty was an evil that eats so deep into the human heart, that even Liberal Institutions could not perceptibly mitigate the evil" (ibid., 139). His diagnosis of the exploitation, poverty, and inequality already visible in the United States leads the novel's Chartist hero to prescribe something more thorough and durable even than what the Charter demands.

And this is not the only place where the novel speaks of the salubrious tonic of revolution; later on, the narrator asks rhetorically, "what is Communism but [. . .] a fresh breathing into the dying clay of past existence, [. . .] a new earth created from the ruins of a former world, purified by the fire of revolution" (ibid., 175). While Wheeler's notion of communism was unlikely to have matched exactly the newly developing ideas of Karl Marx or the Communist League,[13] it does include an explicit indictment of economic competition and of poverty occasioned by a minority's hoarding of capital, as well as recognition that Parliamentary reforms and the right to vote were inadequate to redress those grievances. Thus, while the novel follows Chartism's trajectory, it simultaneously reaches forward to a working-class movement whose demands outstrip those of the Charter, and which therefore must develop new forms of organization to attain revolutionary ends. The theory of organization that emerges is both the novel's most distinguishing feature and its greatest contribution to political theory.

One trait that Wheeler's conception of communism does share with Marx's is the belief that the emancipation of the working class must be the act of the working class, who will gain economic and political power only through their own conscious agency and not through upper- or middle-class benevolence. Contributing what would be a serious advance on existing theories of how to achieve a fair society, Wheeler distinguishes himself from utopian socialists such as Charles Fourier, Saint-Simon, and Robert Owen, who sought to reconcile the interests of the working and capitalist classes, rather than to sharpen class struggle in an effort to abolish rich and poor altogether. Some early utopian socialists made trenchant criticisms of how societies were

---

13. The Communist League decided at its 1847 congresses in London to ask Marx and Engels—new members of the League—to pen on its behalf the *Communist Manifesto*, which it published in London in February 1848. It did not appear in English until 1850 (serialized in *The Red Republican*, the newspaper of Chartist Julian Harney).

organized, as well as putting forward radical ideas about religion, women, human personality, and private property. Yet the fact remains that theirs were mostly generous schemes aimed at improving their social inferiors, dependent on wealthy benefactors rather than the self-activity of poor and working individuals.[14] Wheeler's theoretical innovation—a turn towards working-class agency and the necessity of class struggle—translates into a conviction that working people must form their own political organizations to fight for their interests.

Mistakes and Lessons of the First Chartist Convention

After he leaves school at age fourteen and begins a long apprenticeship, Arthur finds himself on his own financially, since his callous uncle writes to inform him that, on account of the latter's new marriage, Arthur can no longer expect even the meager economic aid he had once received. Arthur successfully completes the seven-year apprenticeship in printing with a "sour master and termagant mistress" who nevertheless cannot find fault with one "so good-tempered, so well-conducted, and inoffensive [. . .] Attentive to his business, simple in his habits, never causing any anxiety or trouble" (*Sunshine and Shadow*, 79). It is in his search for work as a printer that he travels to Birmingham and becomes convinced of the justice of Chartist claims. In the course of his apprenticeship, Arthur had had routine contact with liberal ideas through the printing of a particular newspaper at his shop. Though this wrought a "change" in "the character of his thoughts" (ibid.), shifting him away from his tendency toward abstractions and dreaminess, there remained in his mind a good deal of vagueness about how to effect change. He "longed to have some definite object to do," but his yearning was "for something, of the very nature of which he was yet unaware" (ibid., 80). Despite the haziness of Arthur's new hunger, this episode illustrates a version of what Sanders calls the "appetitive function" of poetry (*Poetry of Chartism*, 10). The unnamed liberal newspaper Arthur helped print undoubtedly contained poetry, and though no particular genre of writing is specified as the content of his reading, the effect Wheeler describes substantiates Sanders's claim that, though it

---

14. William Thompson urged greater working-class self-reliance than many early socialists of a cooperative stamp, especially in the management of Mechanics' Institutes by workers themselves to ensure their catering to working-class interests and needs. See Dolores Dooley's introduction to Thompson's *Appeal of One Half the Human Race* (Cork: Cork University Press, 1997).

did "not alter any specific opinions held by its readers," aesthetic experience effected qualitative change in Chartist activists, the phenomenon his book and mine designate as the Chartist imaginary (ibid., 9–10).

Still, weaned on a newspaper that presumably urged faith in the good will of a Liberal government, Arthur can find in mainstream politics neither a place to utilize his own political energies and intellect nor evidence of any remedy for urgent social ills such as the unemployment and hunger he faced for weeks following his apprenticeship. For these he has to look to Chartism, which "gave form, proportion, and colour to the shadow of his imagination" and taught him that "a love for liberty in name only, without a careful application of its principles, was vain and delusive" (*Sunshine and Shadow*, 91–92). What introduces him to this new political concreteness is his life in Birmingham and his employment there by a Chartist printer. Since the development of his character is tied to the development of the Chartist movement, Arthur's presence in Birmingham at a crucial moment comes as no surprise. To understand the rapid radicalization of his views, one must look at the events that shape them, in particular at the expectations and realities of the first Chartist Convention in connection with the famous Bull Ring riots.[15]

The year is 1839, and Arthur takes up his residence in Birmingham some months before the potentially explosive first two weeks of July, when Parliament summarily dismissed the first Chartist petition with over a million signatures on it, the Bull Ring riots took place in Birmingham, and the first Chartist Convention had moved from London to Birmingham to be closer to the center of struggle. A new conclusion Arthur reaches at this critical stage of his life is that it is vital for workers to form and lead their own independent party, and indeed the Chartist movement *was* the first mass working-class movement in British history. However, as the historical events recounted in the novel demonstrate, to be effective such an organization has to be a highly cohesive one that makes use of a leadership capable of guiding members and sympathizers in united actions.

Such a leadership the first Chartist Convention was not. That significant expectations accompanied its creation in 1839 is evident from the fact that—consistent with the history of its nomenclature—it was conceived of by some as an alternative government to the one sitting along the Thames. If it was a "people's Parliament," the first Chartist Convention was a deeply divided one

---

15. Since this and the following sections of this chapter continually shift between the novelistic and historical accounts of events, I endeavor to maintain some distinction between the two by using past tense for facts culled from histories and the narrative present for those described in the novel.

comprising not only physical and moral force Chartists[16] but also men with and without independent means. Arguably, only 24 of the 53 elected delegates were working men,[17] since few had the resources to quit their jobs and travel to London for some months. There was also tremendous external pressure on the delegates to the Convention, exacerbating its internal difficulties. As the novel explains, dissension leads to disintegration and defection by many "moderate" delegates, and at a critical period shortly before the Bull Ring riots which have a life-altering impact on Arthur, the remnant of the Convention votes to remove itself from London to Birmingham.

It had become the daily custom of Chartists to meet in the Bull Ring and their meetings were "neither riotous nor threatening" (Thompson, *Chartists,* 69), but London's Metropolitan Police had been sent to Birmingham to break up these meetings in early July. This posse attacked a mass meeting of Chartists in the Bull Ring and would, as the narrator tells us, "have speedily met their fate, had they not been sheltered by the military" (*Sunshine and Shadow,* 95). Angered by the police provocation, and again just days later by Parliament's dismissal of the Chartist petition, "the pent-up passions of the mass burst forth like a volcano's lava, scattering flames and destruction around" (ibid.) not only at Birmingham but also in other towns as well in days and weeks to come (Morton, 434–35). This and other clashes indicated a willingness among the masses to confront even armed authority, and reports flooded the Home Office about workers arming and drilling (O'Brien, 30).

The novel suggests that since what remained of the Convention had reconvened in Birmingham, it could have efficiently overseen the confrontations which occurred for several days following the Bull Ring, perhaps even gathering the newly-militant populace into a sufficiently strong force to achieve success (enforcement of the Charter, overhaul of industry, etc.). The ordinary people who made every industry work were "abandoning all sectional pursuits, forgetting all minor subjects of rivalry, actuated by one mighty impulse, [. . .] one grand object—the regeneration of their country.

---

16. "Moral force" Chartists believed their goals could be achieved through moral persuasion—patiently explaining their grievances and relying on the sympathy of the middle class and the willingness of the Whig government to institute reform. Ranged against them in this defining debate within the movement were "Physical force" Chartists, who anticipated the petition's rejection by Parliament and asked what "ulterior measures" should then be taken to force accession to their demands.

17. This is according to the radical Francis Place (O'Brien, *"Perish the Privileged Orders:" A Socialist History of the Chartist Movement,* 28). Chase offers a corrective account by saying that "much has been made of the preponderance of middle-class over working-class delegates. However, when allowance is made for non-attendees and early resignations, workmen [. . .] constituted just under two-thirds of the membership" (*Chartism: A New History,* 58).

Such union, such devotion, deserved, and would have ensured success, had their delegates in Convention" been similarly unified and decisive (*Sunshine and Shadow*, 93). However, the narrator indicates that the divisions among the Convention's delegates prevented decisiveness and leadership for the angry people of that region: its lack of "coherency" "rendered their proceedings a source of discord to their constituents [. . .] reducing their moral and physical stamina, until they fell an easy prey into the hands of the government [which,] paralysed in the first instance, speedily regained assurance" to crush the sporadic, unorganized surges of insurrection in Birmingham and elsewhere and to arrest large numbers of its leaders (ibid.). Arthur witnesses with pain the "mere sectional rioting" (ibid., 95) that occurs, singling out the disunited nature of the actions as the source of their weakness. The narrator tells us that Arthur "would have shed his blood cheerfully in any struggle [. . .] which might possibly result in the emancipation of the masses," but uncoordinated displays of "the pent-up passions of the mass" which "scatter[] flames and destruction around" do not amount to such a possibility (ibid.).[18] The self-activity of laboring men and women is indispensable, but so too, Arthur concludes, is the coordination that the Convention was unfortunately unable to provide.

What might have happened if those scattered clashes with police had been coordinated and disciplined in an unwavering campaign? The expectation among most Chartists that the sight of an overwhelming majority of armed citizens would convince hired soldiers to "lay down their arms and join their brothers" (Charlton, *The Chartists: The First National Workers' Movement*, 20) was not unrealistic.[19] Historian Dorothy Thompson records fascinating evidence that some members of the military were already sympathetic to Chartism and appalled at their orders to shoot at their fellow-countrymen as enemies (*Chartists*, 72–73). What would have been the result if the Convention had clearly, unequivocally urged the month-long general strike (National Holiday) it contemplated but reduced to three days in August?[20] Though

---

18. The "destruction" included some violent confrontations with police as well as arson attacks near the Bull Ring on several shops regarded as strongly anti-Chartist. Items removed from the shops were burned in a ceremonial bonfire at a Chartist meeting place in the Bull Ring (Chase, 95–96).

19. This expectation, along with the call to arms and a month-long general strike, derived from the widely popular *Grand National Holiday*, a pamphlet self-published in London in 1832 by the Lancashire workman William Benbow.

20. Thompson credits Chartist leaders with an awareness that only systematic, planned, disciplined violence could be effective against the Queen's army, citing leaders' efforts throughout the summer of 1839 to suppress sporadic outbreaks and encourage continued drilling. She also speculates that this effort to avoid localized rioting prompted the truncation of the "Sacred Month" to three days. Yet Thompson acknowledges that it was partly their unwillingness "to

Wheeler takes care not to paint all delegates to the Convention with a single brush and he rightly acknowledges their courage and sacrifices, he disparages that body's 1839 failure to take decisive action before the forces of the state did.

The rationale for the Convention's retreat on the "Sacred Month" is somewhat murky, but the account provided by some recent historians would suggest that Wheeler's optimism might have been mistaken. Chase, for instance, points out that 90 percent of workers at that time were not union members and would have neither private means nor communal assistance to sustain a strike, and also that the delegates who gathered first-hand information on workers' readiness for such action discovered some alarming unevenness, so that a top-down decision to go forward might have seemed perilously out-of-touch (79–81). How much of this Wheeler knew is uncertain.

It is significant that the novel moves Arthur from a suburb of London—home to an unresponsive government and his own Liberal ideas—to Birmingham, the seat both of massive popular activity and (temporarily) of the acknowledged leadership of the working-class movement. Placing Arthur in the midst of the agitation and confusion serves the plot in ways I will return to, but more importantly it brings him—and begins to bring readers—to an awareness of the key role of organization and leadership. The balance of the novel will multiply examples of near misses to demonstrate the concrete sources of its theoretical generalization, but from the outset it establishes a firm connection between historic events and the definition of its main character, precipitating out from a misty good will the colder, bracing water of Chartist realism. The interest of his character, and the reader's affection and sympathy for him, mean that his inextricable integration with defining moments in Chartist history lends those moments special weight and appeal. One cannot disregard the political lessons of the first Chartist Convention and of Birmingham without altogether ignoring the first really formative forces that propel the protagonist forward.

DIAMETRICALLY OPPOSED CLASS INTERESTS

Arthur is no mere spectator of the events in the Bull Ring but participates in the action and makes his debut on the historical stage by making his first speech on a Chartist platform. By means of his breath-taking oratory (sadly, it is not transcribed but only reported by the narrator), *Sunshine and Shadow*

---

take the responsibility for calling [the strike]" which occasioned leaders' vacillation, and admits that "this was undoubtedly a point at which Chartism might have taken a very different course" (*Chartists*, 71–73).

begins its case for the incompatibility of working-class interests with those of other classes. Arthur propounds the view that the British working classes of the 1830s and '40s have no similarity of interest with the middle class and insists that social "redemption" will result only from independent working-class action (*Sunshine and Shadow*, 108). He urges workers to organize themselves separately from classes that "would use the[ir] energies [. . .] as the stepping-stone to their own advancement" (ibid., 94), as the middle class had done with the 1832 Reform Bill.

The novel reminds readers that, in 1832, the highest layers of the middle class courted and won popular support at the same time as they warned Parliament that it must pass the Reform Bill in order to placate the "mob" and avert dangerous insurrection. In part to shake off their nightmares of social upheaval, legislators finally passed the Bill whose most important consequence was the enfranchisement of the upper-middle class. Cynically using what the narrator calls "the phantasmagoria of the Birmingham revolution," the capitalist class had thus annexed political power to its economic power (ibid., 91). The novel explains that, still lacking the vote themselves, poor people recognized that they had been the "tools" of a "bourgeoisie" which sought to share political power with the landed class, and workers be damned (ibid.). After reminding his hearers of that infamous betrayal, thereby shredding the "flimsy veil of their [the middle class's] apparent co-operation" and "the bitter mockery of their similarity of interest," Arthur urges his Bull Ring listeners "to cast off all dependence on others, to trust solely to their own energies" (ibid., 94). His message so resonates with and stirs his hearers that no one dares to make further speeches afterwards.

The police reward Arthur for his troubles by seeking to arrest him for inciting the Bull Ring riots and for arson, so he must flee England to escape arrest, but during the outbound voyage his ship founders and many passengers drown. Probably the shipwreck symbolizes the dashing of the hopes Arthur attached to the first petition's presentation and to the surge in working-class militancy in the latter half of 1839. Like those unfortunate passengers on Arthur's ship, many leaders and partisans of Chartism were lost to the movement after 1839, some (like Arthur) through government crackdown and arrests, others through their drift into temperance, educational, anti-Corn Law, and Complete Suffrage Union activities.[21] However, because he is a

---

21. Joseph Sturge and others created the National Complete Suffrage Union in 1842, retaining all six points of the People's Charter but, in its middle-class punctiliousness about respectability, steadfastly rejecting as sullied all versions of the Chartist name. O'Connor and others opposed the divisive move, as also the teetotal Chartist Associations that likewise set themselves up as alternatives to the National Charter Association and were supported by middle-class funds (Thompson, *Chartists*, 260–70).

revolutionary, Arthur cannot long remain in this forlorn condition; after the shipwreck a vessel bound for the West Indies rescues him. His hopes, like his fortunes, must recover and seek new opportunities for fulfillment.

Part of what drives the plot of the novel is this continual renewal of hope following the fledgling movement's mistakes and failures. The grist for *Sunshine and Shadow*'s mill consists not merely in what happened, but what *might* have happened and how. These considerations move the narrative forward, and this constant reconfiguration of historical potential represents much of its generic innovation. This is also why, agree with him or not, Arthur's identity as a revolutionary is essential to the kind of novel Wheeler wished to write. If he had been a John Barton or a Stephen Blackpool, matters would have ended with a pitiful, useless death that could point to nothing more substantial than a wish for better understanding and brotherhood between contending classes. Arthur would drown, there would be some pathos, and readers would wash their hands of him. In such a plot as Gaskell's or Dickens's, there is no room to ask what practical steps might have helped the workers' movement succeed.

The rescue brings Arthur on board a ship where he is pleasantly surprised to find himself reunited with Julia Baldwin, the sister of his childhood friend Walter North, whom he had known in his youth, and who has unwillingly married the governor of a West Indian island, whither she is bound. On shipboard, Arthur holds long colloquies with Julia in which he disabuses her of her illusions about the upper and middle classes, demonstrating that she "judge[s] them too favourably" because she assumes that they must, as she does, perceive the justice of Chartism's claims for humanity (ibid., 107). When Julia asks whether the middle class does not aid the workers because "their interests are similar," Arthur responds with a long speech which begins "No, dear lady, their interests are not similar; they are as distinct as the positive and negative poles of an electric battery" (ibid.). He discusses not only the treachery represented by the 1832 Reform Bill but also the concrete basis of the division between those who own capital and those who do not: "the interest of the working man is to sell his labour at the most profitable rate; the interest of the other is to reduce it down to starvation point; the one is benefited by the whole of his order being well employed and well paid; the object of the other is [. . .] to cause a redundancy of labour in the market, that he may [. . .] purchase their labour at his own price" (ibid.).[22] Nothing could be clearer

---

22. Arthur (like Marx) does acknowledge that some shopkeepers and small tradesmen share interests with those below them economically, but says that, due to ignorance or force of circumstance, they do not usually recognize this and so cannot be relied on as allies in struggle (*Sunshine and Shadow*, 107).

than this statement of the economic necessity of class division created by the capitalist organization of production. No matter how kindly intended or conscientious, each employer is compelled by the imperatives of competition for profits (and survival) to exploit employees, who are equally compelled by the prospect of starvation to resist the worsening of such exploitation. In the face of such arguments, the lady can hardly disagree: "Julia replied not," the narrator observes, "but sighed deeply" (ibid.). The novel's narrative voice will brook no rebuttal.

Well might Julia sigh and have sympathy with Arthur's grievances against the middle class, since she herself has been victimized by its mercenary marriage system and its immoral morality. The subplot of Julia's coerced marriage partakes of a common motif in working-class literature of the time, making *Sunshine and Shadow* representative in this respect.[23] Her forced marriage also resonates with the novel's critique of the bourgeoisie, and it therefore merits a moment's consideration. Julia has rejected an offer of marriage by Sir Jasper Baldwin because she is half his age, she does not know the man—or knows him only well enough to discern that she would be miserable if married to him—and because marrying the governor of a distant colony would mean a long, possibly permanent, separation from her much-loved family. He treats her with cavalier disregard for her wishes in the matter, and the narrator likens Baldwin's instant desire for Julia to the swift, cold dispatch of business inculcated by the slave trade: he makes the nuptial request "with the promptness of a West Indian—in all that related to dealings in human flesh" (ibid., 86).[24]

Declining such crass servitude, Julia accepts an invitation to visit her brother's house in the hope of escaping Sir Jasper but is dismayed to find herself pursued there by him, with her brother's permission. Her brother's connivance is actuated by the bourgeois values of which he is the novel's personification; he ponders how the prestige of the baronetcy and the £4,000 a year "will be of service to me in my matrimonial spec," concluding that "the match [Julia's] must come off" (ibid., 85). The fact that, to her brother Walter North, the procurement of a woman is nothing more than a financial "spec"ulation makes less surprising the repulsive scheme he hatches for Julia's entrapment by Sir Jasper. He sends the servants away one evening, plies Sir

---

23. In addition to Julia in Wheeler's novel, proto-feminist characters and strands occur in other Chartist literature as well, including Ernest Jones's *Woman's Wrongs*, R. J. Richardson's *The Rights of Woman*, and shorter works by Gerald Massey, John La Mont, and others. See chapters 4 and 5.

24. This comparison of economic bondage and black slavery is also common in literature of the day, though Wheeler is more sophisticated than many in his recognition that slave labor and "free" labor can be pitted against each other (as will be evident later in this chapter).

Jasper with drink, and sends him to her bedroom where Jasper rapes her. Thus
they rope her into a "legalised prostitution" more degrading than the actual
trade in sex practiced, and condemned, by middle-class moralists (ibid., 87).
Though Julia is herself petty-bourgeois in status, she sympathizes with the
politics of Chartism because she too has experienced oppression. The rape,
together with the references to marriage as financial speculation and a species of slavery or flesh-trading, forms a strong critique of the hypocrisy and
sexist values propounded by a middle class from which the novel would distance its working-class readers. Wheeler (like some other Chartists) shows his
progressiveness through this use of gender, racial, and colonial oppression as
wedges to split workers off from the rest of the social tree, impressing on them
the distinctness of not only their economic and political but also their social
interests, and further nudging them towards organizational independence.

   Her identification with the justice of working-class claims makes Julia
attractive to Arthur, and despite her marriage the two find themselves in love.
The narrator repeatedly defends their romantic attachment, dismissing "cen-
sorious" and "prudish" critics and frankly stating that "love in her was no
crime, though she was the bride of another" (ibid., 105). Nevertheless, it is not
Julia whom Arthur marries; this the novel does not allow. Julia succumbs to
the tropical climate and dies,[25] leaving Arthur grieved but able—some years
later—to recover sufficiently to marry a young woman of his own class whom
he meets at a Chartist assembly back in England. His erstwhile attraction to
Julia complicates the message of his more general warnings against cross-class
alliance, but his marriage to a shoemaker's daughter whom he meets through
Chartist gatherings and political projects recuperates his spoken convictions.

Uneven Development and the Strike of 1842

The events of 1842 test Arthur's claims about the need for independent working-class organization and throw into stark relief the vital role such a party
would play. In the summer of 1842 Arthur returns to England under an
assumed name (since he is still wanted under the trumped up arson charges
from 1839). Not surprisingly, he travels to Manchester during the height of the
anti-Corn Law agitation.[26]

---

   25. The story of Julia's marriage to the governor of a distant colony and her unexpected
death there reminds one of Letitia Elizabeth Landon's mysterious death in the same year (1838)
that she married and traveled to the African colony her husband governed.
   26. In the early 1840s, middle-class advocates of free trade sought the repeal of the pro-
tectionist Corn Laws, which forbade any importation of wheat when the price of British wheat

The narrator explains that, to enlist the aid of the majority working population against the landowning class, Anti-Corn Law Leaguers promise "cheap bread, high wages, and plentiful employment" as the result of repeal, then try in the most "violent" language to incite workers to "rise and overthrow the tyrant aristocracy" to win the cause (ibid., 143). League orators deliver "inflammatory speeches" and their propagandists issue "tracts and addresses of the most exciting description" containing "threats of revolution" (ibid., 144). After the novel's exposure of middle-class treachery vis-à-vis Parliamentary reform in 1832, this tactic of inciting the lower class in order to threaten the upper classes will be familiar. This time, however, ten years have elapsed during which no benefits of reform have accrued to workers, and now they have their own mass organization, including networks of local leaders and an independent press. The narrator opines that only "the influence of the Chartist leaders" could "counteract the insurrectionary doctrines propounded by the emissaries of the League" (ibid., 143), preventing a bloody revolt on behalf of a class with alien interests. In this instance one can see the positive role of an organized leadership in soberly assessing the interests and abilities of their class and trying to persuade their constituents accordingly.

Though the leaders succeed in dissuading workers from rushing into an as-yet ill-defined conflict with an armed government, strikes and "turn-outs" ensue despite uncertain leadership from prominent Chartists. On Wheeler's account, Anti-Corn Law industrialists, merchants, and shopkeepers collaborate to provoke strikes that will then be used as leverage in the free-trade cause, but they are never entirely successful at convincing the workers themselves that they are striking for repeal of the Corn Laws.[27] Nevertheless, they succeed in provoking strikes and introducing some uncertainty about aims. As the novel explains, from the outset of the work stoppage confusion reigns

---

fell below 80s. per quarter. Keeping domestic wheat prices ruinously high, the law shielded the landowning class from foreign competition but damped the export market for British manufacturers. Therefore, industrial capitalists formed the Anti-Corn Law League in order to secure an expanded market for their exports. They succeeded in this aim: "Thus, as the import of wheat from the Levant increased, so the export of Lancashire cottons rose from £141,000 in 1843 to £1,000,000 in 1854" (Morton, 405). They also anticipated new chances to lower their employees' wages with any fall in the price of bread, which repeal of the Corn Laws might bring. In fact, after the Corn Laws were repealed in 1846, average wheat prices rose from 54s.9d. (1841–1845) to 56s. (1851–1855). See Morton, 404, and Cook and Stevenson, 397, 247.

27. Certainly Friedrich Engels agreed with this view (see his 1845 The Condition of the Working Class in England), as did Feargus O'Connor among many other Chartist contemporaries. Modern historians sound a note of cautious disagreement with them, with Thompson (Chartists, 288–90) disclaiming any concerted League scheme (and admitting that individual League members definitely provoked and exploited the strikes) and Charlton concluding that the League fomentation theory was "probably wrong" (The Chartists, 48).

over the demands strikers should raise: "some say, a rise in wages—some, a Repeal of the Corn Laws—whilst others maintain that the strike is to be continued until the Charter become the Law of the Land" (ibid., 145). One can infer from the array of possibilities that laborers looked in multiple directions for some demand or slogan to unify them and consolidate their strength; they looked to trade union, Chartist, and Anti-Corn Law leaders.

Notably, not everyone even looked to their own class's leaders, since Corn Law agitators were among the contenders. To unify their strike and maximize its potential for success, laborers needed their own independent organization working in the interests of their own class exclusively, and to promote a general strike everywhere, they needed a forum in which to clarify and circulate their goals. However, the novel suggests here that they were unaccustomed to look to their own organization for a clear and timely lead. The strike began without any formal intervention from the National Charter Association (successor to the first Convention); Wheeler notes with frustration that they did not meet until well after (in fact it was two weeks after) the strikes had already begun, and even then they did not provide the certain, unified political direction necessary to marshal strikers' forces quickly and effectively (ibid., 147–48). The novel reveals that, when the executive of the National Charter Association finally did meet in August, the leaders themselves were divided on the question of the strike, so that although they formally voted to support it, O'Connor's newspaper, for example, "was opposed" to it, and in the confusion some workers resumed work while others "were left destitute of any correct information how to proceed" (ibid., 148).[28]

The novel makes it clear that this initial period of uncoordinated effort characterized not only the workers' movement but also their adversaries', and it is this fact especially which makes the disorientation of the strike so poignant (the narrator says that "the chance of centuries fleeted from their grasp" [ibid.]). While the strike was still growing, the courts, the military, and the police mirrored the general uncertainty and took no steps to oppose the march of multitudes from town to town, stopping work wherever they went. When those multitudes marched into Manchester, the narrator explains, they not only stopped the factories there but also took control of the city, giving a new complexion and potential to the strike: "For three days and three

---

28. Bronterre O'Brien abstained; Julian Harney strenuously opposed a national strike because there had been inadequate preparation for it; Feargus O'Connor equivocated, then came out against it in *The Northern Star* by arguing that the people lacked unity of opinion about the strike and were not sufficiently prepared or organized to carry it out; strongly in favor of the strike were Peter Murray McDouall, Thomas Cooper, and James Leach (see Chase, 86, and Charlton, 39). The executive of the National Charter Association did vote to support the strike (after it had already begun).

nights was Manchester entirely under the control of this unarmed mass of people; nearly every town in the district was similarly situated, yet not one act of robbery or personal violence was perpetrated" (ibid.,146).[29] The novel does not specify the exact nature of workers' "control" in Manchester and elsewhere, but it does suggest the wresting of some civil authority since "this state of things was not strictly compatible with [the authorities'] functions as justices and magistrates" (ibid.).

Historians have offered some additional information about the event Wheeler fictionalizes here, including the formation of "Committees of Public Safety" in which strikers handled appeals by employers to be exempted from the strike, and the selection of picket "stewards" who exercised restraint over other citizens who were inclined to violent action (Charlton, 43). At the same time, crowds in the Staffordshire Potteries took into their own hands the representatives of ruling-class power and repression, destroying police stations and releasing their prisoners, pulling down the poorhouses, distributing bread to striking workers, and vandalizing and torching the homes of particularly noxious magistrates and coal owners (Thompson, *Chartists,* 291). The political targets of such actions during the volatile strikes of '42, as well as the appropriation of certain civil authorities and functions, suggest that the stakes of the struggle might have been much higher than either the Charter or Corn Law repeal.[30] The capitalists' delayed response to such actions and aspirations could have cost them more than they yet dreamed.

The novel's introduction of this three-day seizure of Manchester, complete with policing powers, precedes a reference to the strikers' announcing their "determination to persevere in the struggle for political power" (*Sunshine and Shadow,* 147). This determination indicates a new sophistication in their movement, one that combines their political demands with the economic power they possess by virtue of their key role in production; it represents a new and more serious kind of threat to the *status quo.* Wheeler implies that this was the decisive moment when concerted, confident action might have

---

29. Later historians have confirmed Wheeler's account: "There were no killings or serious wounding by the crowds [even when troops fired on them]. The destruction was of property— the property of unpopular people was destroyed, not their lives" (Thompson, *Chartists,* 291). Charlton cites the observations of contemporary William Cooke Taylor, who "several times draws attention to the disciplined conduct of the strikers in relation to property. [. . .] Taylor was also impressed that hordes of hungry strikers passed by an unguarded cherry tree in a factory master's garden without touching a fruit" (*The Chartists,* 43).

30. G. D. H. Cole speculated thus: "The hunger revolt could hope to achieve anything only if it became a revolution. That was what some of the Chartists [. . .] tried to make of it. [. . .] If the Chartists had been united, and O'Connor had placed himself at their head, there might have been at least a widespread rising in arms" (*Chartist Portraits,* 176).

won the day for England's producing class. Facing little opposition from the state in those few days, in the narrator's mind the disenfranchised could have won their struggle for political—and perhaps government and economic— power with minimal loss of life or damage to property. The narrator makes an important remark about the balance of forces between workers and the Queen's police and military at this high point of turbulence; speaking of the rioters in Staffordshire, he says that "their numbers were so overwhelming that the military, fatigued and harassed with marching and countermarching, could not avoid their holding complete possession of Hanley, Shelton, and other towns in the district" (ibid., 149). Here was a dispirited and scattered state force faced with a numerically superior and violently inclined mass of fellow citizens who had already deposed civil authority. As yet the middle class and its government lacked confidence regarding how to proceed.

This was the tense climate in which Chartist leaders finally met, but just a matter of days saw the tide already turning. In the narrator's words,

> All eyes were now turned to the assembling of the Chartist Convention. [. . .] Had this body met a few days earlier, while the authorities were silently gazing around, the energy and enthusiasm they brought into the contest might have rendered it successful; but the crisis was past, through- out the whole district the magistrates were prepared for any emergency— the troops of the whole empire were fast concentrating upon the north [. . .] and the people frightened at their own violence, had once more hugged their chains to their weary hearts. (ibid., 147)

Desperate men and women had shown their willingness to withhold their labor, overturn civil authorities, and clash with armed bodies if necessary for the achievement of their political and economic aims. And that very inter- locking of the economic and political, the use of the strike for the attainment of political ends, marked a promising new maturity in the proletarian move- ment. However, the confusion of the strikers, their loss of confidence, and the hesitation and delay of their leaders gave the forces of repression time to understand what was happening and to mount a united, and successful, offensive against it.

The novel thus affirms that that period of equivocation was the moment to take over the factories, to retain and expand those aspects of state power the masses had seized, to compel the adoption of the Charter's six points and press forward to the many other demands Chartists had articulated.[31] Before

---

31. It is true that this would have required a revolutionary party with a clear sense of work- ers' power via their role in production and the stated aim of abolishing class society, something

the Anti-Corn Law Leaguers realized the true nature (or potential) of the strikes and seizures of cities, before the government's military forces could be moved to the north and concentrated on the few centers of activity, workers' actions allegedly could have spread to several large towns and thus rendered the military weaker by forcing it to be spread too thinly—*if* there had been coordinated leadership already in place and able to move quickly. The novel contends that swift, determined leadership to unify the minds and actions of workers scattered across Britain was the lever that could have catalyzed their political power, but the Convention's delay cost working people the watershed moment. The largest and most militant strike of the nineteenth century faltered, lost its momentum, and suffered defeat. Through his fictional interpretation of this historic event, Wheeler seeks to demonstrate that the struggle of workers for political and economic equality will remain independent and be successful only if it makes use of a coherent, centralized, and disciplined leadership.

Here again the tone of the novel mixes tragedy with the frustrated hopefulness of a new kind of character who can and does conceive of a different, positive outcome. Arthur returns to England at just the moment when this struggle erupts, reversing the emigration patterns in such novels as Gaskell's *Mary Barton* and Kingsley's *Alton Locke*. In both of the better-known plots, working people disappear from the scene while whatever reforms are to be effected—whether in industry or in attitude—will occur under the guidance of the employer class and in the effective absence of agency for the employed class. Alton Locke will never return to England, since he dies upon reaching the US, and the terms of his sudden legacy forbid his fellow Chartist Crossthwaite from returning for seven years, during which the "fraternal union of all classes" is "surely, though slowly, spreading in [his] mother-land" without his help (Kingsley, *Alton Locke Tailor and Poet: An Autobiography*, 389). In contrast, Arthur returns exactly when the upturn in struggle demands his participation and concern. This allows him, and the narrator of *Sunshine and Shadow*, to face squarely what Wheeler saw as the problems and failures of organization Chartism confronted.

Not long after the climax of the strikes in 1842, Arthur travels south to London and there meets and marries Mary Graham, a Chartist activist and the daughter of a shoemaker. They live happily for a while and bear children, but the economic downturn in 1846 means unemployment for Arthur and

---

that was barely conceived by most radicals until several years later. But ideas and strategies change dramatically in struggle, as the example of the proposed general strike—still a new tactic in 1842—vividly demonstrates. And in April 1848 the Chartist Convention decided at its April 4 meeting in London that, if the third petition was rejected by Parliament, it would constitute a National Assembly to take over the government of the nation (Thompson, *Chartists*, 319).

ultimately the death of their first child from malnutrition. Their circumstances improve the next year, but the grief and impoverishment leave permanent marks on Arthur and he throws himself more than ever into political
agitation.

Early in 1848 Arthur travels around England for the purpose of ascertaining the "state of public feeling" and reporting it to those who elected him
their delegate for that purpose (*Sunshine and Shadow*, 182). Social and political unrest stir the continent, and the question of British preparedness for
similar scenes of rebellion is on the order of the day. Arthur finds that the
"seeds of incipient revolution" are abundant, yet crucially "in such profuse
disorder, that, if a struggle came, it needed no seer to foretell the inevitable
result" (ibid., 184). The importance of preparation for upturns in struggle is
one of the novel's parting emphases, warning readers with a direct address in
its final paragraph that if they are not active and alert to signs of revolutionary opportunity, if they have not learned something of their own history, then
"when the time comes, we shall again be found unprepared" (ibid., 192). To
the extent that this novel helps people learn that crucial history, it plays a vital
role in future political history. Its hybridity with historical narrative is, for
Wheeler, what mutates fiction into a catalyst for social transformation.

Implicit here is the notion that there is nothing automatic about revolu-
tions; no recipe of economic circumstances or government provocations or
even European examples could produce the hearty stuff of revolution without the leaven of conscious, organized human intervention. It was because
Wheeler placed such a premium on the subjective component in the changing of history that he wrote this novel; through it he directly addressed the
problems within the movement, contended for the loyalties of his audience,
and sought to prepare them for future upswings in their struggle. In these
ways Wheeler's outlook resembles that of the *Northern Star*'s poetry column
(to which he also contributed) by the end of 1848. As Sanders has shown,
"By the end of 1848 there is a sense [in Chartist poetry] of a pressing need
to interpret the year's events in order to plan future strategy" (*Poetry*, 200).
Strictly speaking, the genre of history presents, rather than interpreting, "the
year's events." But united to the philosophical and ethical possibilities of fiction, history *means,* enables judgment, and provokes action. The generic
hybridity is what infuses the electric potential.

Ironic Success at Kennington Common

Though negative examples of organization and leadership stud the novel with
disturbing frequency, Wheeler deeply respected both his fellow Chartists and

the valiant efforts and sacrifices of their leaders. His decision to include Kennington Common, then, makes sense both because of its importance in Chartist history and because that day was what the novel calls "a bright one in their
annals" (*Sunshine and Shadow*, 179). On April 10, 1848 Chartists planned a
large demonstration at Kennington Common to be followed by a mass con-
veyance of their third and final petition to Parliament. The government had
learned some lessons of its own from the experience of the strikes and rebel-
lions in 1842, so that this time around they would not be caught unprepared
or respond tardily to potentially threatening expressions of mass discontent.
This time it would act preemptively. The narrator tells us that it was a "day
when the middle class of London, and the empire generally, showed their love
for Democracy by arming themselves for its slaughter" (ibid.).[32] Though there
was considerable disagreement among the members of the Chartist executive
about how to proceed in the face of tremendous, and ostentatious, government preparations for the armed crushing of any demonstration, however
peaceable, they did take the lead when that day came and were greeted with
respect and compliance by the organization's rank and file.

The novel lauds the discipline of the people under the direction of the
Convention, which proceeded with the demonstration but called off the
planned procession across London's heavily-guarded bridges to Parliament.
According to Wheeler, members of the Convention decided that it would
be irresponsible to lead an unarmed people "into collision with an armed
force, furnished with every requisite for slaughter," and he compliments not
only the sober caution of the leadership but also the "good organisation and
discipline of the people" in following the Convention's instructions (ibid.).
Curiously, Wheeler suppresses any reference to the disagreement that preceded the Convention's decision, as if to place the emphasis in this case on the
impact of their united front. One can only speculate about authorial choices
and omissions, but it is likely both that he wished to leave readers with at least
one or two positive examples of how a well-organized party can function,
and that he recognized the psychological importance of a retreat of such near
proximity (he began publishing *Sunshine and Shadow* about one year later).
Apparently wishing to stress the point about the positive potential of leadership, even in restraining militant activity, the narrator underlines the power
of an organized movement with a trusted, cohesive leadership:

> It is order, discipline, and a yielding of their own impulses to the com-
> mands of their leaders which shows a determined organisation among a

---

32. *Northern Star,* Saturday Dec. 15, 1849 (chapter XXXIV). Haywood's edition of the novel
erroneously substitutes *this* for *its* in this passage.

people, and when the oppressor sees this he feels that the hour of retribution is arrived; that the handwriting of his destiny is written on the wall
of millions of human hearts, and that they only need a fair opportunity to
achieve their freedom. (ibid.)

Undoubtedly the final rebuff of the Charter made this a dispiriting day for
many Chartists, though it was followed by an increase in Chartist activity
in London and elsewhere before the movement began seriously to decline
(Thompson, *Chartists,* 326).[33] However, the novel makes clear that it was also
a day which showed that ordinary working people are sufficiently self-disci-
plined to form an organization that can act in unison if a timely, clear course
is set out by their delegated leadership, as it seems to have been on that day
at least. For Wheeler and for those who cared about and identified with the
Chartist struggle, it must have been a sad irony that this capacity to lead and
this moment of coordination between leaders and members came only when
Chartism was beginning to wane.

The notoriously harsh repression of Chartist leaders which nevertheless
followed in 1848 means that Arthur has to flee England once again, and the
novel concludes with his living in exile in Europe while his wife and daughter
honor and await him at home. It is fitting that the novel should conclude this
way, given its many other departures from the literary norms of the Victorian
social problem novel. His survival at all contrasts with the fates of Stephen
Blackpool, John Barton, Stephen Morley, and Alton Locke, but his living in
forced exile, with an eager eye to European and British politics and an undi-
minished, unqualified devotion to Chartism, stands out even more starkly.
Further, Arthur neither stumbles onto nor marries an inheritance in this conclusion (unlike Felix Holt, Alton Locke, or Disraeli's Sybil). Instead, two years
after Arthur leaves England "his fate is still enveloped in darkness," and the
narrator says that "what the mighty womb of time may bring forth we know
not" (*Sunshine and Shadow,* 192). As long as the fate of Chartism remains
a question, so too is Arthur's fate unsettled. Martha Vicinus rightly said of
this conclusion that Wheeler "believed in the eventual triumph of revolutionary forces, but since change had not yet come and did not appear imminent, [he] left [his] novel open-ended. The only possible ending is revolution"
(*The Industrial Muse: A Study of Nineteenth Century British Working-Class
Literature,* 133). There can be no "personal solution" for a hero such as Arthur

---

33. Most Chartist demands were eventually achieved in later years, as for example in the
Reform Act of 1867 enfranchising all male householders who paid taxes, the Ballot Act of 1872
granting the vote by secret ballot, and the Parliament Act of 1911 instituting the payment of
members of Parliament at a rate of £400 annually.

because there has been as yet no general solution for the grievances articulated in Chartism—his life is "entwined with the fate of Chartism" (ibid.). As throughout this narrative, his character is integrally tied to Chartist history.[34]

The novel's political argument infuses the plot with a sense of regret for a once-possible but then-receding revolutionary ideal. The very effort to analyze political mistakes through the broad platform of a literary work aimed at the widest possible audience implies the awareness of great potential, the hopefulness, and the disappointment that mingle to give some literary works their tragic undertone. *Sunshine and Shadow* ever intimates, through its advancing of new modes of political organization, that history might have been altered for the better and the fortunes of its characters could have been other than they were. The novel cultivates that capacity to imagine alternative outcomes not only in its narrative tenor but also in the psyches of its readers, simultaneously performing and eliciting the Chartist imaginary. The subtle presence of this tone lends emotional interest to the novel and engages readers at the level of feeling as well as on an intellectual plane, and that feeling is not simple grief. Evaluating the actions of Chartism's leaders as the narrator does presupposes a belief that the results were not inevitable, that the cause they served was not of necessity doomed by some law of nature or Providential preservation of good old English constitutionalism. Arthur Morton experienced hardships and disappointments similar to those faced by other fictional worker heroes, but with the difference that he possessed a psychology that tenaciously clung to the hope of future victory, and therefore confronted what had gone wrong and what should be debated within the movement to take it forward. That very outlook was what made the novel possible, what distinguished its revolutionary treatment of Chartist history and made it into a manifesto for the future of the movement.

Hybridity and Hubris

The audacity of the Chartist movement and the source of its frightening potential to the upper classes consisted to a large degree in its arrogation of the right to national- and self-determination for working people. Demanding legal equality, a share in governance, and the right to education, for instance, seemed to traditionalists to exceed the natural order of things and threaten

---

34. *Sunshine*'s narrative openness here resembles not only *Dissuasive Warnings* and "The Revolutionist" but also the conclusion to Morris's "The Pilgrims of Hope," in which the hero survives the Paris Commune where his wife dies. Faithful to his ideals, he returns home to England to rear his son, nurture the hope of revolution, and prepare for the coming struggle.

society with dire consequences. In some respects they were correct, for the sort of revolution discussed by the authors in this chapter would indeed take Britain beyond any social organization it had known before, and grant new powers to people who had never previously enjoyed or exercised them. Looked at this way, Chartism equaled *hubris,* the ancient Greek word that signified a desire to exceed natural or given limitations, and from which the modern word *hybrid* derives. The gods never granted human beings the power of flight, so they punished the arrogance of Icarus when he appropriated the wings that should belong only to birds. He exceeded natural limitations, and his ambition to fly drew down judgment and death. In fact, he sought to hybridize, to combine distinct genera, violating the prerogatives of those gods who held power over him. The temptation to draw parallels between these mythic and linguistic origins and the generic cross-fertilizing that helped promote Chartist rebellion is strong, but Somerville's radically hybrid, antirevolutionary work urges caution. As with any Victorian formation one can name, there exist in Chartist literature parts that do not fit, that defy generalizations and ruin elegant critical theories. The willingness of recent critics to acknowledge and even embrace that awareness signals both the maturation of Chartist studies and its refusal to homogenize the aspirations and self-expressions of the people it seeks to understand.

· 4 ·

THE GENDER LEGACY

Women in Early to Late Chartist Literature

Chartist attitudes about the position of women in society and politics (also discussed in chapter five) are perhaps less easily discerned from literary than from historical evidence, but there are a number of creative works that directly address the vulnerable position of women in class and industrial society, and it is worth thinking about which views find literary expression and how Chartists imagine these problems and the circumstances that complicate their articulation and solution. This chapter begins by surveying several works from across the range of Chartism's lifetime, to show what they share with each other and with other Victorian literary treatments of the "woman question," and in what ways they are distinctive parts of the larger culture's conversation on this topic. That survey then leads up to and provides context for the chapter's longer, central analysis of Gerald Massey's late Chartist poem "Only a Dream" (1856), of which there has been no prior critical examination in spite of its fascinating structural complexity.

Since the chief purpose of this book is to demonstrate the politics of Chartist aesthetics, it is important to devote to certain works the sort of detailed, literary technical critique customarily afforded to canonical writings. While I clearly think it valuable to subject earlier, more familiar Chartist works to such analysis (as this book does with Cooper's *Purgatory of Suicides,* Wheeler's *Sunshine and Shadow,* and Jones's *The New World,* for example), there is also an interpretive payoff in looking beyond the standard texts and outside the decade or so that was traditionally conceived as defining Chartism's termini. Some critics have significantly improved scholars' sense of the historically contingent texture of Chartist literature, demonstrating differences in the tone, attitude, and preoccupation of its poetry based on the contemporary milieu in which individual poems were composed (see Janowitz and Sanders, for example). This chapter shares a similar orientation by highlighting from the final years of Chartist history a poem that speaks directly to contemporary contests over marriage and women's disabilities therein. Gerald Massey joined Chartism in its later stages, when several of its remaining leaders came from the movement's left flank and were still active because of their ideological commitment to class struggle and radical politics. Those with connections to socialism also tended to articulate progressive views regarding women, and Massey worked closely with that cadre. So although he no longer had any active connection with the dwindled movement by the time his poem "Only a Dream" appeared in 1856, I believe the poem's progressive outlook and its faith in the efficacy of poetry as political intervention result from Massey's radicalization as a late Chartist,[1] making this poem part of the legacy of that movement.

1839: W. J. Linton

There had always been Chartist activists interested in the status of women and the peculiar liabilities they faced, though. In a single 1839 issue of his journal *The National,* William James Linton included two short sketches of his own writing, both of which attack the social hypocrisy that protects patriarchal prerogative over women's lives and bodies. "The Outcast" follows a standard narrative trajectory of the young country girl who elopes to London with her beloved, suffers desertion by him when he learns she is pregnant, unwillingly resorts to prostitution when she cannot support herself and her baby, and dies at age 20. While firmly placing responsibility for this disaster on (the men and women of upper-class) society, Linton more specifically blames patriarchal power: the "Ministers of Religion," who proclaim unnatural sexual standards to be God's law; her father, who wields his power over Rose Clifford by interfering in her choice of a marriage partner; and her lover, whose desertion results less from his having harbored any insidious designs toward her than from his cowardly avoidance of matrimonially allying himself with a woman who—because she became pregnant—would be subjected to relentless moral opprobrium by a canting, judgmental society. Without knowing anything

---

1. His friendship with George Julian Harney led him to become active with the Society of Fraternal Democrats and Harney's *Red Republican,* for instance.

about him, Rose's father rejects the apparently earnest and respectable man of Rose's choice and demands instead that she marry a man he has selected for her, thus "prostitut[ing] herself in 'holy wedlock'" (Linton, "The Outcast," 159). His tyranny and her rebellion set up her father's complete rejection of her once she finds herself in desperate need of aid. His assumption of absolute authority over the women in his family creates the conditions of his daughter's ruin, and his rote adherence to the social forms of morality ("she had disgraced them, and was not entitled to their assistance" [ibid., 160]) seals her death. Perhaps some of her vulnerability also results from the inferior education allotted to women, since Linton mentions that, although Rose had "as much sense" as most people, "those who educated her, did not think that she would ever need such a thing" as a strong mind (ibid., 158).

In "The Free-Servant" Linton turns from women's sexual to their labor exploitation, specifically focusing on the case of a young woman in domestic service, which he renames "domestic slavery" (163). As the eldest child in a large family penally deprived of its father's support, Jane Stephens helps her mother tend the many younger children until she becomes a servant, then a maid of all work, and then a question mark. Sharing a striking feature of some other Chartist narratives,[2] this story leaves its ending and future completely open and undetermined, with the narrator exclaiming "God knows what became, or will become of her" after overwork precipitates a long illness and her loss of employment (ibid.). Again Linton points out the masculinist institutions and customs that render the whole family financially unstable, citing the landlord, legislature, clergy, and jurymen as colluding to impoverish Jane's ploughman father and then to punish him excessively for an unnamed (likely economically impelled) crime, thereby depriving the family of its chief or only source of income.[3] Such institutions operate, the story implies, without regard to their impacts on the women who must nevertheless cope with the consequences (of unequal pay, few options for work, inaccessible divorce, and large families to nurse, feed, and support).

Possible outcomes the story posits for Jane after her loss of work and her friendless urban poverty include begging and prostitution, unless she finds other work. However, even if she does regain respectable employment, the narrator foresees a time when age and hard toil make her ineligible for

---

2. See, for instance, the conclusions of Thomas Cooper's short story "'Merrie England'— No More!" and Thomas Martin Wheeler's novel *Sunshine and Shadow* (both discussed in chapter 3).

3. Ernest Jones's Margaret Haspen makes a similarly incisive point about the impossible position in which government places women by incarcerating their husbands while neither subsidizing the income-deprived wives nor permitting them to regain financial stability by remarrying. See my discussion of "The Working Man's Wife" below.

"service," pushing her to become a seamstress or a char-woman, and when unable to survive in those still more meager vocations, either starving on the streets or bearing the "doom" of the workhouse hospital (ibid.). Though he leaves the story open-ended in this way, Linton does prescribe a specific solution that would liberate such women as Jane from the enslavement of servitude and its bleakly precarious futures: "rich folk and gentlemen" and the "fine Lady" should dispense with servants and "wait upon yourself!" (ibid., 163–64). Families, he proposes, should share the work according to their abilities, taking pleasure in serving those they love. And although the narrator says that "My wife and children wait upon me," he hastens to add that "I help them" and "we know nothing of command and obedience" (ibid., 163). This self-sufficient, more balanced domestic vision is a distinctive contribution to midcentury discourses on the "woman question" because it broadens the scope of which women the "question" includes, indicts the male strongholds that institutionalize women's precarious economic status, and proposes a domestic model that is more egalitarian along both its classed and gendered axes. That Linton intended these two sketches as a radical engagement with gender issues is further demonstrated by the context in which he published them. As Haywood has noted, "the whole issue of the *National* in which the sketch[es] appeared is devoted to feminism," as Linton surrounded these two stories with "extracts from Godwin, Wollstonecraft, and Shelley, all reinforcing the view that conventional bourgeois marriage is superficial, materialist, and ruinous to women" (Haywood, *Literature,* 19). The stories also represent an early instance of a leading Chartist endeavoring to work out how the new movement should address problems specific to its female members.

1842: Mary Hutton

Women themselves were especially active in the movement during its early years, and they likewise wrote creative works preoccupied with the specific ways gender inflected the experiences of women. In one instance, for example, Mary Hutton celebrates the heroic self-sacrifice and mourns the cruel subsequent fate of "Madame Lavalette" (also discussed in chapter 5). Here Hutton perceives a shared experience among women of different classes, temporarily privileging their gender over their social station (as Jones does in *Woman's Wrongs,* discussed below). In this light it is interesting to note the difference between Hutton's version of Lavalette's tale and a version that appeared in the Chartist press at about the time she wrote the poem. Hutton's headnote to the poem says she composed it after reading an account of

Madame Lavalette, and such an account was printed in the *Chartist Circular* for May 2, 1840, showing that Hutton was not the only Chartist interested in the Frenchwoman's story.[4] However, the version presented by the *Chartist Circular* (an abridged extract from Hewson Clarke's account in his 1816 *The History of the War*) makes no mention of the lady's confinement to a "Lunatic Asylum," which is the great overriding concern of Hutton's poem. Hutton emphasizes not only the glory of the wife's substituting herself for her condemned husband but also the fearful permanent consequences of the stress and imprisonment she endured on her husband's behalf. She even opens up the possibility—in both the poem and her afterword—that Count Lavalette was unworthy of his wife's devotion and sacrifice. The poem opines that "A woman's love will firmer cling, / In peril and in pain, / Though often on a worthless thing; / Its treasures are but vain" (lines 22–25). These lines resonate with many Victorian representations of women who are loyal to their own detriment, such as Nancy in *Oliver Twist*, Margaret Haspen in *Woman's Wrongs*, and Dorothea in *Middlemarch*. In Hutton's prose afterword to the poem, she exclaims:

> Oh, when a generous and feeling heart has lavished its affections, and its love, for years, and years, and years, upon a certain object, to whom it has given its confidence, and fondly cherished, and administered to, night and day, in sickness and in health; in sorrow and joy; and lives to see its love and kindness repaid by gross cruelty, and ingratitude, 'tis almost enough to shatter the brain, and destroy the mind, and overturn the reason of the very strongest .... (*Cottage Tales*, 101)

Certainly Madame Lavalette "lavished" her affections and loyalty on her husband in his "sorrow," and though I do not know that she received anything but kindness from her husband during and after his exile, possibly Hutton suspected otherwise, and in any case "her mental powers were entirely overthrown" (ibid., 98). As Kossick has pointed out, the curiously plaintive and personal afterword—cast in unmistakably marital language—hints at Hutton herself having experienced spousal cruelty. Whether Count Lavalette or Michael Hutton was the "worthless thing" (line 24) who repaid prolonged devotion with "gross cruelty" and "ingratitude" (ibid., 101), Hutton's insistence on this part of the story sets her telling apart and intimates her awareness of

4. Since the *Chartist Circular* made no mention of Madame Lavalette's insanity, relying as it did on a source written prior to her commitment, it was probably not Hutton's (only) source. There were other, more up-to-date periodical and encyclopedia sources on which Hutton evidently relied.

the underacknowledged strain placed on women in political households, of whatever class.

Yet while she admires her heroine as brave, brilliant, strong, noble, and even chivalrous, Hutton also seems compelled to load Madame Lavalette with every conceivable "feminine" virtue. She possesses a "too sensitive heart," tenderly and selflessly devotes herself to her "beloved" partner, is a "fair" and "lovely" rose who is as pure as lilies and pitying tears and baby faces, and in addition she is chaste, loving, sweet, generous, loyal, angelic, nature-loving, gentle, ornamental, and good. The poet twice calls her heroine a "fair flower of chivalry" (lines 12, 111), a phrase that neatly encapsulates Hutton's uncomfortably bifurcated characterization of political women: one sees in the phrase both Madame Lavalette's exceptional boldness and bravery and her modest, beautiful delicacy. It is as if the author wants to valorize smart, daring, unconventional women, but then retreats into the shelter of every Victorian cliché of womanhood. She is not alone in such vacillation: she simply anticipates Tennyson's Princess Ida, Brontë's Jane Eyre, and Barrett Browning's Aurora Leigh, for instance. Perhaps Hutton extolled her character's femininity to elicit respect and sympathy for a character whose illness distanced her from most readers, or perhaps she was registering (consciously or not) the ambiguous role of women within the Chartist movement itself. Madness aside, whether one sees the poem's oppositional tendencies as pulling it apart, generating an irreparable breach in which the poem founders, or as accurately representing—in intended and unintended ways—the dilemmas confronting political women, those tendencies form the basis of its interest.

1845: Thomas Cooper

One of the most rousing Chartist calls for a complete overhaul of women's place in society is the opening exordium in book 9 of Thomas Cooper's *Purgatory of Suicides* (1845, also discussed in chapter 2). Like Hutton's poem, this part of Cooper's is also concerned with the plight of a woman whose husband faces execution. In addition, the *Purgatory* here resembles other Chartist works discussed so far in that this woman's solo efforts to sustain her own and her child's life hold little promise of success, given wage inequality and the lack of women's work opportunities, unless she capitulates to prostitution (book 9: stanza IV: lines 1–9). Strikingly like both Madame Lavalette and the beleaguered woman in Hutton's afterword, this almost-widowed wife "forgavest all" her husband's errors, still bestowing on him an "ill-requited love" even though his "wild excess" often "nigh to madness drove" her (9:

V: lines 8, 6, 9). The close resemblances among the women represented thus far indicate the unfortunate likelihood of plentiful models for the trope, and also the desire of authors to create unambiguous sites of reader sympathy to stir outrage in a common cause. Whatever one's position on religion or the Corn Laws or physical force, everyone within the Chartist movement would likely share indignation at the precarious positions which maltreated or single women occupied, especially if they are also directly victimized by middle- or upper-class men. In some respects, evocations of downtrodden women also conferred on poor men the feeling of dignity and manhood that came with assuming the role of protector of the weak. As Schwarzkopf has shown, most Chartist women seemed to share the view that ultimately, their place was in the home, and their exposure to poverty, insult, and insecurity resulted in large part from bad or nonexistent government intervention that their husbands and fathers could correct if they could vote (*Women in the Chartist Movement,* 149).

However, if most men and many women within Chartism subscribed to fairly traditional views of the sexual division of labor, the narrator in the *Purgatory*'s Book 9 decidedly does not. Instead, he furiously attacks how utterly "Man, the tyrant" controls women's fate, affections, and sexuality (9: VI: line 4). The woman gets a voice here too: in a reference to workhouses and the 1834 Poor Law, the grieving wife herself speaks bitterly about how unnaturally cruel the wealthy are in separating poor mothers from their children (9: X–XII), a fate she likely dreads after her husband's imminent execution. In spite of such severe handicaps (jealously domineering men and the deprivations of poverty and class legislation), even poor women nevertheless contrive to rear famously great children. And if, the narrator contentiously asks, women's sons now can be so great, how much greater will they be "when / Man looks on thee no longer with the tyrant's ken?" (9: XV: lines 8–9) Importantly, though, women should seek their liberation not merely in order to be conduits of *others* who are great, but to be great in themselves: "when thy mind matures / In freedom, and thy soul can make its choice, / Untrammelled, unconstrained" (9: XVI: lines 5–7), then women's intellectual achievements will proclaim "that Mind is of no sex," as the sense, skill, music, and reason of works by Maria Edgeworth, Joanna Baillie, Felicia Hemans, and Germaine Necker (Madame de Staël) already demonstrate (9: XVII: lines 1–6). Cooper envisions the time when "Woman's intense / Inherent claim" to intellectual equality, "befoiled / No more by Man" (9: XVII: lines 7–9), will reveal her "truest dignity; no more / A slave, no more a drudge, no more a toy!" (9: XVIII: lines 2–3). What is distinctive about Cooper's peroration is its assertion that men (both working class, such as this woman's husband, and politically and economically powerful men) share responsibility for maintaining women's oppression. Women therefore require not only that their laboring (male) peers gain social freedom, economic parity, and a political voice, but that they do too. To the extent that his intention is to advocate for gender equality in more than abstract terms (i.e., women should receive the same education as men and be entitled to vote, for example), Cooper differs here from many, though not all, of his Chartist peers,[5] but he also demonstrates that Chartism was not uniformly conservative on women's issues, as has sometimes been supposed.

1852: Ernest Jones

Representing a later time in Chartist history, Ernest Jones's *Woman's Wrongs* (1852) is often referred to as a novel, but it is better described as a collection of tales related by their shared purpose of showing "what [woman] suffers" "through all the social grades" (1). Jones accordingly includes five stories[6] focused on women from the lowest classes through the merchant class and up to the leisured class, in each case revealing the burdens placed on women by various—but consistently oppressive—social norms and economic constraints. For the sake of brevity I will mention only two of the stories, which, nevertheless, will give some flavor of the work as a whole: "The Working Man's Wife" and "The Tradesman's Daughter." Though the female protagonists of these two stories have first and last names, their more generic designation in the titles signals their symbolic function; the titles also signal their derivative status in relation to their husbands and fathers, a fact of paramount importance in each woman's life.

In keeping with the standards normalized by the rise of the middle class (and ascribed or aspired to by many working-class families as well), Margaret Haspen, as a married woman, is not remuneratively employed until her working-class husband is transported. Significantly, the reader's introduction to her

---

5. Feargus O'Connor, for example, opposed female suffrage and emphasized the auxiliary and secondary nature of women's support for Chartism. As if in rebuttal to the opponents of Chartism who ridiculed the presence of women at Chartist events, the *Northern Star* for 2 July 1842 reported of one Chartist lecture that its auditors were "a very attentive audience, composed not of women and children, but of intelligent adults" (1). Chartist educationalists such as William Lovett viewed women's instruction in overwhelmingly domestic terms: as necessary to prevent their opposition to husbands' politics and for the enhancement of their housewifely functions as makers and menders of clothing, as bakers, and as child-minders (Schwarzkopf, 193–94).

6. The series originally included four stories, but Jones added a fifth story, "The Girl with the Red Hands," when he republished the collection in 1855.

in "The Working Man's Wife" occurs while she is in the act of childbirth, and the climax which leads to her hanging happens when she is arrested in the quintessential domestic activity of mopping (in fact she is arrested *because* she is mopping—her effort to remove the evidentiary blood implicating her husband for murder makes her an accessory to the crime). Her economic dependence on her husband John poisons the very activities that are supposed to define and "bless" her femininity: her childbearing angers and alienates him, and cleaning her house covers her with his crime and guilt. Her economic dependence also means that she dares not oppose him even when he beats and abuses her. Jones thus shows how bourgeois notions of respectable masculinity (measured as the ability singlehandedly to support one's family) subject women to gross injustice and even distort their supposedly sacred maternal powers into a pretext for blame.

The couple's class status does matter here, as the economic thumbscrews that make John so resentful of more mouths to feed, for example, would not bear down the same way on men of higher rank, but the financial pressures only exacerbate sexist attitudes shared by men of all classes. Despite his status as an unskilled workman, John Haspen subscribes to a conception of wives as protected and provided for by men and also to the paradoxical view of wives as servants: he looks on "his wife merely as a servant without wages, whom he found it convenient to prepare his meals, and make and share his bed" (ibid., 4). Whatever class they occur in, attitudes such as these restrict and punish women in every direction.

Margaret is not an entirely passive victim, however. In one episode of awful domestic violence, she finally hits back, striking John's face and shoulder with a hatchet and threatening to do more. Unfortunately her rage is entirely maternal, aroused not by her husband's repeated violence against her, but by his once striking their daughter after standing by to let her catch fire and burn. Margaret's violence is certainly justified, but why is it only as a mother, and not as a self-respecting human being, that she acts? One explanation could be that Jones wants readers' sympathy for her to be uncomplicated by any acts on behalf of the self. But the episode is still, in my view, a capitulation to the demand or belief that women behave selflessly and maternally, doing for others what they have not been willing or able to do for themselves.

In another instance, Margaret uses language, reasoning, and irony instead of a hatchet to protest her victimization, although there is again an emphasis on the needs of her children as motivating her interrogation of the legal system. In a very interesting dialogue between her and the lawyer who, early in the story, unsuccessfully defends her husband for robbing his erstwhile employer, the beleaguered wife poses a number of astute questions highlighting how obtuse the laws are with respect to economically dependent women. To the counselor's glib pronouncement that by imprisoning him, "society" is protecting her from her husband's "rough" treatment, she asks if "society will take care of [her] children," since it deprives them of their only breadwinner (ibid., 23). The lawyer condescendingly explains that society must punish those who hurt a member of society, as by stealing someone's property. To this Margaret responds with wonder over why she and her children should be punished by starving, when they have never done harm to a member of society. She reasons that, in prison, her husband *will get plenty of food; we shall be at liberty, and there we shall die of hunger.* D'ye see, we shall be worse punished than he!" (ibid., emphasis in original) Rather stunned and "at a loss for an answer" to this and her claim that it would be better if the law killed rather than imprisoned her husband, because then she could seek a new husband to provide for them, the lawyer tries to throw dust in her eyes with this: "Your husband is civilly dead. [. . .] If you had children by him now, they would be bastards. If he earns money before he dies, you wouldn't inherit it. Henceforth, society looks on him as dead" (ibid.). Possibly feigning innocence, Margaret retorts "Oh, then I can marry again, sir, can't I, if I find anybody who'll work to give these children bread?" She defeats the lawyer utterly at this point, and he stalks off muttering about how "stupid these working-people are" (ibid.). Of course, she is not stupid; she has used the Socratic method to expose the complete absurdity and cruelty not only of the legal system that incarcerates and disinherits without opening doors for remedy but also of the impossible, even deadly, position of women rendered helpless and dependent by bourgeois patriarchy.

Jones was too experienced to expect—as some of his contemporaries seemed to do—that wage-earning alone would liberate women from such difficulties (Margaret's labors as a publican, subsequent to her husband's incarceration, do not save her from execution or her daughters from likely prostitution). At least two other tales[7] in *Woman's Wrongs* show women earning wages and still suffering harm from gender bias at the levels of society, employment, and sexuality. It is unclear whether Laura Trenton in "The Tradesman's Daughter" actually earns any wages, though she certainly works hard keeping all the accounts, prices, and stock exchange rates relevant to her father's grocery business. It is easy to see this story as an attack on the relentlessly prosaic and unimaginative drudgery of middle-class money-getting, but it also critiques the other extreme of self-indulgent romanticism in the person of Laura's cousin Edward Trenton, who chafes at the "wooden" tradesman

---

7. "The Milliner" and "The Girl with the Red Hands."

and is instead "full of enthusiasm and overwrought poesy" (ibid., 71), a point I will return to below. What is most important for Jones is that the men on both sides of the dichotomy he thus constructs completely overlook or misapprehend who Laura Trenton is or might be, based largely on their willful blindness and arrogant assumptions about women.

Laura's father treats her as a clerk who mechanically labors punctiliously and, apparently, for free. She has "never known the joys of childhood" (ibid., 72), or the playful exercise of her body that would give it some grace and strength, or the mental stimulation of any literature beyond a "cheap weekly publication" borrowed from a servant and occasional copies of Established Church periodicals (ibid., 74–75). For these reasons, cousin Edward scarcely bothers to initiate conversation with her, given his "habitual disregard of Laura's intellectual powers" (ibid., 74). He even holds her in contempt, exclaiming that "it's impossible to remain in such a house" after quizzing her on the monotony of her inert, drudging imprisonment in that house where, when she is not keeping accounts, she knits (ibid.). Edward's petulant protest and assertion that rather than lead such a life he will "give up trade" and "go away" has everything to do with the fact that a male has the freedom to make such a choice, seek other employment, and travel to other places; he forgets that a woman does not. He does, however, loan some books to Laura, and unknown to him, she begins secretly borrowing his books and literary periodicals, under the influence of which she palpably changes.

Then, however, her father announces that he and his junior partner Mr. Ellman have settled that Laura shall marry the younger man, and by this means Mr. Trenton basically transfers the business to his partner. Laura is both the medium of transfer—as women almost universally are in polite literature—and a piece of the property so transferred: the account-keeper goes with the accounts. In this way Jones exposes how women of Laura's class suffer their own kinds of prejudices and cruelties; they are not the same as those borne by her social inferior Margaret Haspen, but even without poverty and domestic violence, Laura undergoes her own, gender-delimited tragedy.

What is most intriguing about this story is its configuration of Laura's deprivation in terms of her engagement with creative writing. Because she is a woman, no one dreams that she could have any yearning after visions or ideas or characters beyond the smallest possible round of her mercantile life. Hardly does she perceive any such thing in herself. But once exposed to "the best literature of the day" (ibid., 77), she develops a hunger for the same and an increasing discontent with her status as machine and chattel to her father, and eventually, her husband. After she marries, she performs less clerkly labor, reads books openly rather than clandestinely, and shows "continual evidence of soul, intellect, and feeling" (ibid., 84). This brings her and Edward to a mutual confession—too late of course—of love.

While Edward pursues his ambitions of authorship, Laura's jealous husband removes her to a home in Cumberland. It is ironic that her unfeeling merchant husband should take her to live, of all places, to the Lake District so associated with the Romantics, while Edward vainly pursues authorial success in the swindling literary marketplace of Victorian London. But the narrator pointedly contrasts the healthful, sustaining exertion Edward can feel himself to be making as a sublimated service to their love, with the mournful, docile endurance of monotonous "nothingness" Laura patiently suffers (ibid., 93). Of the pair the narrator says "He could fly out in the sunshine—she, like a brooding dove, must fold her wings, and sorrow in the shade" (ibid., 89). In youth and womanhood, in labor and in love, in discovery and in loss, the woman is fenced in and constrained by male assumptions of superiority, authority, and entitlement on every side. Even in death, her fate contrasts with Edward's, for while he is free to travel to the neighborhood near her and there die, the reader's last sight of her places her in "marble silence" in her drawing room, surrounded by the usual worthies of country life, as confined as she ever was (ibid., 99).

If that scene in her drawing room is supposed to show readers the moment of her death, it is very ambiguously narrated. After receiving an envelope containing a ring she knew to be from the then-perished Edward, she put the ring on "and then fell senseless on the ground," with no additional comment or notice by the narrator (ibid.). The natural supposition is that she has fainted. She reacted in an identical fashion when her father told her she would marry his business partner, as she turned pale "and then fell senseless to the ground" (ibid., 81), so there is no reason to suppose anything catastrophic in the later, drawing room scene. Yet when some months pass and a family friend sends a handsomely bound edition of Edward's works to Ellman Cottage, where Laura lived, Jones writes that "Alas! There was no one then in Ellman Cottage, who read poetry" (ibid., 100). This is a startling, highly unusual manner in which to disclose a protagonist's death: "the extinction of the ability to read poetry," as Haywood aptly describes it (*Chartist Fiction, Vol. 2*, xxiv). It is cryptic, since it records the dearth of an audience rather than the death of an individual, but at the same time it effects a transfiguration of Laura from pure body ("a moving anatomy of penmanship and arithmetic" [*Woman's Wrongs*, 69]) to pure mind, perhaps the ultimate vindication of the claim that "she, too, could think" (ibid., 84).

With one hand, the story credits Edward for thawing and awaking Laura's frozen intellect and soul, though with the other it points out his repeated failures to perceive her as other than his "prejudice and folly" toward female intellectual capability represent her (ibid., 86). Perhaps her deafness here to his posthumously published poetry is a fitting reversal of Edward's careless deafness to her through most of the story, summed up in his early avowal that her mental and moral darkness means "you never hear her voice" (ibid., 71). Neither a retired life in the *locus classicus* of Romantic poetry nor the status of tragic muse to a politically obtuse holdover of a Romantic poet (he is sensationalized as "ANOTHER CHATTERTON!" [ibid., 99]) can liberate Laura, who is literally guarded and censored by her husband and surrounded by the stifling conventionalities of middle-class rural life (whist with the local clergyman, for instance). Mental death is death, Jones contends, and the remedy for women such as Laura must be structural, addressing their education, domestic labor, and disposal by male authorities in their lives.

1856: Gerald Massey

The cold and darkness outside the Greenwich Society for the Diffusion of Useful Knowledge were increasingly broken by the gusts of warmth and light which accompanied repeated openings of the door to the crowded hall. Each time the door opened on that November night in 1874, groups of six or eight angry people stomped out into the snow to protest what they considered blasphemous and indecent contentions made by the visiting lecturer, for whose wisdom they had paid sixpence. At the podium stood a five foot, four inch man with the temerity to pronounce the biblical account of the "fall of humanity" a mere "lying legend" and a libel against women, inasmuch as it placed on their shoulders all the weight of humanity's severance from God (Shaw, *Gerald Massey: Chartist, Poet, Radical and Freethinker*, 161). After similar claims on behalf of women and humanity prompted uproarious verbal sparrings among supporters, detractors, and a handwringing secretary to the Society, Gerald Massey found himself with only a third of the audience which had greeted him earlier that evening, and he quietly but confidently delivered the remainder of his lecture. The erstwhile Chartist earned a precarious, sometimes insufficient living through lecturing during the latter third of his life, but is best known as a poet[8] and earned most of his plaudits for love lyrics and exaltations of marriage (Cross, *The Common Writer: Life in Nineteenth-*

---

8. Massey's poetry has begun to be anthologized in such sources as Brian Maidment's *The Poorhouse Fugitives* (1987) and Peter Scheckner's *An Anthology of Chartist Poetry* (1989), and even in *The New Oxford Book of Victorian Verse*.

Century Grub Street, 158–9).[9] Yet some of his poems on love and marriage were less celebrations than examinations of the negative impact those institutions had on women, revealing an innovative view of gender relations that, when brought to the interpretive table, modifies readers' understanding of the contributions of Chartism to civil society in mid-nineteenth-century Britain.

Just one year before the Matrimonial Causes Act reduced the cost of divorce by granting access to it through civil means (rather than through church courts or Private Acts of Parliament), Gerald Massey published his 1856 *Craigcrook Castle* containing the long poem "Only a Dream." In the poem, the main character Charmian—trapped in a hateful marriage— "drag[s] [her] burthen to a nation's throne, / And pray[s] deliverance from this Tyrant's power" (lines 249–50). This and other references in the poem make clear that this is an extended poetic appeal for divorce, and its audience is not only a reading public but also a legislating one. As I will argue, however, the manner of that appeal is not simply a thematic entreaty to readers who will feel moved by the portrayal of a suffering woman. Rather, through its careful exploitation of linguistic multivalence, medieval poetic tropes, and concentric structure, the poem radically expands its protofeminist polemic, demanding that readers become aware of their agency as interpreters of people and literature and as makers of social change. The aim of this section is to show how these literary techniques themselves interpellate readers, forge links among various subaltern groups, and give rise to the conjecture that poetry as a genre was uniquely positioned by midcentury to be the literary icon of marginalized groups.

Since Massey's literary work has garnered little critical attention,[10] an analysis of "Only a Dream" requires a brief summary of the poem's 367 lines. It begins with a narrator describing how he falls asleep and, in a dream world, realizes the true condition of Charmian, a woman he had believed was happy.

---

9. Examples include "The Golden Wedding Ring," in which a lonely woman is revived and completed by marriage, and "Wedded Love," where a poor wife and husband declare their exceeding love for each other. "The Bridal" describes a joyous wedding between a modest bride and a strong, gracious groom (again of small means), and "O Lay Thy Hand in Mine, Dear!" celebrates the continued love of an aging couple.

10. Though he is briefly and generally discussed in Martha Vicinus's *The Industrial Muse* (1974) and Nigel Cross's *The Common Writer* (1985), until recently the only sustained treatment of his poetry was the unpublished 1942 thesis of Harvard doctoral student Buckner Trawick. Mike Sanders's "Constellating Chartist Poetry: Gerald Massey, Walter Benjamin, and the Uses of Messianism" in *The Poetry of Chartism: Aesthetics, Politics, History* (Cambridge: Cambridge UP, 2009), 203–24, provides a modern correction to such neglect. David Shaw published a useful biography of Massey in 1995, and a revised edition in 2009; it does not explicate his poetry (*Gerald Massey: Chartist, Poet, Radical and Freethinker*).

The bulk of the poem that follows consists of her speaking directly to describe how she was torn from her true, but propertyless, lover, and "sold" to a rich man in a degrading and morbidly agonizing marriage. She paints a lurid picture of the hell she shares with "the phantoms of the dark, / The Grave's Somnambules" who were "so wronged" by marriage in life that they cannot rest after death (lines 162–65). When she realizes her husband has impregnated her, she hopes in spite of all to find happiness in the child. However, whether because the baby comes out looking like her true love or for some other reason,[11] her husband hates the child, separates it from its mother, and allows it to pine for her until it finally dies. The poem then turns to allow the first-person speech of her lost lover, who recalls his happy past with Charmian and wonders if she still thinks of him, too. Following his words the narrator closes the poem with about thirty lines expressing bewilderment at how, now that he is awake, Charmian once again appears "in her summer-sumptuous beauty!" (line 343). However, the image of her marriage-tortured self remains in his mind and concludes the poem.

When the narrator thus completes the frame tale, he says that upon waking he read "the letter of [his] Dream" (line 342). That phrase captures much of what I want to posit in this section because a shadowy narrator figures an act of reading that suggests much about one's own reading of the "Dream" letter just transmitted—the poem itself. Upon reaching the end of the poem, one discovers that what one has been reading is some sort of (intentional) letter, not just the (alphabetic) letters of a poem. The difference matters: it is not necessary to rehearse the discussion of letters and words as traces of absent signifieds, familiar to poststructuralist readers; the valences attached to those humble units of signification render them arbitrary, purely relative deferrals of any "real" meaning. But the notion of *a* letter, for most readers, still implies an intentionality and personal address which loads onto the shoulders of the mere "letters" an immediate significance, and loads onto the shoulders of readers a near-irresistible urge to pay attention, read on, even write back.

When the narrator finally reveals that the poem itself is a letter (or perhaps an envelope one has to open to read a letter), one brushes up against

---

11. During her pregnancy Charmian cherishes the memory of her lost working-class lover and so, in accordance with Lamarckian theory, the baby takes on his image. Many working-class thinkers favored Lamarck's 1809 hypothesis that offspring acquired traits based on the associations and environment of their forebears (perhaps because it allowed one to hope that one could alter the future) until Darwin's theories refined and superseded it toward the end of the nineteenth century. For a brief discussion of the French naturalist's theories, see the essay on "Evolution" in Sally Mitchell's *Victorian Britain: An Encyclopedia* (New York: Garland, 1988), 274–76.

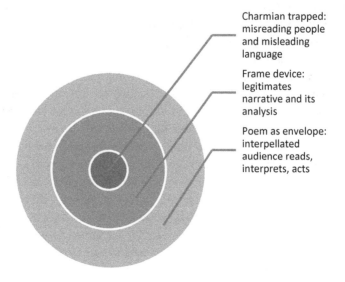

Charmian trapped: misreading people and misleading language

Frame device: legitimates narrative and its analysis

Poem as envelope: interpellated audience reads, interprets, acts

Figure 3. Concentric Structure of Enclosure in "Only a Dream"

the outermost layer of what I conceive as a trileveled concentric structure of envelopment in the poem (see figure 3). Innermost in this structure is Charmian, enclosed and shrouded in numerous explicit ways; the intermediate level consists of the framing device of the poem, whereby both Charmian's and her lover's words exist within a boundary set by the narrator's voice; and most broadly, the poem itself as bearer of the "letter" of a dream becomes an envelope readers must open for themselves and respond to appropriately. Such an elaborate formal pattern of sheathing collaborates with the poem's self-definition as a letter to allure readers, to demand their attention, to habituate them to an interactive experience of reading and, more ambitiously, of the world. Readers simultaneously feel hailed by the poem's letter qualities and "get the hang of" opening envelopes, be they characterological, literary-technical, or semantic. Three broadly defined tasks or roles correspond to the poem's three concentric layers of enclosure: inculcating an awareness of the slippery potential of language, legitimating narrative and the effort to analyze it, and exercising audiences in their essential role as readers and interpreters, actors not only on texts but also finally on the world. I will take up each of those roles as they arise in the discussion of each expanding circle of enclosure.

BIOGRAPHICAL, LITERARY, AND POLITICAL CONTEXT

Like other autodidacts to whom Chartism had given inspiration and a practical utility for their talents (as poets of the movement, journalists, speakers, and organizers), Massey sought a continued livelihood in public speaking after the Chartist movement's demise. By most accounts Massey was an accomplished lecturer, and it was by this labor that he supported himself and his family for much of the latter third of his life. The living was always uncertain, much as his living had been during his days as a reviewer for the *Athenaeum,* as a poet, as editor of the *Edinburgh News,* and as bookkeeper to the publisher William Chapman, among other means of employment. Before his 1850 marriage to Rosina Jane Knowles, daughter of a shoemaker in Bolton, Massey had labored as a draper's errand boy, as a shop assistant, as secretary to the Working Tailors' Association in London, and, when a child, as a straw plaiter and as a silk thrower at the silk mill in his home town of Tring, where his illiterate father, a laborer and boatman, lived in poverty until his death in 1880.

To complement what he could earn through his lecturing and literary pursuits (which included scholarly studies of Shakespeare's sonnets and of the Egyptian origins of human civilization)—and sometimes in lieu of any earnings therefrom—Massey was constrained to apply for grants from the Royal Literary Fund and the Civil List Pension, as well as loans from his acquaintance William Stirling, MP. He was also the occasional beneficiary of Lady Marian Alford, who favored Massey with financial assistance and, during a certain period, rent-free housing on her estate in Berkhamsted. There were occasions on which Massey's resources were insufficient to prevent seizures of his furniture and effects for debt and to prevent his children from suffering the cold which adequate clothing would have mitigated (Shaw, *Gerald Massey: Chartist, Poet, Radical and Freethinker,* 104, 107).

At times his wife Rosina Massey contributed income to the family through her public demonstrations of mesmerism and clairvoyance, but her mental illness and alcoholism presented some financial difficulties as years passed. She required supervision and could not be trusted with the care of their children, so that the Masseys had to hire a housekeeper or Gerald Massey had to take her with him during his lecture tours and pay for the additional accommodations.[12] Doctors pressed for her commitment to a mental hospital, but Massey

---

12. Massey mentions these facts in letters to William Stirling, held by the Strathclyde Regional Archives in the Stirling of Keir Collection, Mss. TSK.29/8/79 and TSK.29/8/30, quoted on page 97 of David Shaw's *Gerald Massey.* See also Shaw, 82–83. Rosina Massey did, however, sometimes contribute her skills to her husband's public appearances, reading and reciting his

resisted, and they remained together until she died at age 33 (apparently of heart disease), after nearly 16 years of marriage.

The nature of Rosina Massey's illness seems to have been largely depressive, but it also included fits of violence and delusions, all perhaps exacerbated and self-medicated by her addiction to alcohol. The question of why doctors urged her consignment to an asylum gathers interest when one considers Mrs. Massey's public and private demonstrations of her paranormal powers.[13] Neighbors' suspicions that she was a witch likely prompted the family's removal from a cottage to a more remote farmhouse on Lady Alford's Ashridge estate, and Victorian cases of other spiritualist women being committed for "lunacy"—and fighting back—are well documented.[14] Whether Gerald Massey's resistance to her incarceration stemmed from a steady affection for an admittedly ill wife or from a suspicion that doctors too readily dismissed women who wielded public and/or spiritual power (or from both) is a matter of speculation.

Given Rosina Massey's lifelong influence on her husband's thought, though, despite her early death and his remarriage, it seems logical to infer that she not only permanently converted him to spiritualism but also helped shape his progressive consciousness with respect to women. British interest in spiritualism arose during the same years as "the woman question," and the two phenomena overlap in important ways. Since Victorian spiritualists believed anyone could be a medium of communication with the spirits of the dead, and that women possessed special talents in this regard, the movement not only provided a forum for female authority and public presence but also attracted large numbers of women to its ranks. Here some women found professional opportunities, social prestige, and personal validation and respect.[15] Owen argues for the "subversive" potential of spiritualist cul-

poetry to appreciative audiences.

13. Gerald Massey first met Rosina Knowles when he went to see her public demonstration of clairvoyance, and after their marriage she continued to perform in public as her health permitted and family finances required (Shaw, chapter 2).

14. Alex Owen details the 1870s case of the spiritualist Louisa Lowe, who in courts of law and the public press tirelessly protested her earlier, wrongful incarceration. Lowe also campaigned through the Lunacy Law Reform Association to protect others—in particular women with unorthodox religious views—from being similarly warehoused. Owen also mentions other women and details the history of Julia Wood, a spiritualist sympathizer who was consequently detained in an asylum for many years, despite Lowe's efforts on her behalf. See *The Darkened Room*, 154–201.

15. As one example, "Towards the end of the 1880s a rival to the London [spiritualist] presses appeared in the form of the highly successful *Two Worlds*, which was published in Manchester. Under the editorship of the talented and well-known medium, Emma Hardinge Britten, *Two Worlds* adopted a progressive and crusading stance which won it an enthusiastic readership amongst provincial and reform-minded spiritualists" (Owen, 24).

ture which could, in certain circumstances, "provide a means of circumvent-
ing rigid nineteenth-century class and gender norms" (*The Darkened Room:
Women, Power, and Spiritualism in Late Victorian England*, 4). Viewed this
way, spiritualism's appeal to progressive men and women who actively agi-
tated for women's rights is unsurprising, and many of the prominent figures
among the 24,000 signers of Anna Jameson's and Mary Howitt's 1855 Petition
on Married Women's Property, for instance, also showed considerable interest in spiritualism.[16] Connecting her husband to communities more interested
in and open to the elevation of women's status and authority, Rosina Massey
might well account for Gerald Massey's increasingly progressive stance on
women's issues.

In his own and in his reviews of others' poetry, Massey showed an interest in women's social, economic, and political status, as when he reviewed
Tennyson's *The Princess*. Speaking there of the inadequate education afforded
to women, Massey in 1847 wrote that "the hallowing wretchedness of this
inequality is often a very hell in its torments" (qtd. in Shaw, 50). In later years,
he believed women required not only education but also access to the parliamentary franchise as an absolute essential if they would begin to enjoy
full equality with men. Perhaps more controversial than these opinions, long
advocated by activists such as William Thompson, Anna Wheeler, and Barbara Leigh Smith (Bodichon), Massey dedicated his poem "A Greeting" to
Annie Besant, whose 1877 prosecution for disseminating birth control information and whose vehement support for the striking Bryant and May match
girls in the following decade won her a notoriety with which not all progres-
sives wished to associate themselves. Nevertheless, Massey's poem hails her as
a "brave and dear" fellow fighter for the right causes (Shaw, 164).

The Masseys married in 1850, and by the time he published his protofeminist "Only a Dream" in 1856, the Petition on Married Women's Property had
circulated, and Barbara Leigh Smith and Caroline Norton had each published
very influential works about the legal disabilities marriage imposed on wom-
en.[17] The legislation proposed by the 1855 Petition on women's ownership of
property mostly disappeared under the twin initiatives of (a) a co-optive and
unfulfilled promise by the Government to initiate its own measure on mar-

16. Howitt herself, for example, as well as Elizabeth Barrett Browning and Harriet Marti-
neau.

17. Barbara Leigh Smith published in 1854 her *Brief Summary, in Plain Language, of the
Most Important Laws of England concerning Women*, and Caroline Norton published her *Letter
to the Queen on Lord Chancellor Cranworth's Marriage and Divorce Bill* in 1855. For an excellent
analysis of Victorian law and literature respecting women, see Kristin Kalsem's *In Contempt:
Nineteenth-Century Women, Law, and Literature* (Columbus: The Ohio State University Press,
2012).

ried women's property and (b) the Divorce and Matrimonial Causes Act of 1857,[18] which addressed some of the worst abuses married women suffered while still not granting women the control over their property that they would later gain under the Married Women's Property Acts of 1870 and 1882 (Perkin, *Women and Marriage in Nineteenth-Century England,* 300–02). That a pre-emptive governmental promise and the clamor over divorce should temporarily drown out the agitation for married women's control of their property suggests just how vocal marriage's critics had become when Massey published his poetic appeal for women's freedom from unwanted marriages.

However, midcentury voices on marriage and divorce were hardly harmonious. While Elizabeth Barrett Browning's 1856 *Aurora Leigh* put forward strong arguments in favor of women's independence from men and marriage, Coventry Patmore's epic of perfect domestic harmony presided over by a wife of otherworldly selflessness and purity began publication in 1854. Patmore's *The Angel in the House* represents one of the most conservative poetic statements on the marriage theme. At least one critic has claimed that, in this work, Patmore rebelled against Tennyson, whose position regarding women and marriage was less conservative than Patmore's (Saintsbury, *Historical Manual of English Prosody,* 190–91). Nevertheless, Tennyson's intellectual, initially separatist heroine in *The Princess* (1847) was only slightly less conservative than Patmore's "angel." After holding a child awakens her to the duties of maternity and womanhood, Tennyson's princess abandons her educational mission in order to marry the prince.

Tennyson espoused these conservative views also in his rendering of Arthurian legend in *The Idylls of the King* (1862–72), which blames Guinevere's illicit, extramarital love of Lancelot for leading the world astray and destroying the Round Table. The poem retails the scandalous rumors of a wicked queen whom her husband Arthur reproaches for her forbidden love. Comparing Tennyson's depiction of Guinevere to William Morris's is instructive because the latter poet's more liberal treatment of an unhappily married woman represents a position farther left on the spectrum of poets' views I am outlining. Morris wears his position on his sleeve, so to speak, by entitling his poem "The Defence of Guenevere" (1858). More as a victim than a cunning schemer (as she is in Malory's original), Morris's Guenevere was almost

---

18. This Act permitted divorce by civil means (rather than through church courts and Private Acts of Parliament) and cheapened the cost of obtaining a divorce (though insufficiently to benefit the working class). At the same time, it unfortunately codified a sexual double standard whereby men could obtain divorces on the ground of a wife's adultery alone, whereas women had to prove not only their husbands' adultery but also one of several aggravating offenses such as rape, incest, cruelty, desertion, sodomy, or bestiality (Perkin, 303).

tricked into choosing a conventional, loveless marriage to Arthur and suffered "hell" as a result (line 38), and though she admits guilt for her illicit relationship, she launches a defense that focuses readers less on the details of what transpired between her and Launcelot than on the fact that her love for him is altogether good, on a spiritual level. All of these poems, published within about a decade of each other, fill in some details of the literary landscape in which Massey published "Only a Dream." His poem staked out a position which was arguably more feminist than any of those to which I have referred, and it was not anomalous within his poetic corpus.

Others of his poems also scrutinized how love and marriage might have a negative impact on women, particularly when women bore children without the sanction of marriage or the aid of deserting men. Such seems to be the scenario in "A Ballad of the Old Time," sung by a pregnant woman anxiously, hopefully, and it appears, futilely awaiting her lover's return. In a hope the poem subtly renders sadly naive, the abandoned woman believes he will come bearing a wedding ring in token that "He never will lightly me" and so that "Base-born his Babe shall not be." And in an especially interesting quartet of poems entitled "Deserted," "Desolate," "Doomed," and "Dead!" Massey progressively tells the story of a suicidally depressed woman who has been deserted with a child.[19] The first two poems are spoken by the woman herself, whose baby dies in the second poem, and in the third a narrator describes her as a victim who has been "stain'd and trampled" before she kills herself. In the final poem the ghostly woman gruesomely, relentlessly (and I must say satisfyingly) haunts her "Wronger." Thus the poem on which the rest of this chapter concentrates is not exceptional in Massey's *oeuvre*.

INNERMOST CIRCLE: DECIPHERING LINGUISTIC AND MARITAL CONCEALMENT

In "Only a Dream," the first layer of envelopment is at the level of narrated characters within the poem: the primary speaker Charmian is herself trapped inside a marriage she likens to live burial, *and* her true state of affairs is obscured to the frame narrator's eyes until a dream reveals it to him. Introducing Charmian's self-narration is the observation that her voice "stifled half its pathos not to hurt" (line 53), indicating that even the words she will utter in this dream are muted. What she does tell us, though, is that she resembled "the

19. "Dead!" was originally published, without the other three poems, in *Craigcrook Castle* under the title "In the Dead Unhappy Midnight." In his collected *Poetical Works* (1861), however, the four poems appear together.

sheeted dead" (line 103) when she married, that she afterwards felt "bound, and buried alive" (line 139), and that with 50 other women,[20] she "struck, and beat" (line 135) on the earth above her and "cried, and cried" (line 141) in an effort to escape, but remained trapped and went unheard. The "woe" suffered by these marriage victims is "unutterable" (line 171), and within the space of four lines we learn that their hearts are "drownéd," their agonies "stifled," their lips "struck dumb" by brutal husbands in the "curtained bridal-bed," and they have endured "silent tortures" and "shrouded deaths" (lines 173–76), so that even the language describing silence and enclosure becomes crowded and gives readers a claustrophobic feeling.

Charmian indicates later in the poem that her anguish rends the "bridal-veil," allowing her to call on her auditors to "Come see what ghastly wounds bleed hidden here!" (lines 245–46). But her concealment extends beyond what *she* experiences in her nightmarish marriage and makes it difficult for *others* to apprehend her true condition as well. This innermost portion of the poem's tripartite form in fact doubles the enclosure: Charmian is "shrouded" and "curtained" in marriage, and the very fact of her misery is hardly disclosed without concentrated penetration beyond appearances and language. When not revealed by the narrator's dream state, Charmian appears to be all beauty, a voluptuous, proud, and "serene" woman with dimpled cheeks and "large lotus eyes" and musical laughter (lines 20–25, 343–47). The narrator thus calls attention to the differences between his perceptions of Charmian when he is waking or sleeping, implying that readers also should beware of what is below the surface, even of language.

It seems important that the narrator portrays himself here as a follower and learner whose initial interpretations had been faulty. In a disarming pedagogical gesture, the narrator is represented as someone who, once needing leadership and correction, is now in a position to welcome and lead the inexpert reader, diminishing any gap between himself and those he would instruct. The frame narrator not only initiates and guides his readers in practices of correct interpretation but he is himself guided by Charmian. The beginning of the poem describes how "a hand reacht thro' the dark, and drew

---

20. She mentions assistance from "a hundred hands" (line 136), which probably means there were 50 other women, a number significantly corresponding to the number of the Danaides. The 50 daughters of Danaus absolutely opposed marrying their 50 cousins and fled to Argos, where they were pursued by the men ready to fight to possess them in marriage. The Argives defended the women and explained that they "would allow no woman to be forced to marry against her will" (Hamilton, *Mythology: Timeless Tales of Gods and Heroes*, 281), but when the marriages finally occurred 49 of the brides murdered their husbands on their wedding night. They were afterwards condemned to hell. See Edith Hamilton's *Mythology: Timeless Tales of Gods and Heroes* (New York: Mentor, 1969).

/ [His spirit] gliding silent on," until the narrator follows Charmian and hears her tale (lines 8–9). The poem thus performs for its Victorian readers a teaching function that shares some qualities with medieval tradition (more about the poem's medievalism later). In the *Divine Comedy,* for instance, the narrator—guided by Virgil and receiving instruction from various mentors among the shades—then guides his readers (through apostrophes) to apprehend the allegorical meanings of his poem and to learn what he has himself been taught. Thus Dante makes "clear that the task of understanding is ultimately the same for himself and the reader" (Spitzer, "The Addresses to the Reader in the 'Commedia,'" 162). Massey, however, seeks to pass on his instruction not through authoritative, direct apostrophic address, but through the successively layered form of the poem itself. His indirect, structural approach subtly alters the learning dynamic from one in which the reader somewhat passively interprets according to direction (narrator's apostrophe), to one in which a second order of deciphering (linguistic and structural decoding) intervenes between instructor and student, making greater demands on the reader and rendering him or her more nearly self-taught. Welcoming nonexpert, active, semi-independent readers to join the narrator on his journey, Massey formally democratizes the literary sphere in the same way that he means to democratize the political sphere. Through the formal structures of the poem, he enfolds workers almost simultaneously into the projects of reading/interpreting and of intervening in public affairs; this is the Chartist imaginary at work in the aesthetic nuances of the poem.

Massey democratizes the literary not only by summoning his readers to active participation with the poem but also by writing Chartists into a literary history that could itself be a smothering, confining force (like Charmian's marriage). Inasmuch as certain styles, diction, and familiarity with literary heritage largely defined social status and cultural clout, those shibboleths contributed much to working people's exclusion from cultural and political power, burying them under a weight of literary tradition as Charmian is buried under social and legal traditions. Massey reworks those traditions as a gesture of intellectual equality, speaking in and revising accepted forms much like Charmian speaks out against her powerlessness. At the same time, he also engages in a sort of pedagogy, bringing his Chartist readers into the experience of the literary tradition (regardless of whether they are aware of that tradition), enabling them to encounter for themselves dream visions, frame narratives, imaginative otherness, the startling effects of oxymoron, and other linguistic and rhetorical devices. Whereas many working-class readers might not recognize the names of Dante or Petrarch, and might experience literary dream visions as forays into alien historical, philosophical, or religious ter-

ritories, they might very well know the need for divorce or the frustrations
of voicelessness, and feel the jarring effects of a phrase such as "warm snow."
Infused with the content of women or workers or other disempowered characters, established literary tropes might be transformed from exclusionary
cultural devices into experiences and imaginative projections for new groups
of (uninitiated) readers. This is a literary education which occurs in tandem
with the overt political education that urges workers to take seriously the
plight of women in restrictive, abusive marriages.

Elaborating the poem's contention that people cannot trust what they see,
either on the page or when they study other people, are numerous linguistic
peculiarities throughout "Only a Dream." On several occasions the diction
of both the frame narrator and Charmian raises questions about language,
as when the narrator describes snow as "white and warm" (line 2). What was
that? Warm snow? (This particular oxymoron also underscores the poem's
medieval debts by alluding to Petrarch's pervasive "icy fire" conceit.) Charmian also surprises readers later when she declares that she should have worn
"The white [. . .] weeds of widowhood" instead of bridal attire when she was
married off to her hated husband (line 101). Victorian standards of mourning
for rich and poor alike required black clothing, not white.[21] In both cases the
adjectives are exactly opposite to what we would expect, alerting readers to
the potential for inaccuracy, or at least slippage, in the medium of Charmian's
history.

A more complex example of how the poem heightens reader awareness
of linguistic nontransparency, moderating one's faith in the word as written,
comes from a passage in which Charmian seeks to impress on her listeners
that her husband "was a cruel Tyrant, just too mean / To murder" (lines 124–
25). For just a moment, one has to puzzle over whether this is a delightfully
withering insult (her husband is so insignificant that she would not squan-
der the energy it would take to murder him) or a statement of his paucity of
resources (he himself would not murder because he is deficient in the requisite courage and determination), semantic alternatives with quite different,
indeed oppositional, implications. Has she contemplated murdering him? Or
has he contemplated murdering her? Arguably this radical divergence of possibilities is foreclosed by the remainder of line 125, which makes the sentence
read "He was a cruel Tyrant, just too mean / To murder, altho' pitiless as the
grave." Now the prevailing sense is that, though he is "pitiless," he lacks the
spirit to be a murderer. Or is it? If readers imagine Charmian as the potential

---

21. For mourning customs including duration of mourning, wakes, and proper clothing
(including colors and materials) for widows, see the helpful compendium on 160–63 of Sally
Mitchell's *Daily Life in Victorian England* (Westport: Greenwood, 1996).

murderer, they have (probably unconsciously) inserted an understood phrase in the white space between the lines. The mental revision reads "He was a cruel Tyrant, just too mean [for one] / To murder, altho' pitiless as the grave." In that case, the adjectival phrase which completes the sentence and would otherwise make clear that her husband is the potential murderer becomes a modifier of the understood "one": Charmian. She would not murder him because, no matter how pitiless she might become, he is still too base to kill. So the sentence never quite comes clean, however much that final phrase seems to clinch the intention and import of the sentence. That Charmian calls her husband a "Tyrant" invites readers to see in her tormenter a figure for the target of radical political discourse since at least 1789. Early Chartist poetry, in particular, abounds with indictments of selfish aristocrats, corrupt legislators, ruthlessly exploitative employers, and religious and military powers as "Tyrants" whose powers must be checked or destroyed by the new movement's popular muscle. This is one of several instances throughout the poem where the straightforward meaning of Charmian's suffering complaint gains additional layers of political signification.

The degree to which language might conceal, rather than reveal, the truth that dreams manifest emerges in this passage from the poem's opening:

> Portentous things which hid themselves by day,
> Sweet-shadowed 'neath her sunning beauty-bloom,
> Came peering thro' the dim and sorrowy night.
> (Massey, "Only a Dream," lines 29–31)

In these lines, the frame narrator draws a sharp contrast between how one might perceive Charmian by day or by night, but her beauty is not the only veil which might block readerly apprehension of or access to "portentous things." Hyphenated nouns such as "beauty-bloom" are common in early nineteenth-century poetry and most readers would take the cue that "bloom" is a noun when they see the hyphen. However, especially in poetry, what readers hear is as important as what they see, and it is impossible to read these lines without becoming aware of "bloom"'s latent double identity as both noun and verb.[22] Because of the potential uncertainty here about what part of speech "bloom" functions as, indicators that her story is ominous might

---

22. For a memorable prose example of the importance of what one hears as s/he reads, see Garrett Stewart's *Dear Reader: The Conscripted Audience in Nineteenth-Century British Fiction* (Baltimore: Johns Hopkins University Press, 1996), 242–49. See also Stewart's *Reading Voices: Literature and the Phonotext* (Berkeley: University of California Press, 1990), the spirit of which informs my discussion in this portion of the chapter.

be "shadowed" or concealed under her beauty-bloom or they might, on the contrary, bloom, albeit in a shadowy fashion, beneath her beauty. Of course, Massey's hyphenating "beauty-bloom" puts the weight of interpretation on the side of the former, with "bloom" as a compound noun obscuring the presence of portentous things, but the "portentous things . . . bloom" construction— having once stepped onto the field of possibility through the gate of one's mental ears—leaves an aural trace, an unmistakable impression, a footprint, so to speak, on the reader's mind. The simple technique of lineation deepens the impression by keeping at bay the true predicate for portentous things: "came," which arrives on the scene only after readers have hesitated between the subject-verb status of "bloom," kept out of sight just long enough for the pun to sink in.

If one doubts, even momentarily, whether her beauty hides the ambiguous "portentous things" or causes them to blossom out into something else, then one loses some confidence in language (and possibly in Charmian) and should consider himself warned that conventions regarding marriage are not the only agents in a cover-up. Readers have to penetrate more than the "bridal-veil" to understand all that this poem seeks to convey. Charmian's burial both within marriage and under the language in which she endeavors to express that marital entrapment represents a first locus for reader awareness of the poem's call to scrutinize characters and linguistic expression.

INTERMEDIATE CIRCLE: FRAME NARRATIVE AS READER INTERPELLATION

Backing out to a slightly larger circumference, readers can detect the poem's second pattern of envelopment at the level of the narrative framing of the poem: the narrator's frame encloses Charmian's telling of her own tale and also encloses the first-person meditations of her true lover. The key point here is that the frame self-reflexively calls attention to its own status as narrative at the same time as it posits the validity of narratives and the importance of their proper reception. This intermediate circle of the poem's structure then implicates its readers in the drama of literary exchange, writing them into the script and thereby directing their interaction with literary "scripts" in general. Though distinct from the direct, apostrophic mode of reader address prevalent in other Chartist poetry, Massey's technique here shares an immediacy that actively, explicitly hails readers and demands a political response.[23]

---

23. For example, Linton's "The Gathering of the People" enjoins its readers to "Gather ye silently" on their "hill of right" in order to "burst on the plain," overwhelm their erstwhile mockers, and "reign." In Cooper's *The Purgatory of Suicides* the poet addresses workers thus:

There has been some disagreement about what a literary frame is and whether it should be regarded as a simple (disposable) relay to the "real," embedded narrative or rather as a narrative in its own right "in relation to which the embedded narrative takes the position of an indirect object" (Jeffrey Williams, *Theory and the Novel: Narrative Reflexivity in the British Tradition,* 100).[24] My own view more closely approximates the latter than the former account of the frame's function. The frame is not a mere bridge between the reader's world and the fictional world, a mediator that is almost nonfictional since it treats the embedded plot as "the story" and seems to stand outside that and comment on it, and something one properly forgets once s/he has settled in to what the work is "actually about;" instead the literary frame serves as a miniaturized pattern for the exchange of narrative, with particular emphasis on its reception. Frames often depict not only a narrator but also auditors who express a desire for narrative and a situation to which storytelling seems like the natural, ideal response. Examples of these characteristics occur in Boccaccio's *Decameron* and Chaucer's *Canterbury Tales*—in which people exiled from a plague-ridden city or on a religious pilgrimage tell tales to pass the time—and Brontë's *Wuthering Heights,* in which Nelly relates to Lockwood the history of Wuthering Heights while he recovers from illness. As these instances demonstrate, the conditions for narrative seem perfect since there are no distractions or other demands to compete with, and in fact the circumstances for any activity *other* than narrative are inconducive. Not every literary frame exhibits all of these characteristics, but they are sufficiently common to warrant their inclusion in a definition of frames.[25]

"Slaves, toil no more! Why delve, and moil, and pine, / To glut the tyrant-forgers of your chain?" Appealing to rural and urban readers on behalf of the Charter, Jones concludes his "The Factory Town" with "Then up, in one united band, / Both farming slave and factory-martyr! / Remember, that, *to keep the* LAND, / The best way is—*to gain the* CHARTER!" These and many other examples of the use of apostrophe in working-class poetry are collected in Peter Scheckner's *An Anthology of Chartist Poetry: Poetry of the British Working Class, 1830s–1850s* (London: Associated University Press, 1989).

24. William Nelles engages in an elaborate dissection of narrative theory in an effort to provide precise terminology for the definition of frame narrative in *Frameworks: Narrative Levels and Embedded Narratives* (New York: Peter Lang, 1997). For accounts of frame narratives as forgettable or merely extradiagetic see for example Mieke Bal, *Narratology: An Introduction to the Theory of Narrative* (Toronto: University of Toronto Press, 1997), John T. Matthews, "Framing in *Wuthering Heights,*" *Texas Studies in Language and Literature* 27 (1985): 25–61, and Bernard Duyfhuizen, *Narratives of Transmission* (Rutherford: Fairleigh Dickinson University Press, 1992). In contradistinction to many views proffered by those authors, Jeffrey Williams regards frame narratives as "moments in which the act of narrative itself is depicted and thus thematized or called into question" (*Theory and the Novel,* 1).

25. My characterization of frames here borrows much from Jeffrey Williams's *Theory and the Novel: Narrative Reflexivity in the British Tradition* (Cambridge: Cambridge University Press, 1998).

Following the convention of frame narratives that auditors be in ideal circumstances to receive the tale, the narrator of "Only a Dream" slumbers. Since in sleep one's attention cannot be directed to any activities, demands, or interests except the dream, this frame not only sets up the seductive power of narrative but also enforces a sense of its aptness or opportuneness. What else should one do during sleep but dream? Far from just establishing contact or opening up a channel through which to transmit the narrative of Charmian's life, the frame dramatizes the consumption of narrative as natural, desirable, and opportune, and narrative itself as valuable and authoritative. The frame asserts the interest and worth of the narrative-to-come but also performs what the reader's response to Charmian's tale should be by figuring for us someone else's reception of (and submission to) narrative in the framing scenes. Readers see the narrator clamoring after what others have to tell him and infer that they should clamor after what he himself has to tell them.

Massey's frame differs in some respects from his models mentioned above because "Only a Dream" makes use of both the framing device and the dream vision device, which adds some features by virtue of its own technical norms.[26] In this poem, as in many dream visions, the narrator himself becomes the auditor who craves narrative, drawn irresistibly toward his guide and the story she has to tell: "lo, a hand reacht thro' the dark, and drew / [His spirit] gliding silent on" (lines 8–9). If the narrator were not already an eager listener, the mysterious, disembodied hand stretched out to grip him like some ghost of Christmas past is likely to capture his attention as well as himself. The convention of dream visions stipulates that the dream comes as a fulfilment of some psychological need in the narrator, dovetailing with the frame narrative's self-valorizing portrayal of the value and desirability of narrative. Instead of a circle of listeners who model how readers should respond to literature (more typical in frame narratives), in "Only a Dream" we are confronted with a narrator whose feminized spirit goes "out to meet her Bridegroom," seduced by his music and "clasp[ed]" by him (lines 5–7). The narrator depicts himself as pursuing and captivated by narrative. In modelling this powerful double attraction, the poem urges readers to seek out stories, which will embrace them with an ardor akin to a lover's—the normative heterosexu-

---

26. Dream visions typically include a narrator who experiences some restlessness or incompleteness that the dream addresses, often with the help of "authoritative figures who impart some revelation or doctrine." And they mix the past, in which the naive narrator lacked whatever the dream imparted, with the present, in which a now-wiser narrator writes retrospectively about the dream vision. The frames of most dream visions indicate the season, time of day, location, environment, and the solitude and neediness of the narrator (Alex Preminger and T. V. F. Brogan, eds., *The New Princeton Encyclopedia of Poetry and Poetics* [Princeton, NJ: Princeton University Press, 1993], 311–12).

ality of matrimony unmistakably casts such a reader/text relation as natural, even necessary.

But whose necessity is it? For the fact is that, to the extent that Charmian and the narrator are fictional characters in a long poem, neither exists and the only real ground of their being is the mind of the reader who encounters this text. Arguably, this symbiotic relation is why the poem performs its structural gymnastics and provides this hybrid of the frame tale and the dream vision (see chapter 3 for more on generic hybridity in Chartist literature). The reader's imaginative engagement is the existential basis of the entire utterance, but because the reader is always outside the text, beyond its entire control, the narrative attempts to inscribe its auditors within itself and thereby contain or direct their decoding of what will come. Right from the beginning, then, the poem offers an analogue of eager reception as a means of forcing on readers a recognition of the self as seeker, as earnest consumer and interpreter of the tale it has to tell. Thus it is no accident that the devices of the frame narrative and dream vision apparently situate the reader's proxy *outside* the story of Charmian's true love and her marriage, as if he too were exterior to and beyond the reach of her narrative. His casual acquaintance with Charmian has led him to see her as contented, but he quickly falls within her sphere of influence and revises his erroneous reading of a text he will now share with readers, who also seem to be outside the text. He has deciphered what really lay in her story, and the textual effect of the reader's metaphoric incorporation into this narrative is that s/he, too, must listen (or rather read)—and that not casually—to discern properly. This is how the text secures itself an attentive readership; if frames function as fences delimiting the possibilities of text or canvas,[27] this frame would circumscribe readers themselves and rope them into the textual fold.[28]

The narrator's usual hunger for dream stories (like the ones his spirit seeks out each night) reaches a higher pitch when Charmian appears in order to guide him and draws our surrogate out to hear the tale she has to tell. And

---

27. In Tennyson's *The Princess*, for example, the frame narrative (clearly more conservative than the embedded tale of Princess Ida) shuts down social possibilities, as when Little Lelia removes her shawl from a male statue that she had converted into a man-woman in the opening frame by wrapping him in her garment. She accompanies her action with a request to her superior, Oxford-educated brothers to "tell us what we are." In numerous nineteenth-century British novels (*Frankenstein, Wuthering Heights, Dr. Jekyll and Mr. Hyde,* and *Dracula,* for instance), "it is precisely the human extremity of death that is circumscribed and packaged, made manageably phantasmal" and tamed by the frame device (Stewart, *Dear Reader: The Conscripted Audience in Nineteenth-Century British Fiction,* 271).

28. For a sophisticated treatment of reception theory using fiction as its site of investigation, see Garrett Stewart's *Dear Reader.*

she is not a mere diversion, but a "Spirit" (line 51), an imposing figure with a vast, "sea-like" soul and a divinely transfigured "white, lit face" (lines 38, 28), suggesting the authority of her words. Compliments of the frame's closing bracket, she reappears as this same larger-than-life figure at the poem's conclusion, in a last effort to command the reader's regard. Awakened from his dream, the frame narrator still sees her "Holding the great Curse up to heaven for ever, / To call God's lightning down, altho' it kill / Her with her wedded Curse" (lines 357–59). One of the poem's final descriptions of Charmian, these lines allusively associate her with two biblical figures noted for their superhuman authority and strength: the prophet Elijah and the judge Samson. Elijah's authority was vindicated when he called down fire to burn not only the sacrifice offered up to God but also the altar and the water with which Elijah had drenched them. Interestingly, Charmian is a prophet with a twist, for she calls down lightning while she holds "up to heaven" a "great Curse," rather than a slain animal or a prayer for the humiliation of competing prophets (1 Kings 18:25–41). Samson avenged himself for his captivity and blinding at the hands of the Philistines through one last show of strength: he pulled down the pillars of Dagon's temple, collapsing the structure and killing himself and his enemies (Judges 16:23–31). Charmian is similarly fearless for her own safety in that she is so set on the abolition of women's captivity in unwanted marriages, she calls for its destruction "altho' it kill / Her with her wedded Curse" (lines 358–59). She differs from Samson in her less selfish motives, so that while she is identified with the authority and strength of both these biblical heroes, her aims are unalloyed with the swaggering, pettiness, and vengeance of those men. By summoning and revising them, what the frame distills from these intertexts is the valor, the courage, and most important for my discussion, the sheer status of an authoritative speaker whose "hand reacht thro' the dark, and drew" the narrator—with readers in tow—irresistibly to hear the story of her curse (line 8).

OUTER CIRCLE:
EPISTOLARY AND THEATRICAL ADDRESS TO THE READER

Finally, at the level of the poem's being itself an envelope or an enveloped letter, one perceives the third and broadest circle of enclosure in the poem: the narrator says at the end "And I with marveling eyes had broke the seal / Of slumber, read the letter of my Dream" (lines 341–42). In the most literal sense, it would seem that slumber is the wax seal affixed to the envelope of a dream, and that the conscious interpretive act on waking constitutes the "reading" of content or meaning, the opening of an enveloping dream to get at its "letter." The dream we have been reading in the form of this poem turns out to contain an urgent letter, and the narrator's "read[ing] the letter of [his] Dream" performs for us what the appropriate response to that letter is: we too must read the letter of this poem/dream and take steps to change the law. The narrator complains that "The kings and queens of prospering love go by, / And little heed this Martyr by the way" (360–61)[29] and Charmian herself calls on "all good people" (read: readers) with the vocative "ye" to "Behold where all the Tortures of the Past / Are stored by Law, and sanctified for use" (lines 251, 247–48). Her interlocutors should "behold" and "heed" both Charmian's torture and the laws which "sanctify" it. How readers receive and respond to this "letter" clearly matters. The injunctions here to examine both letters and laws would have resonated for Victorian readers with the Christian New Testament's distinction between the "letter" and the "spirit" of the religious laws inherited from the Jewish tradition. In the new dispensation, Christian believers are taught to outgrow literal-minded observance of the letter of the law in favor of a more perceptive observance of its spirit. In this poem, by implication, the nature of society's engagement with the laws of marriage crucially depends on its felt apprehension of the suffering and torture, the *spiritual* impact, of that which the laws sanction.

The poem's self-designation as letter is the reason that the narrator calls so much attention to acts of reading, looking, and listening throughout the poem. The sense, if not the grammar, of line 9 is that he "look[ed] up" into Charmian's face, at which time he "read her look" (line 11) and began to follow her to hear her tale. And tales, as the discussion of frame narratives above demonstrates, are not to be ignored. With a prophetic authority whose urgency resembles that of the story Coleridge's Ancient Mariner has to tell, "The golden legends on Night's prophet-brow" in this poem "burn[]" (lines 16–17). Legends here command attention by virtue of their prophet status, burning as divine things do[30] and also burning to be told in the way prophets' messages do (recall, for example, how God compelled Jonah to deliver the story entrusted to him for that purpose). So readers are reminded from the outset to regard stories as urgent, powerful, and demanding attention, a reminder effectively buttressed both by the narrator's misreading of Charmian

---

29. Since Charmian earlier mentions that she "drag[s] [her] burthen to a nation's throne" (line 249), this reference to royalty whose idyllic love makes them complacent about others' marital suffering might well refer to Prince Albert and Queen Victoria, to whose throne were directed such appeals for divorce law as Caroline Norton's.

30. I am thinking, for example, of Moses's encounter with God in the burning bush (Exodus 3) and of God's leading the Jews out of Egypt by appearing to them "in a pillar of fire" (Exodus 13:21–22).

and by the multiplied visual and reading references that fill out this opening section of the poem.

As it progresses, this portion of "Only a Dream" makes readers aware that the narrator's impression of Charmian merely as a beautiful, sensuous, carefree woman is a misreading of which he is disabused when he perceives her "sorrow," "anguish," and the withering of her life's "luxuriant flower" into "ashen dead-sea fruit" (lines 21, 34, 26–27). He becomes conscious of his mis-apprehension through the new imperative to read which dreams bring to bear. Notice how insistent is the visual in these lines:

> Diaphanous in the moonlight grew her life
> With all its written agony visible;
> Down the dark deep of her great grief I stared,
> And saw the Wreck with all its dead around.
>   (Massey, "Only a Dream," 44–47)

Since it means sheer or almost transparent, "diaphanous" is a distinctly visual adjective with which it is appropriate to introduce the metaphor of reading which follows. Her agony grows "visible" when the narrator not only "s[ees]" but also "stare[s]" into what he represents as an ocean entombing a shipwreck. Clearly the emphasis is on the ocular, and not only as a passive reception of images but as focused, active concentration on unpleasant subjects: he stares. However, the really curious word choice here is the adjective describing her agony as "written," which one might regard not only as incompatible with the shipwreck metaphor but also as simply a strange descriptor for an emotional state. The double jarring produced by the diction helps insist on the episto-lary character of this agony, which makes itself known through the letter of a dream and, ultimately, through the letter of this poem. It is the letter as poem at which readers must "stare," and we are cautioned not to misread the letter as the narrator originally misread Charmian.

The interpretation implied in correct reading is the reader's first, and cru-cial, act, but it entails a second act if opening this final envelope is to be com-plete. For if those in power fail to address the pressing need for divorce reform (recall the heedless "kings and queens" of lines 360–61), readers should not only "read the letter of [this] Dream" but also take action on its contents and "drag [the] burthen to a nation's throne" as Charmian herself does. Perhaps an emphasis on action is what Massey means by giving the poem the dismissive title "*Only* a Dream" (emphasis mine), as if to say that, though the text mat-ters, finally what readers do with it and their world matters more. The poem's concluding lines forcefully demonstrate such a contention:

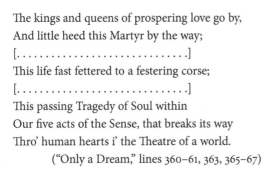

The kings and queens of prospering love go by,
And little heed this Martyr by the way;
[. . . . .]
This life fast fettered to a festering corse;
[. . . . .]
This passing Tragedy of Soul within
Our five acts of the Sense, that breaks its way
Thro' human hearts i' the Theatre of a world.
        ("Only a Dream," lines 360–61, 363, 365–67)

Before moving to its final admonition to readers, which I will discuss momentarily, the poem graphically reminds them of the urgent need for divorce reform. In one of the most densely reiterative lines of the poem, Massey variously alludes to and repeats the ancient punitive practice of strapping together the bodies of (living) murderers and their victims. Massey alters the image to suggest that the victim Charmian is horribly tied to the corrupting dead weight of a bad marriage. "Festering" chiasmically alliterates "fast fettered" and is also a portmanteau word which contains and echoes traces of the earlier pair. The portmanteau in fact gives a creepy performance of just how intimately bound are the decaying and the living bodies: the very description of being "fast fettered" folds over onto itself and merges into the rank image of "festering." The parts of speech in this line also chiasmically fold over onto themselves, as the adjective-noun phrase "festering corse" redoubles, in reverse, the earlier noun-adjective (phrase) construction "life fast fettered," subtly adding another bond between the decomposing and the living. The redundancy of the alliteration, use of a portmanteau word, and chiasmus in a single line form a gripping prelude to the poem's, and this outermost circle's, final hailing of readers to read the letter of this poem and then act based on its contents.

The theatrical references to the genre of "Tragedy," the dramatic structure of "five acts," and the thespian forum of a "Theatre" in lines 365–67 tie together the poem's various insistencies that people attend (to) and watch the story of women such as Charmian as they would a play. But more than this, readers of this poem, watchers of such tragedies, must themselves become the vehicles for their gaining a wide audience. Notice how the "five acts" double as not only the standard divisions of classical plays but also the five human senses; they are "our" five acts "of the Sense," as if human beings themselves are the play and their perceptive faculties the mechanism of its unfolding. Before encountering that line, one might be lulled into thinking that "This passing Tragedy of Soul within" is a purely individual one. The deictic "this" anaphorically points to some tragedy about which we must already know: Charmian's—it is her tragedy and not ours. And it is a tragedy "of Soul"—stressing its internal, personal, spiritual nature—which occurs "within," an almost defensively private preposition. But this line coupled with the following one represents a splendid example of double grammar,[31] in which readers make sense of a line as a complete grammatical unit but have to revise that sense once they round the corner into the next line. Turning the corner, we realize that this Tragedy takes place not just "within" Charmian, but "within / Our five acts of the Sense," a radically different meaning. The new grammar shifts the play from Charmian's interior to an outside, public, collective awareness (not just "my" senses but the collective pronoun "our" senses).

The poem's final line takes this turning inside out even further, beyond the five senses of even a group of people. The plight of women trapped in hymeneal misery bursts onto the theatrical stage "of a world," and I believe Massey's use of the indefinite article "a" instead of the more usual "the" before "world" transforms the prepositional phrase from a simple (possessive) genitive to an equative genitive.[32] The theater of "the world" could imply possession: the world owns a theater and that is where Charmian's terrible drama is staged. The theater of "a world" more strongly suggests an equivalence: the whole world is itself a theater.[33] The possessive relationship implied by "the" would relegate the theater to some subsidiary position (optionally viewed) in the world, whereas the metonymic relationship invoked by "a" renders the theater inescapably, pervasively public. But importantly, the conduit through which such drama reaches the theater of a world is still "human hearts." These final lines of the poem underline the degree to which a literary narrative (or drama) requires the medium of humanity to be realized on a broadly social stage, far beyond their own five senses. By definition, drama is a genre of action, written to be acted, produced, and not just read. This is why I say that the poem calls on readers not only to consume narrative but also to act, based on it, in "a world." Such a reader-text interaction would almost literally turn

---

31. Though now rarely used, the term "double grammar" remains quite useful as a descriptor for a common effect of poetic lineation, often exploited to potent effect. It was coined by William Empson in his 1930 book *Seven Types of Ambiguity*, in the context of a discussion of Shakespeare's sonnets.

32. Also called a genitive metaphor, in which the prepositional phrase establishes an equation, not subordination, of the metaphor's vehicle and tenor. In the example "the eye of the sun," "of" functions as a fulcrum across which eye and sun are equated: the metaphor means the sun *is* the center or eye, not that the sun possesses an eye or a sun spot.

33. Unquestionably Massey, who would later publish a study of Shakespeare, has in mind the famous lines from *As You Like It*: "All the world's a stage, / And all the men and women merely players" (Act 2, scene 7).

inside out "the letter of [this] Dream," inducing readers to unleash its contents on the world through the medium of their own consciousnesses and deeds.

There could hardly be a clearer illustration of the view that the relationship between art and reality is human action. But crucially for *The Chartist Imaginary*, some of the most persuasive, effective means of connecting art and human action are those of form. The outermost ring of the poem's concentered enclosures completes the formal trajectory from character and language to genre to allegory. It is a sort of final frontier of figuration, the place where having to penetrate language and recognize the seduction of narrative culminates in skillful reading and calls for decisive behavior. One is reminded of Brechtian literary theory, in which the form of a work should "alienate" the audience in order to make it aware of its own agency, of the artificiality of (literature and) society and therefore its susceptibility to *change*. It is as if the formal exercises literature calls on readers to perform train them not to be passive registers of presented reality, but to accept responsibility for the imperative to interpret and act on reality, changing it and themselves in the process.[34] "Only a Dream" is not a simple didactic tale or exercise (relying on themes to teach readers to look "deeper" into social practices), but achieves its summons to agency precisely through its concentric form.

Conclusion:
Medievalism, Gender, Genre, and Epistemology

"Only a Dream" registers the wider mid-Victorian fascination with the medieval discussed in chapter 2 on epic. In particular, Massey incorporates literary devices such as oxymoron, the frame tale structure, and the dream vision made famous by Boethius, Petrarch, Dante, Boccaccio, and Chaucer. By means of his concentric structuring of the poem and especially his concluding references to "the letter" of his dream, he also nods to the famously Italian poetic trope of *congedo* ("envoi" or "envoy" in Old French and in Britain). This device of closure has the poet (usually) apostrophize the preceding poem by bidding it to go out into the world and say or do some specified thing with

---

34. Brecht is not, of course, the only author or the only Marxist to conceive of literature this way. P. B. Shelley held that since "The great instrument of moral good is the imagination" and "Poetry enlarges the circumference of the imagination . . . ," therefore "Poetry strengthens the faculty which is the organ of the moral nature of man, in the same manner as exercise strengthens a limb" (Shelley, *A Defence of Poetry*, 1076). Writing of art, Trotsky said that "it refines feeling, makes it more flexible, more responsive, it enlarges the volume of thought in advance and not through the personal method of accumulated experience, it educates the individual" (*Literature and Revolution*, 168).

respect to its readers. *Congedo* very self-consciously emphasizes the act of communication and the process of transmission.[35] Although Massey's poem does not include such a formally demarcated device, his concluding stanza unquestionably gestures at *congedo* by sending the poem out into the world to solicit specific responses from its readers, and he explicitly refers to the foregoing poem as a letter to be interpreted and as a drama to be acted in "our" human hearts. In this way, the poem self-reflexively thematizes both the act of communication and the summons to readers to act *on* the matter so communicated. He concludes by addressing, not the poem, but "us" (implied by the collective first person pronoun "our"), bidding readers to alter women's position in society and in marriage.

Massey's nod to *congedo* furthermore prompts consideration of just what is at stake in the particular erotic encounter of Charmian, her proscribed true love, and her husband. Without the outward-focused conclusion and the concentric interpretive model, the poem would as likely as not be read in a purely lyrical mode, as one woman's cry against romantic travesty. But its close connections to medieval poetic customs turn the lyric inside out (from inward- to outward-looking), a project in which Massey's contemporary Victorian poets were also famously engaged. Arguing for an explicit association between poetic device and political function, Keen observes how Italian poets in exile frequently used the *congedo* to superimpose the political onto the romantic.[36] The trope that Massey echoes and modifies, then, served historically to "open[] up to political interpretation what would otherwise be read as a purely erotic poem, in which imprisonment and separation would be taken as conventional amorous metaphors" (Keen, 190). In "Only a Dream," what broader concerns does Charmian's particular experience represent? Certainly part of the answer is the status of women more generally in loveless marriages. But I contend that another part of the answer is the relatively disempowered position of working people, and of worker writers, in Victorian Britain.

For reasons already mentioned, the weight of literary tradition could be repressive for such political and literary aspirants as numbered among the

---

35. Catherine Keen describes this function as making "both author and audience [. . .] aware of shifting from the fictional space of the lyric back to the world in which its words are read or spoken" ("'Va,' mia canzone': Textual Transmission and the Congedo in Medieval Exile Lyrics," 184).

36. Regarding Re Enzo's lyric "Amor mi fa sovente," for example, Keen points out that its erotic theme seems unrelated to anything political until the *congedo* mentions imprisonment and pleading with a powerful lord. The final stanza also names (in order) the regions of the Italian peninsula through which the poem must travel to reach Enzo's beloved, strongly implying the poet's position in Bologna, where he was a political exile for twenty-three years.

Chartists, helping to enforce their disenfranchisement much as Charmian's rigidly traditional marriage subjects her to silent suffering. Chartist writers such as Massey might very well identify—and be identified—with Charmian due both to their intellectual labor as poets and to their class status as working men. Criticizing Tennyson, for example, as lacking "manliness" in the "emasculate floridity" of his style ("The Faults of Recent Poets," 74), Victorian critics were notoriously uncomfortable with what they saw as the feminizing influence of certain poetry.[37] "Only a Dream" would certainly have earned a similarly gendered dismissal, yet Massey ventriloquizes Charmian's voice over the bulk of the poem, prompting speculation that he is self-feminizing in solidarity with oppressed women and in order to draw an analogy between them and workers more generally. He also explicitly genders the narrator's "Spirit" as a female going forth "to meet her Bridegroom in the night" when the dream state begins in the poem's opening lines (lines 4–5).

Massey's choice and handling of genre associate him with female subjectivity, but his class status too could powerfully link him with the objective definition of womanhood in the middle-class dispensation. Cultural historians have shown how, with the rise of the industrial middle class and the shift of labor away from cottage industry to factory production, an important marker of manhood and status became the capacity to go out (of the home) to work and earn an income sufficient to provide for a dependent wife and family who remained in the domestic space.[38] A key complaint of the Chartists was that mechanization and capitalist competition deprived men of their masculinity by paying below subsistence wages (necessitating employment of wife and children) and by sometimes depriving men of jobs at all (leaving them at home to be supported by wives who formed a cheaper work force).[39] Critiquing the assumptions underlying such complaints, Schwarzkopf avers that

> Chartists responded to the upheaval in gender relations by attempting to
> revert to pre-industrial patterns of sexual power, at the workplace, in the

---

37. Thaïs E. Morgan explains that "Victorian male poets inhabited an ambiguous cultural space: as poets, they were expected to express deep feelings and explore private states of consciousness, yet this was identified in domestic ideology as the preserve of the feminine" ("The poetry of Victorian masculinities," 204). See also Adams's *Dandies and Desert Saints: Styles of Victorian Masculinity* (Ithaca, NY: Cornell University Press, 1995) and Sussman's *Victorian Masculinities: Manhood and Masculine Poetics in Early Victorian England* (Cambridge: Cambridge University Press, 1995).

38. See, for example, Bivona and Henckle's *The Imagination of Class: Masculinity and the Victorian Urban Poor* (Columbus: The Ohio State University Press, 2006) and Davidoff and Hall's *Family Fortunes: Men and Women of the English Middle Class, 1750–1850* (London: Routledge, 2002).

39. See Schwarzkopf, 34 and *passim*.

family as well as in politics. [. . .] In fact, Chartist opposition to women's exploitation was embedded in a conception of a woman's proper social position that put her more firmly in her place by cementing her dependence on man. (*Women in the Chartist Movement*, 77)

Conceding the validity of this line of criticism (also discussed in chapter 5 on female Chartist poets), at present my chief concern is not an evaluation of male Chartists' perceived feminization but simply a notation of its reality, however complicated. To the degree that pre-industrial or middle-class criteria of successful manhood shaped perceptions and self-perceptions of working people, laboring men experienced their diminished power as feminizing. Thus although Charmian's self-representation is principally aimed at specific marriage law reforms on behalf of women, its layers of related meanings include other disempowered people (the working class, Chartist poets, men seeking the vote, for example).

Charmian's own misery as a woman forcibly separated from her true love and trapped in a diabolical marriage neither requires additional meanings to confer significance nor serves as a mere window that disappears as readers gaze through it to the analogous circumstances of workers and Chartist writers. Yet in the voice of the socially and legally constrained, yet self-representing woman, it is hard not to hear as well the voices of culturally excluded, electorally disqualified worker-writers seeking the right of political self-representation. As categories of subalternity, these groupings overlap and share similar positions in relation to hegemonic powers.

Importantly, though, the subject of Massey's poem both hears the outside world ("the sounds above me far away; / The feet of hurrying Life, and loitering Love; / Rich bursts of music, hum of low, sweet talk" etc. [lines 142–44]) and *speaks* at length about her own experiences in this poem, thus insistently injecting the individual, the inconvenient, and the historically excluded into the prefabricated institution of marriage. Likewise Massey and other Chartist writers infuse the protests, hopes, and realities of women and the poor into literary traditions from which they had been largely excluded. As a figure for other oppressed women and for stifled workers more generally, Charmian's self-representation metonymically represents the disruption not only of marriage but also of political exclusion and literary elitism.

As many have pointed out, poetry in the nineteenth century became an increasingly marginalized genre. To explain this, Felluga examines the century's paradoxical demands on poetry in terms of class and gender that are especially useful here: on the one hand, critics said that poetry should strive to maintain a place "above" the taint of the present, with its mass market commodities (such as novels) and lower-class consumers. In this view, poetry's unpopularity signified its status as an antidote to low, democratic tastes. On the other hand, some demanded that poetry should not become solipsistic and lose touch with the common world, for that sort of "purity" and self-indulgent privacy leads to an effeminate sensualism. Critics diagnosed the resulting lassitude and artificiality as a *source,* rather than remedy, of social disease. In either case, whether valorized as an elite cure or demonized as a feminizing curse, poetry landed firmly on the margins of society, as something external to the social body. From this fringe, Felluga argues, the genre has "sought to extricate itself ever since" (*Perversity of Poetry*, 3). As antithetical as these prescriptions for poetry were ("separate us from working-class rabble by being unpopular!" and "avoid feminine irrelevance by being popular!"), both took for granted two assumptions: poetry is not an organic part of the social or political body (it is rather a prophylactic or a disease), and poetry has some poorly defined but fraught connections to women and the poor.

In all cases, it is cordoned off as foreign, as exterior to dominant subjectivities, be they male, ruling class, or narrative/prosaic. For these reasons, poetry was uniquely situated as the genre of the dispossessed, the non-normative, the outsider (with plenty of exceptions and qualifications). That could be one reason Chartists (and other agitators) favored it. Viewing the question of Chartism's genre preferences this way places the discussion within aesthetic and literary historical parameters, which should not be divorced from or replace the more usual material explanations of less leisure to write or read literature, access to newspaper columns but rarely publishing houses, and so on. I propose this explanation of Chartism's overwhelmingly poetic output not to displace the other explanations on which this book also relies, but to take seriously, on their own terms, the artistic choices and cultural intuitions Chartist writers evinced when they chose to write poetry.

As an iconically marginal self-representation, "Only a Dream" poses a final, metadiscursive reminder that historical influence is not unidirectional. Those who come after the settlement of major conflicts easily forget that the power relations, roles, and cultural understandings of the contenders (in this case women and men, lower and upper classes) were once unsettled; it is a critical commonplace that the winners of such struggles dictate the terms in which their successors understand the conflict and its resolution. But still one needs reminding of what feminist scholars have shown: categories such as the state, industrialization, womanhood, and class do not in fact possess characteristics and powers distinct from and pre-dating human beings. Rather, ideologies and institutions "are the progeny of human encounters, of women and men who engage, as they occasion, the potentialities and limits of their circumstances of living" (Silverblatt, "Interpreting Women in States: New Feminist Ethnohistories," 154). The winners might dictate terms to posterity, but the losers are not one-dimensional victims who played no role, however obscure(d), in the creation of those terms. Such apparently settled categories as worker and family and poet and citizen bear traces of the push and pull, the resistance and complicity, of those who did not emerge in control of their definition.

Charmian's (admittedly fictional) protest, like the literary self-projection which is the poem about her, represents a counterhegemonic contribution to what would become the accepted, nearly automatic ways of thinking about wives, poets, and workers. The poem grants readers access to how a culturally or legally powerless individual (autodidact, voteless man, feme covert) actually participates in the formation of customs and laws of which we have come to see them as merely the victims or objects. With this access, "woman" and "wife" become historical entities, the outcomes of a gestation to which women and wives contributed. In the same way, "writer" and "citizen" become contested identities shaped also by the uneducated and disenfranchised who left their imprint on the terms of their own exclusion. The epistemological shift to seeing (literary) history this way—as disputed, multiply determined, lived process—is one of the most important consequences of understanding Chartism and its literature.

· 5 ·

The Politics of Cognition in Chartist Women's Poetry

For as long as Chartist literature has been a subject of critical inquiry, the women who wrote for the movement have been more thoroughly marginalized than they were in the movement itself. Admirable exceptions are Ian Haywood's inclusion of a short story by Mary Hutton in his collection of Chartist fiction, and Mike Sanders's discussion of two poems by women in his study of the movement's poetry.[1] But there is more material available, and in addition to providing some gender balance to the picture of Chartist literature, the effort of finding and analyzing it offers some important insights into the positive feedback loop described by Chartism and its literature.

That self-reinforcing loop has as its poles the explicit goal of political self-representation on one side and the (apparently) corollary production of aesthetic self-representation on the other. This chapter shows that three women poets seemed keenly attuned to how, although for some people the political movement was the precondition of aesthetic sensibilities, for others, those same aesthetic sensibilities were the precondition of the political movement. Without desiring to homogenize the writings of Elizabeth La Mont, Mary Hutton, and E. L. E., I argue that each poet's complex treatment of memory, imagination, and psychic stress expresses Chartism's self-perception as the

---

1. Among histories of Chartism, Malcolm Chase's *Chartism: A New History* (Manchester: Manchester University Press, 2007) stands out for its concerted effort to include women's stories, and Jutta Schwarzkopf's *Women in the Chartist Movement* (London: Macmillan, 1991) remains essential reading.

movement for the whole, authentic person, and also implies the belief that poetry helps create the person and the movement so represented.

This chapter focuses on La Mont, Hutton, and E. L. E. because my aim here is to bring to light the names and works of unknown, working-class women poets in the Chartist movement, and at this point, they are the poets whose working-class status and Chartist sympathies I have been able to confirm. Additionally, those three women each published a number of poems sufficient to give some idea of the range of their preoccupations, tone, and style, allowing for a somewhat detailed and comparative consideration of each poet. Mike Sanders includes brief discussions of poems by Elisa Lee Follen and E. H. in *The Poetry of Chartism,* and Timothy Randall gives credence to the claim in Thomas Cooper's autobiography that a Welsh female Chartist composed the universally known anthem "The Lion of Freedom" (*The Life of Thomas Cooper,* 176). However, these considerations and suggestions are tantalizingly brief, in each case with a sample size of one. The similarly slender poetic output of Caroline Maria Williams likewise limits her utility for my purposes, even though she very clearly identified as a Chartist and was active on the movement's behalf. I am aware of only one of her poems, though she probably wrote more,[2] and she published some prose addresses to other Chartist women. However, she was apparently middle class, and although her class status alone would not bar her from inclusion in this book, this chapter seeks to foreground Chartist poetry by unknown working-class women. Of course Eliza Cook wrote some Chartist-themed poetry and a number of her poems appeared in Chartist newspapers, but she needs no introduction to those interested in Victorian working-class writing.

Elizabeth La Mont

One young Scottish woman whose identity I have been able to trace published a handful of poems in the *Northern Star* and other periodicals directed at the working class to which she belonged. "E. La Mont" was Elizabeth Ramsay La Mont,[3] born in Edinburgh in 1821 to Isobell Wilson and Robert Ramsay, who worked as a bookbinder (her birth record spells *Elizabeth* with an

2. In a note to the editor of the *Northern Star,* she says she does not know if he will publish her poetry or prose, but her preference would be the prose. This implies that, though the newspaper did publish one of her poems ("Self-Conceit" in the June 4, 1842 issue, page 3), there might well have been others, despite her deeming them less important than her political speeches. Her poem is briefly discussed on 176–77 of *The Chartist Legacy.*

3. Kovalev incorrectly supplied "Eugene" for the E. in her name, and so the poems included in his anthology, and in Scheckner's after him, were wrongly attributed to a man.

"s" rather than a "z"). When she married John Oatt La Mont, also a book-binder, on New Year's Eve in 1839, she was eighteen years old and living in Edinburgh, although her father's address at that time was in Glasgow. Possibly she was employed in Edinburgh, though in what capacity is unknown. The couple had a daughter (Jean Smith La Mont) in 1840, and between her birth in November and the June 6th taking of the 1841 census, the family moved to London Street in Glasgow, where their neighbors included female domestic servants, clerks, warehousemen, and butchers. So although the 1841 census indicates that Elizabeth was not employed (either because her husband's artisan occupation earned a sufficiency or because she was still nursing her seven-month-old daughter is only speculation), they lived in a crowded neighborhood among fellow members of the working class.

That the couple was actively interested in the Chartist cause is evident from their both contributing to its press. In 1842 John published a piece in the *English Chartist Circular* arguing in favor of women's right to vote as well as men's (vol. 2, no. 33), and he published *The Grave of Genius* serially in *Cleave's Gazette of Variety* (this story was reviewed by the *Northern Star* on Nov. 4, 1843; the review also mentions a work by John called *The Rebel Revolt*). By the summer of 1841, John was working as a reporter for the short-lived Chartist newspaper the *Scottish Patriot,* a post he had left by the following winter when he became editor of the radical *Dundee Chronicle.* Also indicating that he was known beyond his own immediate circle is the fact that, after he died in February 1844, the *Northern Star* published a memorial poem about him (James Syme's "Lines on the Death of John O. La Mont" in its March 16, 1844 issue).[4] Elizabeth published five poems in the *Northern Star,* plus one each in the *Chartist Circular* and *Cleave's.* Unfortunately I have not been able to locate any trace of Elizabeth (or her parents) after 1844, when she lived in London at the time of her husband's death there.[5]

The content and role of memory pervade La Mont's poems, three of which were published in 1840 while the Chartist movement anxiously watched the

---

4. References to his work as a reporter and editor occur in the *Northern Star* for 07 August 1841 and 26 February 1842. An announcement of his death, at age 29, ran in the *Colonial Times* of Hobart, Tasmania, Australia, on Tuesday, 27 August 1844, evidently because he had a sister who had emigrated there. An entry in the General Records Office Index records the death from consumption of John Oat [sic] La Mont, aged 28, in Islington, London, on February 13, 1844. Elizabeth La Mont lived with him there at 19 Park Place, and John's death certificate lists his occupation as a commercial clerk.

5. Their daughter Jean married R. J. Fowler on Sept. 18, 1869, at the British Consulate in Paris. The event, announced in a Quaker newspaper published in Glasgow, identifies her as "Jeanie Smith" La Mont, "eldest daughter of the late John Oatt." This indicates that John and Elizabeth had another daughter after Jean, in the few years remaining between her birth and her father's death. See pages 258–59 of the *British Friend* for October 1st, 1869 (vol. XXVII, no. X).

government reprisals following the Newport uprising. The poems also exhibit caution regarding the use of violence, in keeping with the Scottish variety of Chartism.[6] As Mike Sanders has pointed out, the works in the *Northern Star*'s poetry column at this time demonstrate ambivalence about the use of violence by workers. La Mont's "'The Land of the Brave and the Free!'" represents the "people" who have been oppressed and enslaved as "rais[ing] their shackled hands" in groans and prayer to "peace and freedom's God," a complaining but passive gesture that relies on supernatural intervention to right their wrongs (lines 16–17).

At the same time, their "Despair" and "Shame" in comparison to their "honoured" fathers (who spurned servility) generate an ominous sound: "the distant tramp of armed men, / Or the moan of swelling seas" (lines 25–26, 11–12). Their brows burn, and the angry irony of the final two lines expresses a sneering bitterness toward Britain's self-congratulatory belief that others look to them as models of bravery, freedom, and plenty: "Ah! Britain, where's thy boasted strength? / And where thy 'glory' *now?*" (lines 27–28). This direct question, plus the title's placement of "The Land of the Brave and the Free" in quotation marks, undermines by ironizing the identity of the nation, and casts any impending conflict as a patriotic effort to restore the principles that have distinguished Britain historically. In this way, memory helps justify violence, and even potentially compels it by shaming her contemporaries who have submitted to "the tyrant's rod" (line 14). Still, the vague threats remain limited and "distant" (line 11), while the pacific people raising their hands in agonizing prayer occupy the poem's foreground.

La Mont clearly has Newport in mind in "Universal Liberty—The Chartist Reaction," also published in 1840, and this poem uses the language of class antagonism rather than peace and conciliation. Here "the children of toil" stand in military opposition to their oppressors who have "laughed at our cries, and they mock'd at our pain" (line 22). The "sons of oppression" still pray (now to a "smit[ing]" rather than a peaceful God) for vindication, but the martial tone is unmistakable in the "unfurl'd" banners, the "foes" of their "CAUSE," and the giving of "the signal" to act in defense of that cause (lines 1, 10, 20, 19). The speaker summons readers to be "up!" and to "rouse thee! Then rouse thee!" in an effort to "Win freedom or death! and be slaves no more!" (lines 19, 22) Reminding toilers that they have suffered "Too long" in having their demands met with "the scaffold, the block, or a foreign grave" (fates faced by the Newport Chartists), the poem accuses rulers by describing how

6. See Leslie Wright's *Scottish Chartism* (Edinburgh: Oliver and Boyd, 1953). A contrasting view is presented in W. Hamish Fraser's *Chartism in Scotland* (Pontypool, Wales: Merlin Press, 2010).

"our land has been drenched with the blood ye have spilt" (lines 12–13). The forms La Mont uses here likewise sustain the military tone and energy: the relatively short tetrameter lines hasten along in the rising, galloping rhythms of anapests, while the couplets' swift return of rhyme sounds lends a feeling of tightness and cohesion suggestive of the closed ranks in a military formation.

The anger brimming in this poem likely resulted from Parliament's rejection of the first Chartist petition in 1839 as well as the state's vindictive reaction to Newport. Indeed, vengeance has an ambiguous provenance in "Universal Liberty," for it could be the vengeance of the people against their cruel oppressors, or it could be the vengeance those oppressors will take if the people do not rise up and strike their blow for freedom quickly enough. After invoking the "voice of liberty" which carries "The resolve of a people to conquer or die," she urges Chartists "Then up! for behold, on the wings of the blast, / The spirit of vengeance is hurrying fast; / And the cloud that now darkens our once happy isle, / Shall burst on the foes of the children of toil" (lines 6–10). In the context of conquering or death and of furious storms breaking on their "foes," the balance of probability tilts towards the people wreaking vengeance on their rulers, a somewhat surprising position to take in the context of the more usual repudiations or cautious defenses of (self-defensive) violence in Chartist poetry at this time.

It is true that the people have prayed and now expect God's "mighty arm" to "smite" the tyrants, and that "our glorious CAUSE has the sanction of Heaven" (lines 18, 20), but these assurances are meant to embolden the activists, not replace their efforts. By noting how the people are already resolved to "conquer or die" and "Win freedom or death" (lines 6, 22), and by repeatedly calling on them to "come" and "rouse" themselves and "rise," La Mont also urges human action, and much more emphatically than in her previous poem. Here she combines anger at the remembered and present sufferings imposed on her class by those in power, fervent aspiration for "freedom" and the triumph of their "CAUSE," and an agitational summons to agency in realizing those desires.

Given such a combination of memory, desire, and action in the poem itself, the title "Universal Liberty—The Chartist Reaction" appears somewhat at cross-purposes because of how it casts Chartists as reactive rather than proactive. Based on that title, one might expect a narrative poem describing how the movement perceived some already-accomplished granting of political freedom. Instead, this is a vocative poem calling on its auditors to "conquer" at the behest of "the glad voice of liberty" (line 2). The key distinction is between "liberty" as a *fait accompli*, a pre-existing state of affairs over which Chartists now simply rejoice, and "liberty" as the personification of democratic reform, a metaphoric force whose urging Chartists must obey. Clearly this latter understanding of what Chartists react or respond to (a call) dominates the poem, as it should to effect its agitational intent, but the title's latent duality of reference highlights what sets poetry apart from other, nonaesthetic uses of language. Strictly functional or communicative language can, of course, also contain ambiguities and *double entendres*, but its principal orientation is toward intellectual apprehension rather than affect, imagination, and association, as poetry's is.

As La Mont evidently understands, in order for people to take seriously a call to action, they need to be able to imagine the future toward which they are asked to strive. For this poem, conceptualizing the achievement of liberty (as already accomplished) motivates responsiveness to the personified ideal of liberty (as presently calling). It is not only in the density of poetic language that this double effect inheres; the effect results to a significant degree from the ways of thinking that poetry makes possible, as Armstrong and Sanders, for example, have theorized.[7] By exercising the creative, imaginative capacities of writers and readers,[8] Chartist poetry calls on innate powers which form an important basis of human self-definition, affirming the shared humanity and hence dignity of "the children of toil" ("Universal," line 10). Moreover, conceiving of conditions or realities different from one's own fosters the awareness, hope, and expectation that the world (living and working conditions, relations among humans and to nature, one's range of emotions, etc.) can be different than it is. That cognitive breakthrough, coupled with what Sanders calls the "appetitive function" of Chartist poetry (e.g., its inciting of a thirst for more poetry, more knowledge, more emotional experience), generates a "psychic structure" (Sanders, 10), that is a way or pattern of thinking, which could and did lead numbers of men and women into the movement that represented "more": Chartism.[9]

What is most powerful about the Chartist imaginary, this privileging of the imaginative, aesthetic experience as a potential gateway to political consciousness and action, is its recognition that creative activity is not ornamental or secondary to social humanity's existence but utterly fundamental, not

---

7. See Armstrong's *The Radical Aesthetic* (Oxford: Blackwell, 2000) and chapter 1 of Sanders's *The Poetry of Chartism: Aesthetics, Politics, History* (Cambridge: Cambridge University Press, 2009).

8. As mentioned in chapter 4, both P. B. Shelley before the Chartists and Trotsky after them famously focused on the benefits conferred by the cognitive workout effected by literature's imaginary. See Shelley's "A Defense of Poetry" and Trotsky's *Literature and Revolution*.

9. See Jacques Ranciere, *The Politics of Aesthetics* (London: Continuum, 2004). Thinkers such as Ranciere have noted that such a progressive political outcome does not necessarily follow from the impact of the aesthetic.

only as expression of the self or group but also as that which structures consciousness in politically enabling ways. La Mont thematizes acts or practices of imagination in "Thoughts by Moonlight. A Simile." Here "Memory" is in the ascendency, inviting people to "ponder on the fairy joys / Of childhood's fleeting years" with a "dreaming" forgetfulness of present hardships and the world's ills (lines 13, 17). Such thinking can serve multiple purposes, including offering consolation to workers surrounded by noise, cramped conditions, illness, and death by placing before them earlier, happier times less burdened with the experiences and responsibilities of adulthood (whether or not such times actually ever occurred in the lives of many working-class people—she does call these earlier joys "fairy" ones, perhaps acknowledging that even such "memories" result from a fictive creativity). In addition, this reverie might suggest to La Mont's peers that there can be beauty and goodness in the world even if there seems to be little or none at present: "So fair a world can hold no ill— / Earth seems an hallowed spot" (lines 18–20). That world would be something worth striving for, much as it forms a contrast to the world in 1840 with all its "ills," "cares," and "tears" for individuals and for Chartism itself, then undergoing its hardest challenges to date.[10] Encouraging such a striving accounts for the rather hackneyed reminder that "The darkest hour in all the night / Is that which heralds morn" (lines 23–24), as the once-cloudless sky suddenly obscures the moon in preparation for the triumphant arrival of the sun.

The sun plays an equivocal role in "Thoughts by Moonlight," since the poem has devoted most of its time to conjuring up and celebrating the quiet solitude and restorative fantasy accompanying the soft and peaceful moonlit hours. The concluding quatrain tells us that "Soon morning breaks, and from the east, / The monarch of the day / Comes riding forth, and chaseth night, / With all its dreams, away!" (lines 25–28) Given how fondly the speaker describes the ideals that arise with the moon, calling the sun a "monarch" that "rid[es] forth" as to battle and "chaseth" away night implies a dominance tainted by harshness and responsible for loss. Yet historically the trope of dawn overwhelmingly figures a positive, hopeful condition of clarity and renewed energy. Interpreted this way, the sun's arrival revises readers' understanding of the foregoing imaginative indulgence, and invites them to make a comparison between the sun's appearance and the dawn of a new era under Chartism's vision of a truly democratic society. After all, La Mont's subtitle "A

---

10. The rejection of Chartism's first petition to Parliament, the bloody suppression of the Newport uprising, and stringent government reprisals in its aftermath occurred in 1839. The early 1840s brought organizational competition from the newly formed Complete Suffrage Union and Anti-Corn Law League.

Simile" directly appeals for a figurative reading of the poem and insists on its not being only a meditation or reverie. Instead, it tells readers to compare its subjects to something else. Thus the experience of reading the poem becomes double; it offers consolations in the temporary escape from present troubles, hopes in the reminder that the world has not always been painful and is susceptible of change, and it offers encouragement and a spur to action by figuratively casting Chartism as a powerful, ascendant, promising new light on the world. Though not named, the Chartist movement seems the likeliest tenor for this simile's vehicle, that which permits the rest and dreaming of night but then demands a move beyond merely backward-looking nostalgia.[11] Reading the poem then occasions an active imaginative excursion, as readers dreamily cast their memories back to a (possibly imaginary) time of beauty and joy, feel the contrast of that time with the care-laden present, and conclude by revising their initial sense of the poem and engaging in nonliteral thinking that conceives of Chartism as a strong light which forbids mental stasis and will take the world forward into a new day. Treating dreams, imagination, and memory as its central themes, this poem provides a concrete example of my contention that aesthetic, and particularly poetic, language is a precondition of political consciousness. One cannot, or at least should not, struggle to bring about a world of which s/he has no imagination.

Of the four other poems La Mont published in 1841–42, the most obviously political is "The Honest Working Man.—A Character."[12] As the title announces, the 32 lines that follow extol the "toil-worn man[]" as the repository of the freedom and virtue sought by some unspecified addressee. Although the laborer recognizes the oppression and injury done to himself and his country by the overbearing and proud wielders of the "iron hand," he is a "Patriot" who seeks social amelioration rather than individual retribution (lines 14, 24, 21). La Mont's invocation of the "patriot" label links her poem to the prevailing rhetoric used to describe the variously punished Chartists since the winter of 1839–40, only some of whom had been recently freed from prisons around the UK when this poem appeared. Like the transported Chartist heroes for whom the movement continued to agitate in the months preceding this poem, this man's "spirit melt[s] / For his injured native land" (lines 21–22). He is a disinterested, religious, tender, faithfully married,

---

11. Mike Sanders has argued for a dialectical recuperation of *nostalgia* from the persistently pejorative notion of it since postmodernism. Countering Zlotnick's claim that Chartist poetry is basically nostalgic (and therefore lacking accurate, specific historical memory) and antimodern, Sanders shows that Chartist memory can be "a necessary starting point for a critique of the present" (*The Poetry of Chartism*, 163).

12. This poem was originally published in the *Northern Star* of Aug. 21, 1841, and then reprinted in *The Penny Satirist* of Oct. 30, 1841.

humble, forgiving, and hardworking man glimpsed in a tableau scene with his wife and children gathered around him, kneeling in prayer. In a conventional but politically pointed comparison, he forms a stark contrast to the institutions of the church and state, where "sin" and "guile," "envy, malice, strife, and hate" reside (lines 6, 8, 11). "The Honest Working Man" clearly aims to correct misapprehensions and prejudices about the lower classes as selfish rabble whose only concern is the satisfaction of their gluttonous appetites, stereotypes persistently leveled against workers as justifications for their exclusion from the franchise.

"Life's Dream," "The Old Maid's Scarf," and "Lines to a Mother" address human needs that were also important to Chartist men and women, ranging from the fleeting nature of human pains and pleasures and the evanescence of ambition's goals, to the remembrance of old friends now scattered and gone, to the purity and consolations of a mother's love and her power to shape a child's mind. Each of these more contemplative poems focuses on occurrences common to early Victorians, familiar as they were with the loss of loved ones to disease and accident at home, catastrophes at sea, and colonial emigration, for example. These are not peculiarly working-class experiences (though they might be more common to workers), and perhaps they are not meant to be, since it is precisely their shared nature that asserts the emotional range and dignity common to all regardless of class status. In this respect the poems retain a political complexion, at the same time as or because of their affirmation of the full humanity of the poor. La Mont's poems resonate with others in the Chartist press at the time that express "opposition to the distortion and degradation of the human character by representing Chartism as a movement which preserves and affirms authentic, human feelings" (Sanders, *The Poetry of Chartism*, 153). Importantly, her poems do this by foregrounding the perceptions and roles of women, both married and single.

She does cast the mother in the traditional roles of giver of comfort and love and molder of young minds, and the old maid as unfashionable and lonely (though it is not a maudlin, sentimental depiction of her as simple object of pity), but these are no less conventional depictions of women than are poetry's portrayals of men as hardworking and upright. More to the point, representations of women in terms of their familial roles characterized much Chartist writing as a way to defend their involvement in politics and the public sphere. As Jutta Schwarzkopf has shown, Chartists "claimed that, precisely because [women's] conduct was primarily motivated by familial concern, it forced them to leave the confines of their homes and to attempt to improve their families' lot by joining a political struggle in the public arena," and this "family discourse" enabled "the women to speak about the private and the public simultaneously, help[ing] them carve out some space in the male realm of politics" (*Women in the Chartist Movement,* 114, 99). Recourse to this "pose," as Schwarzkopf terms it, ultimately brought with it some significant limitations to women's independence of action by accepting both the propriety of feminine domesticity (and the exceptional nature of their political intervention) and the relational sources of women's identity. Nevertheless, since laws such as the 1834 New Poor Law directly attacked poor families, the conditions of industrial labor split up even those families living in the same dwelling, and families provided much of the meager emotional consolation to be had in the largely alienated factories and cities which must have been such a shock to laborers of the 1830s and early 1840s, defending the family was a mode of resistance to the impacts of the capitalist organization of production.

Mary Hutton

One poet who seems to have embraced a slightly enlarged public identity is Mary Hutton, the Sheffield Chartist now known to specialists for both her poetry and fiction.[13] She also wrote a fairly long autobiographical preface to one of her three volumes of stories and poems,[14] in addition to some lectures on political topics, which were printed in the Chartist press. After receiving her "Thoughts on Universal Suffrage" (published Feb. 24, 1839), the *True Scotsman* invited more from her pen, saying that her thoughts were very much to their (Chartist) taste. That essay argues for universal suffrage, fair remuneration of labor, and peaceful tactics while condemning the 1832 Reform Bill as a "complete delusion, and as arrant a mockery" as could be imagined. Her references to those present leads me to believe that she publicly delivered her "Lecture on Equal Rights," also published by the *True Scotsman* (May 11, 1839). This more fiery speech explicitly names the Charter as the means of addressing a variety of problems including the oppression of the Irish, child labor, the Poor Laws and Corn Law, and the death penalty. The tone of this speech, when compared to her other writings, is actually quite startling and puzzling, and not because she calls for religious freedom and a system of national education (which she does). Here, after declaring that

---

13. Haywood includes her short story "The Poor Man's Wrongs" in *The Literature of Struggle* and Kossick introduces some of her poems with a biographical headnote in vol. 2 of *Nineteenth-Century English Labouring-Class Poets* (London: Pickering & Chatto, 2006).

14. *Sheffield Manor, and Other Poems,* ed. John Holland (Sheffield: J. Blackwell, 1831); *The Happy Isle; and Other Poems* (London and Sheffield: n.p., 1836); and *Cottage Tales and Poems by Mary Hutton* (Sheffield: J. Blurton, 1842).

class interests are "diametrically opposed" and the monarchy is useless, she calls for "death to aristocracy." To appreciate how uncharacteristic this is for her, one need only know that the preface to her 1842 *Cottage Tales and Poems* includes her self-defense against criticisms that her writings sometimes fawn on the high of the land. Her *oeuvre* does include poems and stories praising generous royals, lamenting their deaths and celebrating their marriages, and—congratulating Queen Victoria on her escape from a second assassination attempt—asserting that God has appointed her to her exalted destiny and that anarchists and civil war should be forever banished from England. Can these two writers be the same Mary Hutton?

I cannot conclusively account for the contradictions, but some possible explanations do emerge. One pressure Hutton certainly felt was financial and editorial: she very reluctantly undertook the excruciating task of soliciting subscribers in order to publish her books,[15] and as Kossick has noted (*Nineteenth-Century English Labouring-Class Poets, Vol. 2*, 25), the 1842 volume garnered a remarkably meager list of them, with the Queen Dowager Charlotte heading the list. Economic dependence on aristocratic largesse promotes thematic conformity, even sycophancy, although resistance jostles alongside conformity in the book. Moreover, Hutton's editor for *Sheffield Manor* (1831) calls attention to the "correctness" of sentiment therein, as if to allay fears that a poor and unknown woman would air the sort of insurrectionary miasma of which Reform Bill proponents made so much at the time this book was published. Such assurances give only a faint trace of the kinds of pressure women writers, especially those in the working class, had to negotiate in order to gain an audience. Florence Boos's observation about the ephemeral nature of laboring women's publications applies to volume issue as well: the majority of these women "published most of their work in pamphlets or local or regional newspapers, whose editors' preferences for poems on the rigors of winter and redeeming consolations of family life (say) amounted to an amiable form of censorship" (*Working-Class Women Poets*, 15). In Hutton's case, her editor's stated preference for sentimentally conventional writing, as well as that most awkward need to secure the favor of their names and financial commitment from her superiors, inevitably pressed her books into somewhat different molds than they might otherwise have found. Her more confrontational writings for fellow Chartists, however, met with a warm welcome, if the remark cited above by the editor of the *True Scotsman* (and the fact that several of her pieces garnered front page placement therein) is representative.

---

15. Introducing *Sheffield Manor* in 1831, Hutton describes the "harsh and rude" refusals she often received (vii).

As numerous better-known Chartists amply demonstrate, people also simply change their minds and moods over time, and there is no reason Hutton might not have done so too, although viewing her work diachronically reveals no clear patterns of change. Each of her volumes contains both the flattering eulogistic poems and the more acerbic, political ones. The two essays cited above as evidence of her public and political persona both appeared in the tense months immediately preceding the presentation of Chartism's first petition to Parliament (when there was talk of arming and drilling and a national strike, the Chartist leader Henry Vincent was imprisoned, and the government commenced spying on and intercepting the mail of delegates to the newly convened Chartist Convention [Chase, 57–79]). Hutton's prose and poetry in those months partakes of and helps generate the nervous energy of the new phenomenon of a massive, national working-class movement.

A less materialist, more speculative and tenuous theory to explain the radically bifurcated tenor of her work is that it is the linguistic signature of a turbulent but impalpable psychic dissonance. In multiple places—fictional, nonfictional, and poetic—Hutton openly expresses her anxiety that her mind will fail to retain its grasp of sanity under the strains of her life (among them lifelong illness and poverty, profound disappointments and frustrations, and possibly spousal or other familial cruelty). "On Reading the Distressing Account of John Clare's Aberration of Mind" (*Cottage Tales*), for example, observes of Clare that "mind, and lyre, are both unstrung" before expressing Hutton's pity, solidarity, and fear: "A broken spirit mourns thee, Clare, / And sheds a pitying tear for thee; / For soon she may thy prison share, / A victim to insanity" (lines 22, 27–30). Her publication of this and similar confessions seems quite brave. It is not my intention to suggest that she ever did break down or that her writing must be the work of someone deranged, but merely to take seriously her own stated concerns as they might (or might not) have influenced her self-presentation.

Hutton's perception of how much she had been harmed by circumstances certainly led to an awareness of and sympathy for others who suffered in similar ways. Her attentiveness to the intellectual and emotional effects of hardship informs a significant number of her poems. For example, in "Written on Seeing a Poor Miserable Sweep" (*The True Scotsman* of May 18, 1839 and *Cleave's Gazette of Variety* of June 8, 1839), she notes that the abused child is "Wounded in heart, and mind, and limb—" (line 21). "The Factory Lord's Daughter and the Factory Slave" (*The True Scotsman* of June 1, 1839) builds its dramatic contrast partly on the ways in which a lifetime of grinding overwork and poverty has mentally dehumanized the young female factory worker. "She vegetates in toil and fear," the narrator says, because "She must to labour, labour keep, / With scarcely time to eat or sleep— / No time at all to pray or read" (lines 89–92). The constant anxiety and labor which exclude essential imaginative activities (reading, sleeping, praying) render her not just tired or bored or resentful, but "vegetat[ive]," so that by age sixteen her "strength of mind [is] forever gone" (line 98). Having begun her work at age seven, the girl labors in a "Cimmerian night," and here the classical reference is particularly poignant. For while readers might be lucky enough to know that for the Greeks the Cimmerians represented all that was dark and unknown about the afterlife, the girl herself could not understand this allusive metaphor precisely because of the mental darkness for which it stands.[16] For her, "Perpetual labour at the mill" has simply "Destroy[ed] the energies of mind" (lines 110, 112), and it ultimately destroys her body as well, for she dies at age sixteen.

In this poem Hutton's recursive emphasis on the intellectual toll of overwork simultaneously represents Chartism as a movement appealing to the whole person and thematizes the redemptive power of literature as that whose reading rescues one's mental "energies" and "strength of mind." Moments such as this provide concrete examples of the personal and political agency of Chartist poetry; by stressing the crushing effects of imaginative deprivation, the poem valorizes its own reading and enacts or performs Chartism's integration of the social and private selves.[17] As she says in "On Reading a Letter in Frazer's Magazine" (*Cottage Tales*), "And such is genuine poetry; / It dignifies humanity" (lines 19–20). Reading poetry becomes an act not only of political expression but also of personal salvation.

However, while these and others of her poems highlight the intellectual and emotional harm inflicted by industrialism, Hutton elsewhere specifies the less general form such harm might take: insanity. She pities the titular figure of her poem "Madame Lavalette" (*Cottage Tales*) not only because of her heroic self-sacrifice to free her husband from prison and execution but also because her mental powers seemed utterly "overthrown" and she was confined to a "Lunatic Asylum." Hutton follows the poem—as much about insanity as about Madame Lavalette—with a very interesting statement about people wrongly supposing that the insane do not feel, and she claims that "I know well, that if a little more tenderness, humanity, and endearing kindness, had been shewn towards them at home, upon the first symptoms of an unsettled

---

16. In Homer's *Odyssey* the Cimmerians inhabited caves at the earth's western extreme, believed to be the entrance to the Underworld. They were associated with the oracle of the dead.

17. In *Victorian Poetry as Social Critique* (Charlottesville: University of Virginia Press, 2003), E. Warwick Slinn examines poems by canonical authors in terms of speech act theory.

mind [. . .] thousands and thousands might have been saved from the dreadful privations and cruelties of a madhouse" (100–01). Regardless of whether her suggestive "I know well" signals personal experience and anger, the poem and its prose accompaniment maintain that, at least as much as any organic cause, environment profoundly affects mental illness, and the poor suffer harsher conditions not only domestically but also in treatment facilities.

The class dimension Hutton introduces into her etiology of disease in "Madame Lavalette" comes to the fore in two other poems from her 1842 volume. "On Reading the Distressing Account of John Clare's Aberration of Mind" laments the "hunger, woe, and scorn" which beset the laboring poet, whose talent "sinks" for lack of the "dew" required to nurture it and to soothe the "despair" caused by "deep afflictions" (lines 37, 24–26, 39). That those "afflictions" include economic as well as emotional "privations" is explicit in "On Reading a Letter in Frazer's Magazine, for Sept. 1836; Said to be from the Ettrick Shepherd" (line 24). After discovering that Edinburgh's literary elite preferred to encourage the rural poet from a comfortable social distance, James Hogg returned to the country in the hope of supporting his family on what funds he could generate through farming and hack writing. Hutton identifies with the beleaguered bard, noting that "when to them [working-class writers] is richly given / Poetic wealth, with poverty, / Deeper they feel their misery" (lines 39–41). Kossick rightly claims that Hutton's "experience offers a salutary corrective to the assumption that the poetic muse is a compensatory gift, ennobling poverty and transfiguring pain" (26). In fact the poet's anger over the barriers obtruded on poor writers flashes out in "On Reading a Letter" in a rare moment of bitter sarcasm:

> The poor should ne'er attempt to rhyme,
> Nor even think, nor hear, nor see;
> For in old England's christian clime,
> Our men of gold alone should be
> Endow'd with genius, wit, and sense.
>   (Hutton, lines 9–13)

This mockery of mainstream prejudices against worker-writers indicts their arrogance with a confident, outraged edge she might well have derived from the Chartist movement (and the arguments marshalled against it). Mixed with that bitterness, though, is pain. She grieves over the obscure penury in which Hogg concluded his life, and also over what is lost to the world through its denial of creative opportunity to the vast majority of the artistically inclined poor. She remarks that one will never know what worker-poets' "genius might have dar'd, / Had their privations timely shar'd / The sheltering care of kindly powers" (lines 23–25). Naturally one wonders to what extent she wrote these lines (and these poems) about herself as well as Hogg, Clare, and other stifled voices.

What one gains by analyzing Hutton's poems from the angle of their persistent linkage of economic and mental/psychological impoverishment is a deeper awareness of the mutually reinforcing roles that Chartism and aesthetic expression played: the movement created a forum, audience, and occasion for literary self-expression, and Chartists' taking advantage of those benefits created works that unified, instructed, and inspired the political movement, performing in a smaller arena the very self-representation Chartism demanded in the grander arena. Even the poems that did not rehearse the platform of the Charter (which, in point of fact, broadened considerably with each iteration of the Petition), but confessed anger and anxiety over the stultifying, even maddening, effects of industrialism or personal abuse, for example, were thoroughly Chartist and deserve study by those interested in what I am, with Sanders, calling "the Chartist imaginary." In ways that corroborate Kirstie Blair's thesis about the importance in Victorian poetry more generally of what she calls "the political heart," these poems help create the perception *and the reality* that Chartism represents the whole, authentic, political and emotional human being that workers felt themselves to be.[18] Asserting as much by writing poetry was an essential component of the Chartist political project.

It is possible to overstate the degree to which Chartism created or thought of itself as an arena for public political self-assertion by women, however, and the movement's equivocal position on this matter could also account for Hutton's experience and articulation of sympathy with the distantly patronized (Hogg), the publically smothered (Madame Lavalette), the relentlessly overworked (the Factory Slave), and the starved for encouragement (Clare). Particularly in its strong anxiety over the possibility of insanity, Hutton's poetry registers a fear with peculiar relevance to Victorian women, whose gender itself was a medically recognized cause of insanity and who were sometimes committed to asylums for being "unfeminine" or rebellious. Women such as Hutton who made public speeches doubtless felt pressure not to do so, even within Chartist ranks. Chartism's critics pounced on the mere presence of women at its public meetings as occasions for ridicule, but what must have been the feelings of female Chartists who read of one lecture in their own newspaper, the *Northern Star,* that it was attended by "a very attentive audi-

---

18. Blair, *Victorian Poetry and the Culture of the Heart* (Oxford: Oxford University Press, 2006).

ence, composed not of women and children, but of intelligent adults" (July 2, 1842, page 1)? O'Connor's firm placement of Chartist women in secondary support roles and his opposition to their right to vote, the view of some Chartists such as Gammage that women attended certain Chartist lectures not from intellectual interest but simply because they found the speaker physically attractive (78),[19] and the undermining of female Chartist orators in Wheeler's novel *Sunshine and Shadow* (152), for instance, bear witness to a distinctly antifeminist component within the movement, despite abundant evidence for the simultaneous existence of contrary views as well (discussed in chapters 1 and 4, e.g.). It is not hard to believe that Hutton's poetry expresses more than her own personal discomfort with the experience of patronizing treatment or the prospect of being labeled unfeminine, eccentric, or mad. Especially in "Madame Lavalette," where a (cross-dressed) woman sacrifices her reputation and personal liberty in the service of her husband's freedom and political cause, the analogy with women in Chartism seems uncomfortably close. The latent as much as the explicit tensions within her writing record weaknesses and active contests within Chartism, as well as between it and the larger Victorian culture.

Though Hutton passed her adult life in Sheffield and probably died there around 1860, she was born in about 1795 in Wakefield, Yorkshire. She reveals in her preface to *Sheffield Manor* that she was a twin, and the only twins I have been able to locate in Wakefield in 1795 are George and Mary Benton, so that this might have been her name prior to her marriage to a man who, if I have correctly identified the household in the 1841 Census which included the poet Mary Hutton, was a cutler named Michael Hutton, 25 years her senior. The home included Mary's ten-years-younger stepdaughter, also named Mary Hutton, and the two women appear to have made their home together until the elder's death, even though Michael died many years prior to that event.[20] Hutton refers to their family's having to resort to the parish for relief in her 1842 Preface, though whether that relief required their living in or out of the workhouse is not clear. Interestingly, though, their 1841 Census record shows them living at Cotton Mill Row, a street that was just outside the eastern walls of the Sheffield Workhouse in Kelham Street. Note also the "Asylum" area of this workhouse, in Figure 4.

---

19. R. C. Gammage, *History of the Chartist Movement, 1837–1854*. Vol. 2. 1854. (London: Merlin Press, 1976).

20. The 1851 Census shows the two Marys sharing a home at Bethnal Green Lane in Sheffield, with the elder's occupation listed as "Poetess," while the younger was a "Hair Seater (?)," an occupation at which she still labored in the 1861 Census, by which time she lived alone. I have not been able to locate any record of marriage for Michael Hutton.

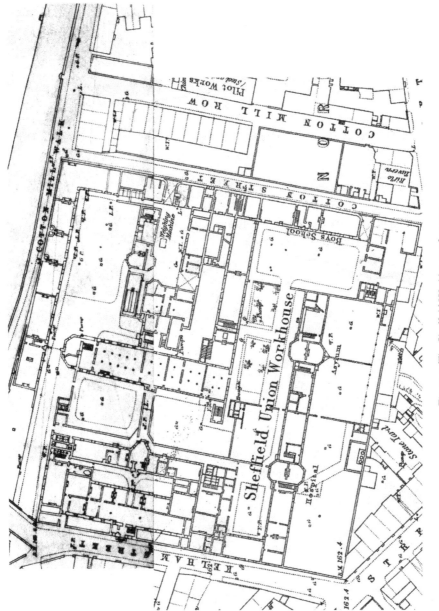

Figure 4. The Sheffield Workhouse after 1829

E. L. E., "A Sempstress"

In some ways more obscure than either La Mont or Hutton, despite her publication of several poems in *Hood's Magazine*[21] and a small volume of poems
in 1848, E. L. E. remains known to us only by her initials, with nothing more
known about her than that she was a seamstress. Despite her never nam-
ing Chartism in her verse or, apparently, sending her work to any Chartist
periodicals, I include her in this discussion for a few reasons, not least her
appropriation by the *Northern Star*'s poetry column in 1851, a point I will
return to. Her work shows her strong solidarity with her own class, including sympathy for how prolonged poverty crushes hope and dignity, subtle
condemnation of the Poor Law—the single most important source of anger
and political activism to usher women into the Chartist movement[22]—and
anger over the powerful's defeat of "the sacred cause" of Justice and "right"
on behalf of which people have struggled in "patriot zeal" ("Song," lines 30, 3,
19).[23] Published some months after Chartism's final presentation of its petition
to Parliament, and using language identical to that of other Chartist poems
discussed in this book, her "Song" in particular seems to be for or about the
Chartist movement.

There is a significant instance of formal aesthetic connection between
E. L. E. and the Chartist movement, as well, and it is a sufficiently peculiar
formal trait to justify calling attention to it for the purpose of my argument.
Her poem "The Fate of Diffidence. An Allegory" consists of Spenserian stanzas that were very unusual in the nineteenth century, although they famously
formed the basis of Thomas Cooper's 1845 Chartist epic *The Purgatory of Suicides* (discussed in chapters 2 and 4). It is hard to imagine that E. L. E. was not
aware of and possibly imitating Cooper's also allegorical book of just three
years before, prompting me to argue that these formal and subgeneric simi-
larities to a stylistically anomalous Chartist classic provide evidence of her
respect for and connection to Chartism.[24]

---

21. "An Elegiac Ode. To the Memory of the Late Thomas Hood" in December 1846, "Oh,
Cancel the Past" and "The Dreamer" in January 1847, "The Old Maid. A True Story" in February
1847, "The Last Fear" in April 1847, and a series of sonnets in June and August 1847.

22. Schwarzkopf notes that "The hatred inspired by the Poor Law provided much of the
impetus for women's commitment to Chartism, which the Anti-Poor Law Campaign merged
into" (105).

23. *Poems, by a Semptress* (London: C. Mitchell, 1848).

24. The working-class Mary Smith composed her epic *Progress* (1863) in stanzas that
could, as Boos says (*Working-Class Women Poets*), have been influenced by Cooper, although
her meter, stanza length, and rhyme scheme do not quite follow Spenser's (and hence Cooper's) distinctive form. Some Romantic poets used this stanza early in the century and Tennyson used a mere handful of them in "The Lotus Eaters" in 1832, but it is most rare in the

On June 13, 1851, the *Royal Cornwall Gazette* published E. L. E.'s "The Toiler's Dream" with this editorial headnote:

> The following remarkable lines are from a Volume of "Poems by a Semp-
> stress," and the production of a poor English girl. It is melancholy that the
> talent, taste, feeling, and resolution which they evince should lead to noth-
> ing better than a scornful defiance of society, and a craving for the rest of
> the grave, though without hope beyond it. (6)

Beyond the unintended humor, this remark is interesting because of its deviation from its source: the *Northern Star*, which published the same poem four
months earlier with a nearly identical headnote. Unsurprisingly, where the
headnotes diverge is after the first sentence, which the Chartist newspaper
follows with "They are indeed beautiful, and, under the circumstances, thoroughly and thoughtfully appropriate" (Feb. 8, 1851, page 3). That the upper-
class, Tory-leaning newspaper copied the poem from the Chartist one seems
clear from their both identically altering the original title ("The Dreamer")
and incorporating the same mistakes with respect to E. L. E.'s original in
Poems. Presumably the *Star* extracted the poem from her book, placing
greater emphasis on its working-class appeal by altering the title to highlight
the "toiler." In any case, its editor viewed the poem as not only "beautiful" but
also "appropriate" in its representation of a poor but defiantly self-respecting
speaker, whereas the editor of the *Royal Cornwall* presented it as a "melan-
choly" cautionary tale.

In the context of this chapter, "The Dreamer" ("The Toiler's Dream")
deserves attention for how its preoccupations with imagination, psychic suffering, and loss of human potential bear striking resemblance to La Mont's
and Hutton's poems. Here, however, dreaming is not a consolatory act, and it
does not lift the speaker's spirit to any thoughts of heavenly care, vindication,
or reward. From start to finish, this is a poem of negations and inversions.
The first word of the poem, and indeed of the first two stanzas, is "Not," as
the speaker negates the usual locales associated with flights of fancy: "Not in
the laughing bowers" and "Not on the couch of ease" does she dream (lines
1, 10). She elaborates by saying "nor where the golden glories be, / At sunset
paving o'er the flowing sea, / And to pure eyes, the faculty is giv'n / To trace
the smooth ascent from earth to heav'n" (lines 6–9). Though nullified, here is
the usual introduction to reverie, with the golden light of sunset inducing one
to "trace the smooth ascent from earth to heav'n," that is to shift one's gaze
from the earthly glories of sunlight on the ocean upward to the visions of a

---

Victorian period.

beatified afterlife.[25] That is the figurative translation supposed to occur when dreaming commences.

But since this dreamer insists on the fact that her translation occurs in scenes quite distinct from those with "Soft light, sweet fragrance, beauty at command" (line 12), her gaze resolutely does not drift from the physically to the spiritually transcendent. Partly this results from her radically different working-class surroundings:

> But where the incessant din
> Of iron hands, and roar of brazen throats,
> Join their unmingling notes;
> While the long summer day is pouring in,
> Till day is done and darkness doth begin;
> Dream I—or in the corner where I lie,
> On winter nights, just covered from the sky;
> Such is my fate, and barren as it seem,
> Yet, thou blind soulless scorner! yet, I dream.
> (E. L. E., "The Dreamer," lines 19–27)

In a noisy, crowded, hot work environment and a cramped, cold, scarcely sheltering dwelling, it can hardly be source of wonder that she feels uninspired. In these conditions the speaker nevertheless contrives to dream, but while the dream includes a world of "just and equal brotherhood" where she might "glean, / With all mankind, exhaustless pleasure keen," it also reminds her of what "I might have been!" in body and disposition "were man more just" (lines 28–34). This is an embittering reminder of how injustice and poverty deform and diminish the best potential of humanity, and it is a startling reversal of readers' dream-poem expectations. In fact, in a tone of astonished disgust the speaker casts the usual expectations of heavenly reward harbored by "the full self-complacent heart, elate, / Well satisfied with bliss of mortal birth" as an obscene greed for even greater indulgence of the already-gorged, who "Sigh[] for an immortality on earth" (lines 16–18).

In an inversion of the opening stanza's image of the "pure eyes" to which are granted the ability to move upward from earthly to heavenly, the penultimate stanza has the speaker "lift mine eye, / Bright with the lustre of integrity, / In unappealing wretchedness on high, / And the last rage of destiny defy"

---

25. "Paving" is a strangely urban intrusion into this scene of nature, possibly testifying to how proletarian living conditions shape notions of the ideal. "Laving" sensibly substitutes for "paving" in the newspaper versions of this poem, but since it is not known that E. L. E. had anything to do with its publication in those venues, which also introduce several errors, the change might not reflect authorial intention.

(lines 28–31). Though her eyes are just as pure ("bright") as anyone else's, they are turned back from the otherworldly to the worldly, from a fantasy of what she might have been to the reality of what she is: "the despised of Fortune" (line 27). What she most vividly sees is not her eternal bliss, but her temporal "wretchedness," so that her eyes emphatically do not make any appeal for indulgence; she implies that since she has never known generosity before, she scorns to expect any hereafter. The poem's ironic doubling here makes the case that whether one's mental "eyes" move from terrestrial to celestial or from fantastic to realistic depends heavily on his or her class position.

As a poor, and apparently unmarried, woman, the speaker harbors no illusions of blessed life or afterlife, and as part of her antimetaphysical defiance, she intends not to subject any others to such a harsh, hopeless life by giving birth: she is "Resolved, alone to live—alone to die, / Nor swell the tide of human misery" (lines 31–32). Breathtaking in its clear-sightedness and energetic anger, these lines assail myths of motherhood as redemptive, or indeed as anything other than cruel under the circumstances, and they cast her choice to remain childless as both humane and aggressively irreverent. For ultimately, she dreams of a sleep without illusions, where "dreams no more shall come" and she can at last enjoy real "Rest" (lines 34, 36). The nature of that rest is a matter of interpretation, but it certainly could be, as the editor of the *Royal Cornwall Gazette* took it to mean when he reproved her lack of "hope beyond [the grave]," the cessation of life rather than some delusive afterlife.

The speaker's insubordination extends to human as well as divine powers, for she tells the "blind soulless scorner" repeatedly "And, yet, I dream" (lines 27, 28, 36, 43), owning that humanizing imaginative power in ways familiar to us from the poems of La Mont and Hutton. In addition, the speaker claims her entitlement to "Rest" as the "Sole remnant of my glorious heritage / Unalienable" (lines 46–48). Affirming inalienable rights as part of a lost "glorious heritage" rhetorically enacts a civic rebellion that complements the metaphysical one. It also echoes the language of Chartist poetry and propaganda, which, for example, cited not only "the government of [their] Saxon ancestors" but also that of their Roman forbears, as having been based on "the principle of universal suffrage" (Kettering Radical Association, "The Just Claims of the Working Classes," 97). With this final inversion of the discourse of inheritance, the poem "broadens" the scope of ancestral heritage from political to personal rights. In a single poem, E. L. E. at once stresses the personal and aesthetic limitations imposed by industrialism, provides a trenchant class analysis of otherworldly dreams, and manages to found a claim to equal human dignity on the practice of dreaming.

There are other women who also contributed to the literature of Chartism, most often anonymously or using only initials. For the *Northern Star* alone, the list of identifiably female writers whose poetry was published is larger than might be supposed. Not all of these women submitted their own works to the newspaper or even necessarily supported the cause, but for the sake of completeness I include them in this list (in addition to La Mont and E. L. E.): E. H. (A Factory Girl of Stalybridge), Eliza Cook, Caroline Bowles, "Two Ultra-Radical Ladies," Caroline Maria Williams, Mrs. Abdy, Mrs. Crawford, Jesse Hammonds, Camilla Toulmin, Mrs. James Gray, Frederika Bremer, "Irish Girl," Adelaide (A Lowell factory girl), Miss Sheridan Carey, Mrs. E. S. Craven Green, "An Englishwoman," Caroline Norton, Georgiana C. Munro, "Aurora" (Glasgow), Mrs. Lydia Huntley Sigourney (Boston, USA), Lady Dufferin, Elizabeth Barrett Browning, Mrs. B. F. Foster, Sarah Parker ("The 'Irish Girl'"), Eliza Lee Follen, Miss A. Samsuda, Mrs. Mary M. Maxwell, Mrs. J. H. Lewis, and Emily Varndell. An extremely useful index of the names and dates of all poems and poets published in the *Northern Star* is appended to Sanders's *The Poetry of Chartism*, greatly simplifying the task of finding these women's poems.

Plato famously banned epic and lyric poets from his projected Republic, not because he disliked poetry (he referred to it throughout his work and seems to have been both attracted and repelled by it), but because he detected in it an emotional power that could be politically dangerous. The Chartist poets of this chapter would suggest that he was on to something. The philosopher described poetry as inciting rebellion because it foregrounds (for dramatic effect) sources of complaint, appeals to the emotions and passions without regard to their rational control, and fosters the imagination of how things might be different than they are. The poems examined in this chapter do all of those things, except perhaps for the disregard of reason, and they do them in the service of a movement seen by Victorians as rebellious and dangerous to the existing state. It was precisely through their appeal to the imagination of how things should and might be different that Chartist poetry fostered personal, intellectual, and political ambition. The poems of La Mont, Hutton, and E. L. E. aim at exactly the sort of psychic integration—indulging all parts of the human being—that Plato denigrates for its tendency (specifically by arousing their emotions) to feminize men. In answering and challenging his former teacher's views, Aristotle mounted a defense of poetry that came down to English literary history through Sidney and then P. B. Shelley. Less obviously and certainly less consciously, but in no way less effectively, that Aristotelian tradition comes down to modern literary history in part through the practice of the Chartist poets.

WORKS CITED

Altick, Richard D. *The English Common Reader: A Social History of the Mass Reading Public, 1800–1900.* 2nd ed. Columbus: The Ohio State University Press, 1998.

Anderson, Amanda. *Tainted Souls and Painted Faces: The Rhetoric of Fallenness in Victorian Culture.* Ithaca, NY: Cornell University Press, 1993.

"Argus." "The Revolutionist." In Haywood, *The Literature of Struggle.* 131–40.

Armstrong, Isobel. *The Radical Aesthetic.* Oxford: Blackwell, 2000.

Arnold, Matthew. *Culture and Anarchy and Other Writings.* 1869. Edited by Stefan Collini. Cambridge: Cambridge University Press, 1993.

Ashraf, Phyllis Mary. *Introduction to Working Class Literature in Great Britain.* 2 vols. East Berlin: Ministerium für Volksbildung, Hauptabteilung Lehrerbildung, 1978–1979.

Ashton, Owen, Robert Fyson, and Stephen Roberts, eds. *The Chartist Legacy.* Rendlesham: Merlin, 1999.

Bagehot, Walter. "Wordsworth, Tennyson, and Browning; or, Pure, Ornate, and Grotesque Art in English Poetry." 1864. In Collins and Rundle, 633–44.

Bal, Mieke. *Narratology: An Introduction to the Theory of Narrative.* Toronto: University of Toronto Press, 1997.

Bates, Crispin. *Subalterns and Raj: South Asia since 1600.* New York: Routledge, 2007.

Blair, Kirstie. "'He Sings Alone': Hybrid Forms and the Victorian Working-Class Poet." *Victorian Literature and Culture* 37.2 (September 2009): 523–41.

———. *Victorian Poetry and the Culture of the Heart.* Oxford: Oxford University Press, 2006.

Boos, Florence S., ed. *Working-Class Women Poets in Victorian Britain: An Anthology.* Peterborough, Ontario: Broadview Press, 2008.

Breton, Rob. "Genre in the Chartist Periodical." In *The Working-Class Intellectual in Eighteenth- and Nineteenth-Century Britain,* edited by Aruna Krishnamurthy, 109–27. Farnham: Ashgate, 2009.

———. "Ghosts in the Machina: Plotting in Chartist and Working-Class Fiction." *Victorian Studies* 47.4 (Summer 2005): 557–75.

Brewster, Patrick. "The Seven Chartist and Military Discourses." In Claeys, *Chartist Movement, Vol. 3*: 215–366.

Bronte, Emily. *Wuthering Heights*. 1847. In *Case Studies in Contemporary Criticism*, edited by Linda H. Peterson. Boston: Bedford, 1992.

Browning, Elizabeth Barrett. *Aurora Leigh*. 1856. Edited by Margaret Reynolds. New York: Norton, 1996.

Buckley, Jerome Hamilton, and George Benjamin Woods. *Poetry of the Victorian Period*. 3rd ed. New York: Harper, 1965.

Bulwer-Lytton, Edward. "The Present State of Poetry." *Critical and Miscellaneous Writings*. 2 vols. Philadelphia: Lea and Blanchard, 1841.

Charlton, John. *The Chartists: The First National Workers' Movement*. London: Pluto, 1997.

Chase, Malcolm. *Chartism: A New History*. Manchester: Manchester University Press, 2007.

Claeys, Gregory, ed. *The Chartist Movement in Britain, 1838–1850*. 6 vols. London: Pickering, 2001.

Clough, Arthur Hugh. "Recent English Poetry: A Review of Several Volumes of Poems by Alexander Smith, Matthew Arnold, and Others." 1853. In Collins and Rundle, 582–97.

Codell, Julie F. "Alexander Somerville's Rise from Serfdom: Working-Class Self-Fashioning through Journalism, Autobiography, and Political Economy." In *The Working-Class Intellectual in Eighteenth- and Nineteenth-Century Britain,* edited by Aruna Krishnamurthy, 195–218. Farnham (Surrey): Ashgate, 2009.

Cole, G. D. H. *Chartist Portraits*. 1941. London: Cassell, 1989.

Coleridge, Samuel Taylor. "The Rime of the Ancient Mariner." In *English Romantic Writers,* edited by David Perkins, 404–13. San Diego, CA: Harcourt, 1967.

Colley, Linda. *Britons: Forging the Nation, 1707–1837*. New Haven, CT: Yale University Press, 1992.

Collins, Thomas J., and Vivienne J. Rundle, eds. *The Broadview Anthology of Victorian Poetry and Poetic Theory*. Concise ed. Peterborough (Ontario): Broadview Press, 2000.

Cook, Chris, and John Stevenson. *The Longman Handbook of Modern British History, 1714–1995*. London: Longman, 1996.

Cooper, Thomas. *The Life of Thomas Cooper*. London: Hoder, 1897.

———. "'Merrie England'—No More!" In Haywood, *The Literature of Struggle,* 53–59.

———. *The Purgatory of Suicides: A Prison-Rhyme*. London: How, 1845.

———. *Wise Saws and Modern Instances*. 2 vols. London: How, 1845.

Cross, Nigel. *The Common Writer: Life in Nineteenth-Century Grub Street*. Cambridge: Cambridge University Press, 1985.

Dante Alighieri. *The Divine Comedy, Vol 2: Purgatory*. c1308. Translated by Mark Musa. New York: Penguin, 1985.

Dickens, Charles. *Hard Times*. 1854. Edited by Paul Schlicke. Oxford: Oxford University Press, 1989.

Disraeli, Benjamin. *Sybil or the Two Nations*. 1845. Edited by Thom Braun. London: Penguin, 1985.

Dooley, Dolores. "Introduction." In Thompson, *Appeal*, 1–21.

Doubelday, Thomas. *The Political Pilgrim's Progress*. In Haywood, *Chartist Fiction*, 17–64.

Duyfhuizen, Bernard. *Narratives of Transmission*. Rutherford: Fairleigh Dickinson University Press, 1992.

E., E. L. *Poems, by a Semptress*. London: C. Mitchell, 1848.

Eliot, George. *Felix Holt, the Radical*. 1866. Edited by Lynda Mugglestone. London: Penguin, 1995.

Engels, Friedrich. *The Condition of the Working Class in England*. 1845. Edited by Victor Kiernan. London: Penguin, 1987.

"The Faults of Recent Poets: Poems by Alfred Tennyson." *New Monthly Magazine and Literary Journal* 37.145 (January 1833): 69–74.

Felluga, Dino Franco. *The Perversity of Poetry: Romantic Ideology and the Popular Male Poet of Genius*. Albany: State University of New York Press, 2005.

———. "Verse Novel." In *A Companion to Victorian Poetry*, edited by Richard Cronin, Alison Chapman, and Antony H. Harrison, 171–86. Malden, MA: Blackwell Publishing, 2002.

Fraser, Hamish W. *Chartism in Scotland*. Pontypool, Wales: Merlin Press, 2010.

Fussell, Paul. *Poetic Meter and Poetic Form*. Rev. ed. New York: Random House, 1979.

Gammage, R[obert] C. *History of the Chartist Movement, 1837–1854*. 2nd ed. 1894. New York: Kelley, 1969.

Gaskell, Elizabeth. *Mary Barton: A Tale of Manchester Life*. 1848. Edited by Macdonald Daly. London: Penguin, 1996.

Gilbert, Pamela K. "History and Its Ends in Chartist Epic." *Victorian Literature and Culture* 37 (2009): 27–42.

Hadley, Elaine. *Melodramatic Tactics: Theatricalized Dissent in the English Marketplace, 1800–1885*. Stanford, CA: Stanford University Press, 1995.

Hallam, Arthur Henry. "On Some of the Characteristics of Modern Poetry." 1831. In Collins and Rundle, 540–55.

Hamilton, Edith. *Mythology: Timeless Tales of Gods and Heroes*. New York: Mentor, 1969.

Harrison, Antony H. *Victorian Poets and Romantic Poems: Intertextuality and Ideology*. Charlottesville: University Press of Virginia, 1990.

Haywood, Ian, ed. *Chartist Fiction*. Aldershot: Ashgate, 1999.

———. Introduction. In *The Literature of Struggle: An Anthology of Chartist Fiction*, edited by Haywood, 1–25. Aldershot: Scolar, 1995.

———. *The Revolution in Popular Literature: Print, Politics, and the People, 1790–1860*. Cambridge: Cambridge University Press, 2004.

———. *Working-Class Fiction from Chartism to Trainspotting*. Plymouth: Northcote, 1997.

———, ed. *Chartist Fiction, Vol. 2*. Aldershot: Ashgate, 2001.

Hutton, Mary. *Cottage Tales and Poems by Mary Hutton*. Sheffield: J. Blurton, 1842.

———. *The Happy Isle; and Other Poems*. London and Sheffield: unlisted publisher, 1836.

———. *Sheffield Manor, and Other Poems*. Edited by John Holland. Sheffield: J. Blackwell, 1831.

Jackson, Virginia. "Who Reads Poetry?" *PMLA* 123 (January 2008): 181–87.

Janowitz, Anne F. *Lyric and Labour in the Romantic Tradition*. Cambridge: Cambridge University Press, 1998.

Jones, D. J. V. *The Last Rising: The Newport Insurrection of 1839*. Oxford: Oxford University Press, 1985.

Jones, Ernest. "Britain's Duty to Her Soldiers." In Saville, 177–80.

———. "The Chartist Movement." In *Notes to the People*, 766.

———. "Ernest Jones to the People." *The Red Republican*. 10 Aug. 1850:64. Rpt. in *The Red Republican and The Friend of the People, Vol 1*. Introduction by John Saville. New York: Barnes, 1966.

———. "The Factory Town." *The Labourer* (1847) 1: 49.

———. "The Fraternity of Nations." In Saville, 86–88.

———. "The German Powers." In Saville, 213–14.

———. "Introduction to the Second Volume." In *Notes to the People*, 513.

———. *The Maid of Warsaw; or, The Tyrant Czar. A Tale of the Last Polish Revolution.* London: G. Pavey, 1854.

———. "The March of Freedom." *The Labourer* (1848) 3: 101.

———. *The New World: A Democratic Poem. Notes to the People* (London) 1851: 1–15.

———. "On Internationalism." In Saville, 215.

———. "Preface." *Notes to the People.* 1 (1851): 20.

———. "A People's Paper." In *Notes to the People*, 753.

———. *The Romance of a People. An Historical Tale, of the Nineteenth Century. The Labourer* 1– 3 (1847–1848).

———. "Soldier and Citizen. To the Oppressed of Either Class." In Saville, 99–102.

———. "A Song for May." *The Labourer* 1 (1847): 193.

———. "Speech at the Annual Banquet of the German Democratic Society for the Education of the Working Classes." In Saville, 92–94.

———. "Taxes on Knowledge." In *Notes to the People*, 357.

———. "To the British Democracy." In *Notes to the People.* 61.

———. "To the Subscribers for and Readers of The People's Paper." *The People's Paper* (8 May 1852): 1.

———. *Woman's Wrongs.* 1851–52. In *Chartist Fiction, Vol 2,* edited by Ian Haywood, 1–177. Aldershot: Ashgate, 2001.

———, ed. *The Cabinet Newspaper.* November 1858–February 1860, Volumes 1–3.

———, ed. *Notes to the People.* May 1851–May 1852, Vol 1. New York: Barnes and Noble, 1968.

Keen, Catherine. "'Va,' mia canzone': Textual Transmission and the Congedo in Medieval Exile Lyrics." *Italian Studies* 64.2 (2009): 183–97.

Kettering Radical Association. "The Just Claims of the Working Classes." In *The Early Chartists,* edited by Dorothy Thompson, 94–114. Columbia: University of South Carolina Press, 1971.

Kingsley, Charles. *Alton Locke Tailor and Poet: An Autobiography.* 1850. Edited by Elizabeth A. Cripps. Oxford: Oxford University Press, 1983.

Klaus, H. Gustav. *The Literature of Labour: Two Hundred Years of Working-Class Writing.* Brighton: Harvester, 1985.

———, ed. *The Socialist Novel in Britain: Towards the Recovery of a Tradition.* Brighton: Harvester, 1982.

Knoepflmacher, U. C. "Editor's Preface: Hybrid Forms and Cultural Anxiety." *Studies in English Literature, 1500–1900* 48.4 (Autumn 2008): 745–53.

Kossick, Kaye, ed. *Nineteenth-Century English Labouring-Class Poets, Vol. 2, 1830–1860.* London: Pickering & Chatto, 2006.

Kovalev, Yuri V., ed. *An Anthology of Chartist Literature.* Moscow: Foreign Languages Publishing House, 1956.

Kuduk, Stephanie. "Sedition, Criticism, and Epic Poetry in Thomas Cooper's *The Purgatory of Suicides.*" *Victorian Poetry* 39:2 (2001): 165–86.

La Mont, Elizabeth. "The Honest Working Man.—A Character." *Northern Star* (August 21, 1841): 3.

_____. "The Land of the Brave and the Free!" *Northern Star* (August 15, 1840): 7.

_____. "Life's Dream." *Northern Star* (September 11, 1841): 3.

_____. "Lines to a Mother." *Cleave's Penny Gazette of Variety* (August 20, 1842): n.p.

_____. "The Old Maid's Scarf." *Chartist Circular* (Sept 18, 1841): 436.

_____. "Thoughts by Moonlight. A Simile." *Northern Star* (October 10, 1840): 3.

_____. "Universal Liberty—The Chartist Reaction." *Northern Star* (September 26, 1840): 3.

Landon, Letitia Elizabeth. "On the Ancient and Modern Influence of Poetry." 1832. In Collins and Rundle, 556–61.

Landry, Donna. *The Muses of Resistance: Labouring-Class Women's Poetry in Britain, 1739–1806.* Cambridge: Cambridge University Press, 1990.

Ledger, Sally. "Chartist Aesthetics in the Mid Nineteenth Century: Ernest Jones, a Novelist of the People." *Nineteenth-Century Literature* 57 (2002): 31–63.

Linton, W. J. *Bob Thin, or The Poorhouse Fugitive.* [London, s.n.], 1845.

———. "The Free-Servant." 1839. In Haywood, *The Literature of Struggle,* 162–64.

———. "The Outcast." 1839. In Haywood, *The Literature of Struggle,* 158–61.

Macaulay, Thomas Babington. *Essays, Critical and Miscellaneous.* New York: D. Appleton, 1861.

Maidment, Brian, ed. *The Poorhouse Fugitives: Self-taught Poets and Poetry in Victorian Britain.* Manchester: Carcanet, 1992.

"Marriages" [of Jeanie Smith La Mont]. *The British Friend* XXVII. X (October 1, 1869): 258–59.

Marx, Karl. *Capital: A Critique of Political Economy Volume One.* Translated by Ben Fowkes. London: Penguin, 1990.

Marx, Karl, and Friedrich Engels. *The Communist Manifesto.* Edited by David McLellan. Oxford: Oxford University Press, 1992.

Massey, Gerald. *Craigcrook Castle.* London: Bogue, 1856.

———. *The Poetical Works of Gerald Massey.* New edition. London: Routledge, 1861.

Mather, F. C., ed. *Chartism and Society: An Anthology of Documents.* London: Bell, 1980.

Matthews, John T. "Framing in *Wuthering Heights.*" *Texas Studies in Language and Literature* 27 (1985): 25–61.

Mill, John Stuart. "'What is Poetry?'" 1833. In Collins and Rundle, 562–70.

Mitchell, Jack B. "Aesthetic Problems of the Development of the Proletarian-Revolutionary Novel in Nineteenth-Century Britain." In *Marxists on Literature,* edited by David Craig, 245–66. London: Penguin, 1975.

Mitchell. Sally. *Daily Life in Victorian England.* Daily Life Through History. Westport: Greenwood, 1996.

———, ed. *Victorian Britain: An Encyclopedia.* New York: Garland, 1988.

Morgan, Thaïs E. "The poetry of Victorian masculinities." In *The Cambridge Companion to Victorian Poetry,* edited by Joseph Bristow, 203–27. Cambridge: Cambridge University Press, 2000.

Morris, William. "The Defence of Guenevere." In Buckley and Woods, 619–23.

Morton, A. L. *A People's History of England.* 1938. London: Lawrence, 1979.

Nelles, William. *Frameworks: Narrative Levels and Embedded Narratives.* New York: Lang, 1997.

Newcomb, John Timberman. *Would Poetry Disappear? American Verse and the Crisis of Modernity*. Columbus: The Ohio State University Press, 2004.

O'Brien, Mark. *"Perish the Privileged Orders": A Socialist History of the Chartist Movement*. London: Redwords, 1995.

O'Grady, Jean. "Laws of Public Worship, Speech, and the Press." In Mitchell, 440–41.

Owen, Alex. *The Darkened Room: Women, Power, and Spiritualism in Late Victorian England*. 1989. Chicago: University of Chicago Press, 2004.

Paul, Ronald. "'In Louring Hindostan': Chartism and Empire in Ernest Jones's *The New World, a Democratic Poem*." *Victorian Poetry* 39:2 (2001): 189–204.

Perkin, Joan. *Women and Marriage in Nineteenth-Century England*. Chicago: Lyceum, 1989.

Porter, Thomas W. "Ernest Charles Jones and the Royal Literary Fund." *Labour History Review* 57.3 (Winter 1992): 84–94.

Preminger, Alex, and T. V. F. Brogan, eds. *The New Princeton Encyclopedia of Poetry and Poetics*. Princeton, NJ: Princeton University Press, 1993.

Prins, Yopie. "Historical Poetics, Dysprosody, and *The Science of English Verse*." *PMLA* 123 (Jan. 2008): 229–34.

———. "Victorian Meters." In *The Cambridge Companion to Victorian Poetry*, edited by Joseph Bristow, 89–113. Cambridge: Cambridge University Press, 2000.

Pugin, A. Welby. *The True Principles of Pointed or Christian Architecture*. London: Henry G. Bohn, 1853.

Ricks, Christopher, ed. *The New Oxford Book of Victorian Verse*. Oxford: Oxford University Press, 1987.

Rose, Jonathan. *The Intellectual Life of the British Working Classes*. New Haven, CT: Yale University Press, 2001.

Rosenberg, John D. *The Genius of John Ruskin: Selections from His Writings*. London: Allen, 1963.

Ruskin, John. *The Library Edition of the Works of John Ruskin*. Edited by E. T. Cook and Alexander Wedderburn. 39 vols. London: George Allen, 1903–1912.

———. *The Seven Lamps of Architecture*. 1849. In Rosenberg, 124–38.

———. *The Stones of Venice*. 1851. In Rosenberg, 139–217.

Ranciere, Jacques. *The Politics of Aesthetics*. London: Continuum, 2004.

Randall, Timothy. "Chartist Poetry and Song." In *The Chartist Legacy*, edited by Owen Ashton, Robert Fyson, and Stephen Roberts, 171–95. Rendlesham: Merlin Press, 1999.

Saintsbury, George. *Historical Manual of English Prosody*. 1910. New York: Schocken Books, 1966.

Sanders, Mike. "'God is our guide! Our cause is just!' The *National Chartist Hymn Book* and Victorian Hymnody." *Victorian Studies* 54.4 (2012): 679–705.

———. "Poetic Agency: Metonymy and Metaphor in Chartist Poetry, 1838–1852." *Victorian Poetry* 39:2 (2001): 111–35.

———. *The Poetry of Chartism: Aesthetics, Politics, History*. Cambridge: Cambridge University Press, 2009.

Saville, John. *Ernest Jones: Chartist*. London: Lawrence, 1952.

Scheckner, Peter, ed. *An Anthology of Chartist Poetry: Poetry of the British Working Class, 1830s–1850s*. London: Associated University Press, 1989.

Schwarzkopf, Jutta. *Women in the Chartist Movement*. London: Macmillan, 1991.

Scofield, C. I., ed. *The New Scofield Reference Bible*. New York: Oxford University Press, 1967.

Shaw, David. *Gerald Massey: Chartist, Poet, Radical and Freethinker.* London: Buckland, 1995.

Shelley, P. B. "A Defence of Poetry." In *English Romantic Writers.* Edited by David Perkins. San Diego, CA: Harcourt, 1967.

———. *The Mask of Anarchy. Shelley's Poetry and Prose.* Edited by Donald H. Reiman and Sharon B. Powers. New York: Norton, 1977.

Shevelow, Kathryn. *Charlotte: Being a True Account of an Actress's Flamboyant Adventures in Eighteenth-Century London's Wild and Wicked Theatrical World.* New York: Holt, 2005.

Silverblatt, Irene. "Interpreting Women in States: New Feminist Ethnohistories." In *Gender at the Crossroads of Knowledge: Feminist Anthropology in the Postmodern Era,* edited by Micaela di Leonardo, 140–71. Berkeley: University of California Press, 1991.

Smith, F. B. *Radical Artisan, William James Linton, 1812–97.* Manchester: Manchester University Press, 1973.

Somerville, Alexander. *Dissuasive Warnings to the People on Street Warfare.* In Haywood, *The Literature of Struggle,* 106–30.

Spitzer, Leo. "The Addresses to the Reader in the 'Commedia.'" *Italica* 32.3 (1955): 143–65.

Stallybrass, Peter, and Allon White. *The Politics and Poetics of Transgression.* Ithaca, NY: Cornell University Press, 1986.

Stevens, William. *A Memoir of Thomas Martin Wheeler.* London: Leno, 1862.

Stewart, Garrett. *Dear Reader: The Conscripted Audience in Nineteenth-Century British Fiction.* Baltimore: Johns Hopkins University Press, 1996.

———. *Reading Voices: Literature and the Phonotext.* Berkeley: University of California Press, 1990.

Sussman, Herbert L. "Novel." In *Victorian Britain: An Encyclopedia,* edited by Sally Mitchell, 549–51. New York: Garland, 1988.

Sykes, Robert. "Early Chartism and Trade Unionism in South-East Lancashire." In *The Chartist Experience: Studies in Working-Class Radicalism and Culture, 1830–60,* edited by James Epstein and Dorothy Thompson, 152–93. London: Macmillan, 1982.

Taylor, Miles. *Ernest Jones, Chartism, and the Romance of Politics, 1819–1869.* Oxford: Oxford University Press, 2003.

Tennyson, Alfred Lord. *The Idylls of the King. The Poems of Tennyson.* Edited by Christopher Ricks. London: Longmans, 1969.

———. *In Memoriam.* In Buckley and Woods, 57–91.

Thompson, Christopher. *The Autobiography of an Artisan.* London: Chapman, 1847.

Thompson, Dorothy. *The Chartists.* London: Temple Smith, 1984.

———. *The Early Chartists.* London: Macmillan, 1971.

Thompson, E. P. *The Making of the English Working Class.* New York: Pantheon, 1964.

Thompson, William. *Appeal.* Cork: Cork University Press, 1997.

Trawick, Buckner, B. "The Works of Gerald Massey." Diss., Harvard, 1942.

Trotsky, Leon. *Literature and Revolution.* 1925. Translated by Rose Strunsky. Ann Arbor: University of Michigan Press, 1966.

Tucker, Herbert F. *Epic: Britain's Heroic Muse, 1790–1910.* Oxford: Oxford University Press, 2008.

Vanden Bossche, Chris R. *Reform Acts: Chartism, Social Agency, and the Victorian Novel 1832–1867.* Baltimore: Johns Hopkins University Press, 2014.

Vargo, Gregory. "A Life in Fragments: Thomas Cooper's Chartist *Bildungsroman.*" *Victorian Literature and Culture* 39 (2011): 167–81.

Vicinus, Martha. *The Industrial Muse: A Study of Nineteenth Century British Working-Class Literature.* New York: Barnes, 1974.

Vickers, Roy. "Christian Election, Holy Communion and Psalmic Language in Ernest Jones's Chartist Poetry." *Journal of Victorian Culture* 11.1 (2006): 59–83.

Vincent, David. *Bread, Knowledge, and Freedom: A Study of Nineteenth-Century Working Class Autobiography.* London: Methuen, 1981.

———. *The Rise of Mass Literacy: Reading and Writing in Modern Europe.* Malden, MA: Blackwell, 2000.

Waters, Christopher. "Morris's 'Chants' and the Problems of Socialist Culture." In *Socialism and the Literary Artistry of William Morris,* edited by Florence S. Boos and Carole G. Silver, 127–46. Columbia: University of Missouri Press, 1990.

Weiner, Stephani Kuduk. *Republican Politics and English Poetry, 1789–1874.* Houndmills: Palgrave Macmillan, 2005.

Wheeler, Thomas Martin. *Sunshine and Shadow: A Tale of the Nineteenth Century.* In *Chartist Fiction,* edited by Ian Haywood, 72–200. Aldershot: Ashgate, 1999.

Williams, Jeffrey. *Theory and the Novel: Narrative Reflexivity in the British Tradition.* Cambridge: Cambridge University Press, 1998.

Williams, Raymond. *Culture and Society, 1780–1950.* New York: Columbia University Press, 1983.

Winn, Sharon A., and Lynn M. Alexander. *The Slaughter-House of Mammon: An Anthology of Victorian Social Protest Literature.* West Cornwall, CT: Locust Hill Press, 1992.

Wright, Leslie. *Scottish Chartism.* Edinburgh: Oliver and Boyd, 1953.

· INDEX ·

Nelles, William, 137n24

"New Move," 6, 54, 82

Newport Rising: purpose and results of, 6, 79–80, 81–82, 154, 155, 157n10

nostalgia, 158

O'Connor, Feargus: 101n27, 102n28; imprisonment of, 81; and Land Plan, 6; and "New Move," 6; as polarizing leader, 6; and women, 118n5, 166

Owen, Alex, 128–29

Patmore, Coventry, 130

petroglyphs, 1

Plato (philosopher), 172

Politics and Poetics of Transgression, The (Stallybrass and White), 39, 39n8

Poor Law, New, 35, 37, 117, 160, 168

portmanteau word, 143

Puebloans, 1

Pugin, A. W. N., 3, 47, 48–49

Purgatory of Suicides, The (Cooper): capital punishment in, 58–60; and "Chartist theology," 44; critique of religion in, 42–64; and Gothic architecture, 3, 47–49; knowledge valorized in 53–58; Spenserian stanza form, 44–45, 59–63, 168; and women, 116–18

Ranciere, Jacques, 156n9

Randall, Timothy, 152

Reform Act of 1832: 161; Chartist disappointment in, 5, 97, 98, 101, 160

religion: and capital punishment, 58–63; critique of 42–64, 65, 66; disbelief in, 169–71; and education, 53–58; and reason, 47–51; and state repression, 58–63

revolution: 74, 109–10; distinct from reform, 90–92; and internationalism, 26, 27–32; opposition to, 74, 76–79; strategy for, 83–109; support for, 80–110

Rose, Jonathan, 56

Rossetti, Dante, 75

Ruskin, John, 3, 39–40, 40n10, 47–48, 75

Samson (Biblical judge), 140

Sanders, Mike: 36n7, 154; and Chartist imaginary, 2, 2n1, 34n4, 58, 92–93, 156; and "Chartist theology," 43–44, 165; and Chartist women writers, 151, 152; and nostalgia, 158n11; "Poetic Agency," 23n5, 23–24; *Poetry of Chartism, The,* 9, 106, 124n10, 156n7, 159

Saville, John, 26n6

Schwarzkopf, Jutta, 117, 147–48, 151n1, 159–60, 168n22

Sepoy Rebellion, 15n4, 68, 69

Shakspearean Chartist Hymn Book, The (Cooper), 63–64

Shaw, David, 124n10

Sheffield, 160, 166, 167

Shelley, P. B., 145n34, 156n8

Silverblatt, Irene, 149–50

Slinn, E. Warwick, 163n17

Somerville, Alexander, 9, 74, 76–79, 80, 81, 83, 109n34

Spenserian stanza: 42, 44–45, 44n14, 59–63, 71, 168, 168n24

spiritualism, 127–29

Spitzer, Leo, 133

Stewart, Garrett, 135n22, 139n27, 139n28

Sturge, Joseph, 97n21

Sunshine and Shadow (Wheeler): ambiguity of hero of, 86–87; epigraphs in, 88–89; genre hybridity of, 83–90, 106; political strategy in, 83–109; as social problem novel, 84–85, 86, 98, 105, 108–9

Taylor, Miles, 12n1, 28n7

Tennyson, Alfred, Lord: 147; *Idylls of the King, The,* 130–31; *In Memoriam,* 49–51; "Morte d'Arthur," 72–73; *Princess, The,* 129, 130, 139n27

Thompson, Dorothy, 95–96, 101n27, 103

Thompson, William, 92n14

Thomson, Christopher, 56n20, 57

Trawick, Buckner, 124n10

CPSIA information can be obtained
at www.ICGtesting.com
Printed in the USA
BVHW070151180720
583903BV00001B/49